CIMA EXAMINATION KIT

Final Level

Paper 14

Management Accounting –

Information Strategy

ISBN 1 84390 128 5

British Library Cataloguing-in-Publication data

A catalogue record for this book is available from the British Library.

We are grateful to the Chartered Institute of Management Accountants for permission to reproduce past assessment material. The solutions have been prepared by The Financial Training Company.

Published by

The Financial Training Company
22J Wincombe Business Park
Shaftesbury
Dorset
SP7 9QJ

Contents

Questions and Answers

Case study questions

Syllabus

Syllabus overview

This syllabus is concerned with the strategic importance of information to organisations in the current and future business environment. It recognises that although many organisations employ IT professionals, Chartered Management Accountants have a key role to play in the provision of information that adds significant value to the ever increasing volume of data that is available.

Aims

This syllabus aims to test the student's ability to:

♦ Identify how information supports business strategy

♦ Evaluate the use of IS/IT to improve the competitiveness of an organisation

♦ Prepare a coherent plan to manage information

♦ Identify the ways in which IS/IT is changing the nature and structure of the working environment

Assessment

There will be a written paper of 3 hours. Section A will contain a compulsory question up to a maximum of 50 marks based upon a scenario. Section B will contain a choice of questions, normally two from four.

Learning outcomes and syllabus content

14(i)   Strategic information management – 25%

Learning outcomes

On completion of their studies students should be able to:

♦ Evaluate the use of information as a key resource in different organisational contexts.

♦ Evaluate information and information systems.

♦ Evaluate the appropriate channels of communication available.

♦ Evaluate and advise managers on the development of knowledge management strategy.

♦ Identify and evaluate the various support systems available for the management of knowledge.

♦ Evaluate the impact of electronic commerce on the way business is conducted and recommend an appropriate strategy.

Syllabus content

♦ Typical information requirements of organisations operating in different sectors such as manufacturing, service and the public sector as well as non-profit making organisations such as charities.

♦ Chief reasons why information is important for organisations.

♦ Process of cost-benefit analysis and how to assess the value of information.

♦ Characteristics of information at all levels of the organisation.

♦ Use of qualitative information by organisations in planning, control and performance monitoring.

♦ Typical methods of data collection in various business sectors (eg bar codes and scanners in retailing).

♦ Various IT systems that deliver information to different levels in the organisation (eg Transaction Processing, Decision Support and Executive Information Systems).

♦ Potential benefits and drawbacks of Internet use by organisations for activities such as data collection and dissemination of information (including the security issues to be borne in mind), as well as the concept of Intranets and their use by organisations in information management.

♦ Concept of electronic commerce and the potential impact it has on the business strategy.

♦ Concept of knowledge management and why it is seen as a key element to an organisation's success.

♦ Use of databases and planning models in assisting the strategic planning process (eg external databases, economic models, forecasting and modelling packages/applications).

14(ii)   Strategic dimension – using IS/IT competitively – 35%

Learning outcomes

On completion of their studies students should be able to:

♦ Identify and evaluate appropriate IS/IT systems and recommend changes to meet the strategic information needs of an organisation.

♦ Evaluate the use of IS/IT to gain competitive advantage and recommend appropriate strategies.

♦ Evaluate the importance of process innovation and reengineering.

♦ Evaluate the strategic benefits of IT and advise managers on the development of an IS/IT/IM strategy.

Syllabus content

♦ Why an organisation needs an IS/IT strategy which is complementary to the organisation strategy.

♦ How organisations can compete through better use of information as opposed to technology eg using a database to identify potential customers or market segments as opposed to creating a barrier to entry through investment in IT.

♦ The link between IS/IT and business strategies and how one supports the other, whilst at the same time, potentially using IT as the key element of the competitive strategy.

♦ The way IT can impact upon an industry by utilising frameworks such as Porter's Five Forces and Value Chain and how organisations can use IT to enhance their competitive position.

♦ How CSFs link to performance indicators and the corporate strategy and how they can be used to drive the information needs in the organisation.

♦ The strategic business use of the Internet and WWW in terms of marketing and sales activities, and utilising the technology to provide enhanced value to customers and suppliers.

♦ Use the applications portfolio to improve IS/IT strategy (McFarlan).

♦ Data warehousing and data mining as tools for managing data and the likely benefits that can be gained for their use, together with the implications of data warehousing.

♦ The concept of business integration – links between strategy, people, technology and operations in determining the role of IS/IT.

♦ The role of IT innovation and Business Process Engineering.

♦ The strategic case for IT investment particularly where the benefits and value of information are difficult to quantify with any degree of reliability.

14(iii)   Planning and implementation of IS/IT strategies – 25%

Learning outcomes

On completion of their studies students should be able to:

♦ Analyse the contents of IS, IT and IM strategies and recommend improvements thereto.

♦ Evaluate the organisation of the IS/IT function within a given organisation.

♦ Recommend strategies for achieving the integration of technical and business staff.

♦ Evaluate and recommend strategies for managing change in an IT context.

Syllabus content

♦ The purpose and contents of IS, IT and IM strategies.

♦ How to develop a plan and implement the various strategies in a positive way.

♦ The potential ways of organising the IT function involving the use of steering committees, support centres for advice and help desk facilities, end user participation.

♦ The argument for and against outsourcing.

♦ The criteria for selecting outsourcing/Facilities Management partners and for managing ongoing relationships, service level agreements, discontinuation/ change of supplier, hand-over considerations.

14(iv)   The social and organisational impact of IS/IT – 15%

Learning outcomes

On completion of their studies students should be able to:

♦   Identify and recommend new working patterns to improve a given situation.

♦   Identify and evaluate the impact of developments in telecommunications.

♦   Recommend ways of achieving coordination of activities via IS/IT in a decentralised organisation.

♦   Explain and interpret the concept of Human Information Processors.

♦   Evaluate the use of "intelligent agents" software.

♦   Identify and evaluate the cultural dimensions of IT acceptance.

Syllabus content

♦   The way IS/IT is changing the method of working and the increase in the knowledge content of many jobs.

♦   The organisational impact of technology, its implications for structure and working relationships, and how individuals may be faced with a role change.

♦   The Human Information Processor and the implications of providing a user friendly interface to gain maximum benefits whilst minimising the potential drawbacks, such as physical and emotional effects, providing the right volume of information, easy retrieval and storage facilities and merging sources of information reaching individuals so that they become a manageable number.

♦   How intelligent agent software can be applied to monitor an individual's use of a system and learn what the user's day to day information needs are.

♦   The growing awareness of remote working and the implication for the individual and the organisation.

♦   The impact of IS/IT on the social aspect of the organisation and implications for organisational culture.

♦   The management of change and potential staff reactions, particularly in respect of actual or perceived role changes.

Meaning of CIMA's examination requirements

CIMA use precise words in the requirements of their questions. In the schedule below we reproduce the precise meanings of these words from the CIMA syllabus. You must learn these definitions and make sure that in the exam you do precisely what CIMA requires you to do.

Learning objective	Verbs used	Definition
1 Knowledge What you are expected to know	List	Make a list of
	State	Express, fully or clearly, the details of/facts of
	Define	Give the exact meaning of
2 Comprehension What you are expected to understand	Describe	Communicate the key features of
	Distinguish	Highlight the differences between
	Explain	Make clear or intelligible/state the meaning of
	Identify	Recognise, establish or select after consideration
	Illustrate	Use an example to describe or explain something
3 Application Can you apply your knowledge?	Apply	To put to practical use
	Calculate/compute	To ascertain or reckon mathematically
	Demonstrate	To prove with certainty or to exhibit by practical means
	Prepare	To make or get ready for use
	Reconcile	To make or prove consistent/compatible
	Solve	Find an answer to
	Tabulate	Arrange in a table
4 Analysis Can you analyse the detail of what you have learned?	Analyse	Examine in detail the structure of
	Categorise	Place into a defined class or division
	Compare and contrast	Show the similarities and/or differences between
	Construct	To build up or compile
	Discuss	To examine in detail by argument
	Interpret	To translate into intelligible or familiar terms
	Produce	To create or bring into existence
5 Evaluation Can you use your learning to evaluate, make decisions or recommendations?	Advise	To counsel, inform or notify
	Evaluate	To appraise or assess the value of
	Recommend	To advise on a course of action

Questions

Question 1

Information Systems

B5 Cars manufactures motor vehicles for sale to the general public and companies. Several other motor vehicle manufacturers operate within the industry, which is highly competitive: there is a trade association, which collects a wide range of information.

B5 Cars has five manufacturing plants and 53 sales outlets in the country in which it operates. Information for the company's executive information system (EIS) is obtained both from internal sources such as the production plants and also external sources such as customers. Internally generated information is sent to head office over a wide area network.

Due to the overall escalating cost of the company's EIS and to the fact that the majority of the information is never used, the board has decided to collect only internally-produced information. This decision has been taken against the advice of the chief information officer.

Required

(a)   Explain why the company's EIS could be becoming expensive to operate.   **(7 marks)**

(b)   Evaluate the decision of the board to concentrate on internally-produced information. Clearly describe the information sources that will be lost and explain the effects on the company's information systems and its products.   **(8 marks)**

(Total : 15 marks)

Question 2

E-mail (Nov 98)

E-mail is becoming one of the most common forms of communication, both for sending messages within organisations and across the Internet.

Required

(a)   Discuss the impact of communication by e-mail on work practices.   **(15 marks)**

(b)   Discuss situations where e-mail would NOT be an appropriate communication medium.   **(10 marks)**

(Total : 25 marks)

Question 3

Monitored Websites (Nov 99)

LMC plc provides advice to a wide range of clients. This advice is based on the internal and external information systems maintained by LMC plc.

As a newly appointed management accountant at LMC plc, you have been reviewing the information produced by the different systems in the company.

A first evaluation shows that information produced from the older systems, including the EIS, is incomplete at best. However, more recent systems including Internet monitoring produce a considerable amount of information.

The Directors are always interested in the actions of competitors. LMC plc has a 24-hour on-line Internet link that monitors over 100 different websites, which are either maintained by competitors or provide information maintained by specialist companies. Any changes in the sites are recorded and reviewed by analysts on a daily basis.

Required

(a)   Explain how the analyst can check whether the information obtained from the monitored websites is accurate.   **(8 marks)**

(b)   The Directors have been concerned that the 24-hour on-line web monitoring mentioned above is expensive to maintain.

Explain how you, the management accountant at LMC plc, can determine the costs and benefits of information produced from the web monitoring activities.   **(17 marks)**

(Total : 25 marks)

Question 4

Information Centre (May 96)

JH plc trades in an overseas country, arranging freight forwarding contracts for up to 2,000 corporate clients. The company's mission is to be the most profitable freight forwarder in that country. The company is very profitable, partly due to its high investment in modern IT systems, and its narrow focus on its corporate mission.

The company's IT systems are supported by its Information Centre, which has a staff of 20. Although large, the centre is always well utilised.

In a recent corporate review, the Board of JH plc noted that the Information Centre was costing the company £4,000,000 per annum with no discernible income. The Board is therefore considering whether to close the Information Centre to improve the company's profitability.

The most recent addition to the computer system is a network that links all departments. It is anticipated that an increasing number of clients will send their requirements direct to the company via the company's gateway to the Internet.

Required

(a)   Write a memo to the Board to justify the continuance of the Information Centre on non-financial grounds.   **(12 marks)**

(b)   Explain how JH plc's Information Centre can provide an enhanced service to the staff of JH plc using the recently installed computer network within the company. **(8 marks)**

(Total : 20 marks)

Question 5

Information Characteristics (Nov 98)

The HZ hospital has recently invested in the most up-to-date computer systems to assist its doctors in making assessments of patients' illnesses. Two of the software packages now available to doctors are:

♦ a Management Information System (MIS), which provides information on the medical history of each patient. It includes detailed factual information on past illnesses and any recurring symptoms as well as the patient's name, address and other personal information.

♦ an Expert System (ES), which is used to assist in the diagnosis of current illnesses. The Expert System is linked to the MIS to obtain details on each patient's medical history. From this information, and symptoms of the current illness, the Expert System provides an initial diagnosis, which the doctor uses in making his recommendation for the treatment of the patient. The diagnosis is stated in terms of probabilities of what the illness could be, rather than giving definite conclusions.

Both systems are accessed and updated via a series of on-line terminals located at key points around the hospital. All terminals are linked directly to a central file server; there are no external communications links due to the sensitive nature of the information being held.

Required

(a)   Explain the differences in the characteristics of information being provided by the two systems.   **(16 marks)**

(b)   Describe three general conditions, which must exist in order for an Expert System to be appropriate.   **(6 marks)**

(c)   Outline three advantages of using Expert systems (other than speed and accuracy).
                                                                                     (3 marks)

(Total : 25 marks)

Question 6

Management Information (May 97)

RG Ltd manufactures industrial glues and solvents in a single large factory. Approximately 400 different inputs are used to produce the 35 specialist outputs, which range from ultra-strong glues used in aircraft manufacture to high-impact adhesives that are required on construction sites.

Two years ago, with the company only just breaking even, the directors recognised the need for more information to control the business. To assist them with their strategic control of the business, they decided to establish a MIS. This is now operational but provides only the following limited range of information to the directors via their networked computer system:

(i)   A summary business plan for this and the next two years. The plan includes details of the expected future incomes and expenditure on existing product lines. It was produced by a new member of the accounting department without reference to past production data.

(ii)   Stock balances on individual items of raw materials, finished goods etc. This report is at a very detailed level and comprises 80% of the output from the MIS itself.

3

(iii)   A summary of changes in total demand for glues and solvents in the market place for the last five years. This information is presented as a numerical summary in six different sections. Each section takes up one computer screen so only one section can be viewed at a time.

Required

(a)   (i)   Comment on the weaknesses in the information currently being provided to the directors of the company.   **(8 marks)**

       (ii)   Suggest how the information may be improved, with particular reference to other outputs, which the MIS might usefully provide to the directors.
                                                                                    (6 marks)

(b)   Explain what strategic information any MIS is unlikely to be able to provide. **(6 marks)**

                                                                              (Total : 20 marks)

Question 7

Meetings (Nov 96)

YK plc operates 20 factories, each of which manufactures and distributes dairy products within its surrounding region. The products are particularly subject to market forces and, as a result, decisions on the pricing and quality of the products are required on a daily basis. Each factory is controlled by a Managing Director and a Finance Director who together take all the operating and managerial decisions for that factory.

Every two weeks, all the Managing Directors and Finance Directors meet in a central location to discuss the results of each factory and to make plans for the coming two weeks. The information exchange is seen to be crucial by the senior executives of YK plc to ensure that the overall corporate strategy is maintained. The Directors also value the meeting because they can discuss various detailed operational problems informally with the Directors of the other factories.

For much of the past year, the senior executives of YK plc had been seeking an alternative to the two-weekly meetings. The reason for this was to avoid the high travelling costs and having all its Directors away from their factories for effectively a whole day, with a consequent lack of decision takers in the factories. As a result of this review, a new e-mail system was implemented with the full approval of the Directors. The result of this is that Directors can share information on a minute-by-minute basis if they want to, and the senior management can communicate strategic information straight to the Directors without waiting for the two-weekly meeting.

Although the implementation of the new systems did have the approval of the Directors, there is now some uncertainty that this was the correct decision. A number of Directors have started meeting Directors from other locations informally even though the e-mail and information-sharing systems should provide all the communication that they require.

Required

Explain the potential problems and benefits of using e-mail in YK plc. Your answer must include an explanation of why the Directors of YK plc are returning to face-to-face meetings on an informal basis.   **(Total : 20 marks)**

Question 8

Incorrect Information (May 98)

JS plc is a large manufacturing company. It operates from 10 different sites and produces a wide range of consumer goods. Within each site, each department (eg sales, production, stock control) maintains its own independent computer-based Transaction Processing and Management Information Systems. The computer systems within a site, or on different sites, cannot communicate with each other. The lack of communication is a result of different system implementation dates, operating systems, hardware platforms and substantial amendment by users of the software being used in each individual department.

JS plc is now experiencing significant increased demand for its products, and all systems, computerised and manual, are working excessively. A number of very large orders have recently been lost because managers made incorrect pricing and production decisions. This was surprising because managers obtained what they thought was up-to-date and accurate information from the company's computer systems when they were making the decisions. Subsequent investigation showed that the managers' decision-making process was not at fault: it was the information in the computer system itself that was incorrect.

Required

(a)   Explain why the information being provided by the computer systems could be incorrect. Make reference in your answer to the problems in JS plc's computer systems and the information being provided by the systems.   **(12 marks)**

(b)   Discuss how an information centre could help the company provide an acceptable standard of information to its managers.   **(8 marks)**

(Total : 20 marks)

Question 9

Information as a Valuable Commodity

PC Inc is an Internet service provider. This means that it allows customers to connect their computers to its own large computer system, normally via the telephone system. Customers then have access to a number of services, as explained below.

The company provides two types of services to its subscribers:

1   Information services

The company has recently established its own Web site, which is accessible by anyone using the Internet. The information provided here includes general information on company share prices, dividends declared etc and specialist information arising from research that PC Inc itself has undertaken. This specialist information is not generally available from other Internet service providers.

2   Communication services

The company also acts as an access point to the Internet. For a small monthly fee, customers can maintain their e-mail box on PC Inc's computer. Customers can access their mailbox or send mail to other people or companies. Access to the full World Wide Web (WWW) is also available. Payment for the WWW is by a combination of monthly fee and on-line access time.

PC Inc competes against other service providers in both of these markets.

Required

(a) Comment on the factors that PC Inc must take into account when setting prices for the information and communication services that it provides. **(13 marks)**

(b) Explain the factors that make information a valuable commodity, which means that a charge can be made for viewing the information. **(12 marks)**

(Total : 25 marks)

Question 10

Information Quality

To be effective, operational decision-makers require information that is of good quality.

Required

Explain why information provided to operational decision-makers may *not* be of good quality. Provide examples from your own experience and/or a business situation with which you are familiar. **(20 marks)**

Question 11

IS/IT Strategy

KLP plc are a large manufacturing company, who have developed computer systems over a number of years in response to business demands. The Managing Director believes that they need to develop an information systems and information technology strategy in order to address the long-term objectives of the organisation.

Required

Evaluate the case for KLP plc developing a strategy for information systems and information technology. **(Total : 20 marks)**

Question 12

IT Strategy (May 98)

Explain FIVE reasons why it is essential for a modern organisation to have an IT strategy. Illustrate your answer with examples of these reasons drawn from your own knowledge and experience. **(Total: 20 marks)**

Question 13

Information Systems (May 99)

The SFA Company manufactures clothing and operates from one location in a major city. It purchases cotton and other raw materials and manufactures these into garments of clothing, such as sweatshirts, T-shirts and similar articles in its factory. There are approximately 20 administration staff, 30 sales staff and 300 production workers. Although the company is profitable, three major concerns were raised at a recent Board meeting about the operations of the company:

(i)   The company does not always appear to obtain the best prices for raw materials, which has decreased gross profit in the last few years of trading.

(ii)   Many garments are made to order for large retail shops, but the company has spare capacity and so it maintains an active sales force to try and increase its total sales. However, the sales force does not seem to be making many sales because of lack of information about the garments in production and stocks of finished garments.

(iii) Some production is carried out using Computer Assisted Design and Manufacture although the company has found limited use for this application to date. The system was purchased in a hurry two years ago with the objective of keeping up with competitors who had purchased similar systems. The Board believes that greater use could be made of this technology.

The Value Chain model produced by Porter provides a good summary of the primary and support activities of the company. An adaptation of Porter's general model is shown below:

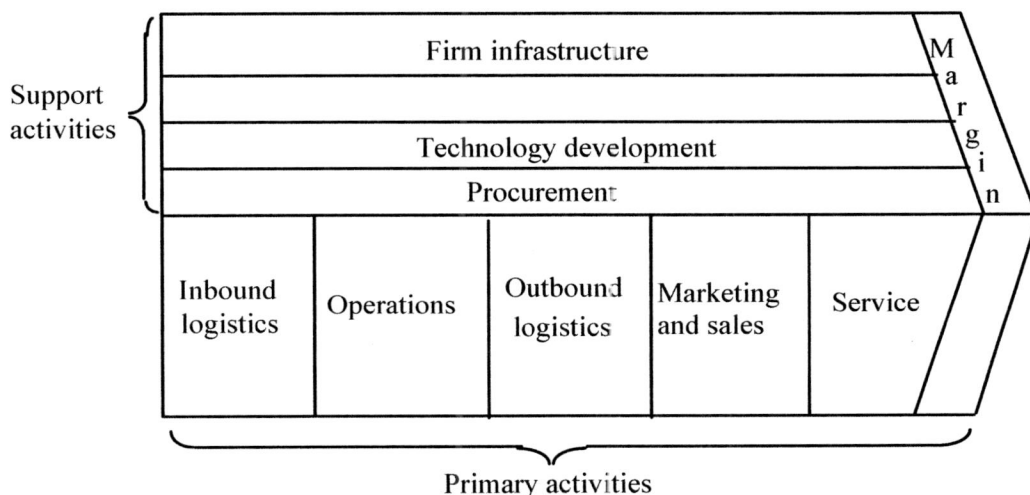

Primary activities

The Board of SFA is currently considering implementing some form of information system or systems, such as a MIS, into the company for all staff to use. Because of the perceived weaknesses in the current systems already mentioned, the directors are particularly interested in the areas of:

1   inbound logistics,

2   marketing and sales, and

3   technology development

Required

Explain:

(a)   what inputs will be needed for the information systems designed to support the operations of the business in the three areas mentioned above;   **(14 marks)**

(b)   what outputs will be required from those information systems.   **(6 marks)**

Note: Do NOT describe Porter's general model.   **(Total : 20 marks)**

Question 14

Website Information (May 99)

SK Products Ltd was established 65 years ago by two entrepreneurs to distribute tools and spare parts to the then small electronics industry. Since that time the company has expanded its product range to just over 100,000 items and supplies electronic and computer components to many major organisations. The components supplied range from small fuses and computer chips to complicated electrical assemblies requiring specialist knowledge to install.

The current directors pride themselves on the organisation's attention to the specific requests of customers and the personal and friendly service that all staff provide. Recent customer surveys show that a significant amount of repeat business is generated by good customer care, even though SK Products Ltd's prices can be higher than those charged by competitors.

The organisation is planning its first website. A review of competitors' sites shows that information provided is little more than an electronic catalogue. Repeat visits to the site are greeted with the same 'home page' whilst most of the information provided appears to be out-of-date.

SK Products Ltd currently supplies a catalogue every four months in paper format.

Required

(a)   Explain the advantages and disadvantages of SK Products Ltd providing information on a website rather than a paper-based catalogue. Ensure that your answer shows how a website can provide a more user-friendly presentation system than a paper-based catalogue.   **(14 marks)**

(b)   Explain what information SK Products Ltd can provide on its website to help customers install and use its products.   **(6 marks)**

(Total : 20 marks)

Question 15

Internet Opportunities

The Finance Director of a small cleaning company has asked you to suggest ways in which the staff might use the Internet to promote and sell the cleaning services.

Required

Outline the opportunities available to the organisation for using the Internet to increase business turnover.   **(14 marks)**

Question 16

EPOS and Database Systems (Nov 97)

HS plc is a large quoted company, which owns and maintains 42 large supermarkets in the country in which it operates. Each supermarket sells a very wide range of food and household goods to the general public.

There is a high level of competition from other supermarket groups.

HS plc has tended to be the industry leader in computerisation and has a corporate objective to offer the best computerised sales service to its customers. HS plc has introduced some computerisation in the stock and ordering systems, although there is no integrated system. Stock levels are high, being three days for perishable goods like milk and up to 28 days for tinned goods. This has resulted in a high stock-holding cost for the company.

HS plc is now considering an investment of over £50 million in the latest Electronic Point of Sale (EPOS) systems to maintain its competitive advantage. The databases associated with the system will be able to store information relating to stock levels of each product line, cash and bankings and even sales by individual customer. Information on HS plc's competitors indicates that they are also considering similar systems, but it will take at least two years to implement them. Because HS plc has already produced the initial feasibility study and systems specification, the company could have its system running within 10 months.

The Board of HS plc is meeting tomorrow to make the final decision on the investment. The Managing Director has indicated that he expects the investment to take place, but he would like to see a list of the benefits of the EPOS system, from both the strategic and operational viewpoints.

Required

Produce the report requested by the Managing Director, which can be used at the Board meeting.

The report must show clearly the strategic and operational benefits of the proposed EPOS and database systems and how these relate to HS plc.   **(Total : 20 marks)**

Question 17

Strategic Planning

Funtours is a firm of travel agents, employing 1,500 people in the UK and overseas. In the past, it has operated only as a broker, selling holidays run by package holiday firms. However, the managing directors have decided to go into the holiday business themselves. To avoid competing directly with some of their suppliers, Funtours will offer a bespoke service to customers who wish to have the flexibility that many package holidays do not have: Funtours will help customers design their itineraries and will do all necessary bookings as they wait. Each office will have a consultant to deal with such enquiries, and also head office will have a team of consultants to deal with enquiries over the phone and the Internet in real time.

The managing director, Sam White, believes that the critical success factors underlying this new business will be the following:

♦   The ability to charge a premium price for the service.

♦   The quality of advice offered by the newly trained consultants. They will have to be knowledgeable, experienced and adequately supported.

♦   Continued access to cheap flights, so that the service is profitable.

♦   The ability to make bookings swiftly.

♦   Efficient communications with hotels, transport providers and local agents in the destination countries.

♦   Identification of customer needs for future business.

Sam is well aware that information technology will be a major factor underpinning the success of the new project, and can also be used in the main travel agency business, which is becoming decreasingly profitable.

Funtours' existing information systems are these.

♦ A mainframe computer sited in the computer centre at head office, which carries out most of the heavy-duty processing (eg, booking, invoicing, payroll, cash book and treasury management, debtors and creditors ledgers). Bookings are processed in real time. Accounting information is batch processed at night.

♦ PCs at each branch, connected over leased lines to the head office mainframe deal with the bookings. Some users have been complaining about the constant delays in the system.

♦ 50% of the costs of the computer centre are charged out to each branch, by the number of bookings. Accounting and treasury processing is just written off as an overhead.

♦ Proposals for equipment and software upgrades are made every year. Most of the time, branches must submit proposals with their annual budget. If rejected in one year, they can be resubmitted to the budget committee.

♦ Information systems are the responsibility of the finance director, although for the new business a comprehensive review is proposed.

You have been employed as a management consultant to advise on the firm's use of IT.

Required

(a) Explain what 'strategic planning' means and why planning the IS/IT strategy is important. **(8 marks)**

(b) What role do information systems play in Funtours' existing activities and how will this change in future? Support your answer with reference to appropriate frameworks. **(12 marks)**

(Total : 20 marks)

Question 18

JD plc

JD plc operates 15 stores in a central European country, selling home improvement materials to individuals and small companies. The IT systems in each store are based on two large mainframes, one being used for all communications with Head Office including e-mail and Internet access (the 'communication mainframe') and the second maintaining all the store's transaction processing and information systems (the 'transaction mainframe'). The mainframes are linked, although this link is active only when the end-of-day backup is made.

Sales are made throughout each day by cash and credit card. Stock balances are updated in real time on the transaction mainframe. However, daily transaction data is stored on the transaction mainframe in RAM before being copied hourly to hard disk and then transferred to the communication mainframe for onward transmission to the backup computer at Head Office.

Staff in all stores have access to the company's internal e-mail system, as well as being able to send external e-mail and browse the Internet.

The existing IT backup and disaster plan for each of the stores includes the following features:

♦ A daily backup is taken from both mainframes at each store and copied offsite via a dedicated landline to a server at the company's Head Office located some distance away. Head Office maintains a system of on-site backup using exchangeable disk storage.

♦ All virus checking is carried out at each store where all external e-mails (ie, those that originate from outside JD plc) and Internet accesses are checked for viruses.

♦ Computers in each store are maintained by an Uninterruptible Power Supply (UPS) with automatic switching to a backup generator in the event of a power loss. Because of the less critical nature of the computer systems at Head Office (very little transaction processing is carried out) there is no UPS at Head Office.

The first annual service of the communication mainframe at one store (providing the backup and Internet access) is due and the computer will be switched off at 3.40 pm precisely. However, the two mainframes at this store were labelled incorrectly when they were installed. The current situation is that the communication mainframe label is on the transaction mainframe, and *vice versa*. This error has not been identified because the computers have never been switched off before (they have to be on-line 24 hours per day) and have never had any faults or problems requiring maintenance.

Required

Discuss the benefits and weaknesses of the IT backup and disaster plan at JD plc and suggest methods for alleviating any weaknesses that you identify. **(20 marks)**

Question 19
SKO plc

SKO plc owns a large number of small, retail shops. None of the shops uses electronic point of sales systems.

Each shop generates a substantial amount of data each week including:

♦ purchase invoices;

♦ copy sales receipts;

♦ details of prices charged;

♦ banking records; and

♦ summaries of prices in competing shops.

In an attempt to manage this volume of information, it is proposed that all documents will be transferred to a central information storage facility located in the middle of the country in which SKO plc operates. The facility will provide a secure environment for the data and also various outputs for use by SKO plc.

None of the shops currently shares data, and there are no plans to introduce any direct communication links between the shops. Each shop will continue to produce the daily reports that it requires. A shop will therefore not need to contact the central information storage facility for any information about its own normal operating activities. Information, such as comparative pricing reports between the shops in the SKO plc group, can be transferred back to the shops as required.

Two outputs from the central information storage facility will be

♦ information on other corporate entities, particularly regarding pricing policy; and

♦ summaries of the information held, including sales by region and estimated market share of each shop which SKO plc owns.

Required

(a) Critically evaluate the proposal to store information in a central location. **(14 marks)**

(b) Explain what action SKO plc will have to take regarding the Data Protection Act 1998 with respect to the two outputs mentioned. **(6 marks)**

(Total : 20 marks)

Question 20

JHD Inc

JHD Inc manufactures a wide range of products in a large number of different departments. Each department is a cost centre. IT is extensively integrated into the company with departments relying heavily on IT systems for their operational activities. The IT Department's work includes the implementation and servicing of equipment as well as central file maintenance.

The IT Department is therefore viewed as an essential service: its costs are charged to other departments as part of company general overhead. No other charge is levied on any department for its use of computer services.

The size of the IT overhead cost (approximately 10% of the total wages bill and 15% of indirect expenditure costs) has been concerning the Board of JHD Inc. Furthermore, some departments have implied that their overhead apportionment is too high for their use of the service and have been obtaining third-party quotes for providing this service. The Board is now re-considering the charging method used.

Required

(a) Contrast, from the point of view of the departmental managers, the alternative policies of charging the costs of the IT Department

♦ as part of company overheads, *and*

♦ on the basis of individual department usage. **(12 marks)**

(b) It is proposed that the basis on which usage of the IT Department is determined will be the amount of network traffic generated by each department. Network traffic relates to the amount of data transferred across the network each day in megabytes.

Required

Explain the problems associated with the proposal to charge the IT Department's cost on the basis of network traffic, and suggest an alternative approach that would solve these problems.

(8 marks)

(Total : 20 marks)

Question 21

KN Company

The KN Company manufactures a wide range of plastic mouldings. The mouldings are used in such diverse products as motor vehicles, garden furniture and children's toys. As a result of this variety, there are six different sales departments, a single manufacturing department and an ordering department. There is a separate IT service department, which provides basic IT services to all the other departments.

The company has established its IT systems within each individual department. Each department has its own computerised records and databases. The IT department of KN has been very successful in previous years in meeting IT systems requirements and in providing a high quality of service to each user department.

KN now wishes to set up one central sales database that can be used by all departments. The database will include, amongst other things, details of goods, customers and debtor analysis. This will mean that the individual databases in each department will be amalgamated into this central database.

Required

(a)   Explain the relative merits of the KN Company concentrating its data and information on individual departments compared with centralising its database.   **(14 marks)**

(b)   Evaluate the problems that the IT department may experience in amalgamating the company's data into one central database.   **(6 marks)**

Note: Your answer must concentrate on the data held by the company. Comments concerning hardware or the physical location of the database are NOT required.

(Total : 20 marks)

Question 22

Technological Infrastructure

Gerrard and Jones (G&J) is a specialised manufacturer of allergy-free cosmetics and toiletry products such as soap, shampoo and shower gel. Products are sold directly to account customers who largely comprise independent retail chemists and specialist health stores. G&J field sales staff periodically visit each customer, negotiate a stock replacement order and then enter the product order details on to a customer order sheet.

Order details are processed at G&J's computer centre and in due course the products are despatched to the customer using G&J's own fleet of delivery vehicles.

G&J is facing severe competition from the larger cosmetic manufacturers who are moving into the allergy-free cosmetic market and are targeting the larger retail outlets, which form part of G&J's customer base. The competition is offering lower costs, own branding if required, and a fast two-day order delivery facility. A number of key accounts have already been lost. The marketing director at G&J believes that the sales ordering system is acting as a major handicap in holding on to key accounts.

The existing method is very expensive, involving as it does a visit from a sales representative. Indeed on some of the smaller accounts a representative can drive for several miles to pick up a very small volume order. At the end of each day the sales representatives despatch the order sheet to the computer centre for batching, data input and subsequent processing. As so many orders from the retail outlets involve only a small number of product items, the distribution department has been holding processed orders until a large enough delivery batch is achieved to justify a visit to each customer area. The result, in some cases, is an order-to-delivery cycle of over five weeks leading either to stockouts at retailers or retailers keeping larger stock levels than should be necessary.

The marketing director is now of the view that a major strategic shift in information technology applications is essential for the longer-term survival of G&J. However he is not sure how this shift should be managed. For example: how prominent should be the role of G&J's existing computer staff?

Required

(a)   In the light of the marketing director's concern that IT is failing them, examine the view that the information technology used within G&J is far too important to be left only to computer specialists.   **(10 marks)**

(b)   Provide a briefing paper to the Marketing Director of G&J, which identifies the benefits to them, arising from the close integration of strategic planning and the supporting technological infrastructure.   **(15 marks)**

(Total : 25 marks)

Question 23

Facilities Management (Nov 99)

The directors of DS are not satisfied with the GDC Ltd facilities management company, which was contracted two years ago to run the IT systems of the company. At that time, the existing in-house IT development and support department was disbanded and all control of IT systems handed over to GDC Ltd. The appointment of GDC Ltd was relatively rushed and although an outline contract was agreed, no detailed service level agreement was produced.

Over the last few weeks, the number of complaints received from staff regarding the service has been increasing and the provision of essential management reports has not been particularly timely.

A recent exchange of correspondence with GDC Ltd failed to resolve the matter. Staff at GDC Ltd recognised the fall in standards of service, but insisted that it had met its contractual obligations. DS's lawyers have confirmed that GDC Ltd is correct.

Key features of DS's contract with GDC Ltd - a facilities management company:

The contract can be terminated by either party with three months' notice.

GDC Ltd will provide IT services for DS, the service to include:

♦ Purchase of all hardware and software

♦ Repair and maintenance of all IT equipment

♦ Help desk and other support services for users

♦ Writing and maintenance of in-house software

♦ Provision of management information

Price charged to be renegotiated each year but any increase must not exceed inflation, plus 10%.

Required

(a)   Explain, from the point of view of DS, why it might have received poor service from GDC Ltd, even though GDC Ltd has met the requirements of the contract.   **(12 marks)**

(b)   Explain the courses of action now available to DS relating to the provision of IT services. Comment on the problems involved in each course of action.   **(8 marks)**

(Total : 20 marks)

Question 24

Overcoming Barriers (May 97)

The Board of JH Ltd has become aware that there is no IT strategy in place within the company. A decision has therefore been made to establish a working group to produce an outline IT strategy. The group members are:

Senior manager - He does not have much knowledge of IT because he has avoided IT in general as he sees it as not providing him with any benefits for his particular job. He is actually quite fearful of IT. He is very task-orientated and dislikes wasting time on non-essential work. He is very good at producing overall policy directives.

IT professional - She has an excellent knowledge of mainframe computers and enjoys being in charge of a large IT department. Her knowledge has arisen from 20 years in computing. She has tended to ignore the recent shift towards end-user computing, believing that 'IT' is best handled by specialists. Although she has some knowledge of PCs, this is not complete. She has very little contact with the users of the information that the IT department produces. She believes that users should accept the information given and not make difficult demands on the department.

IT user - trainee accountant - He is a Final Level student, who has been working in various roles within the accounts function: this is his first major assignment. His agenda is to try and ensure that IT is used effectively and that all staff within the company can therefore use PC applications to support their work. He is already well-read on IT matters and is now looking to advance rapidly in the company by being the IT 'champion'.

Required

(a)   Comment on the disadvantages that could arise for JH Ltd by not having an overall IT strategy in place.   **(8 marks)**

(b)   Explain how the background of each individual in the working group may present barriers to the production of an IT strategy as required by the Board. Suggest how these barriers may be overcome.   **(12 marks)**

(Total : 20 marks)

Question 25

JBCC

JBCC, a local administrative authority, provides a range of services to individuals including welfare provision. JBCC has a total workforce of 2,450.

In the welfare department, JBCC employs 30 staff who visit individuals to assess their welfare requirements. This job means visiting individuals, who are normally low paid or facing difficult family circumstances, to find out whether they should receive financial assistance (sometimes termed 'benefits') from JBCC.

The area covered by JBCC has a very low population density. Staff may have to travel many kilometres between each appointment and may not return to their central office for days at a time.

Rules that determine whether people are entitled to financial assistance are complicated, with over 6,500 separate rules and 170 different forms to complete. These rules change frequently; three rules changing each week is not uncommon. Consistent application of rules is difficult because of benefit fraud, human error, constant changing of rules and time delays inherent in the system itself. Staff retention is low because of poor morale.

The existing IT system is a mainframe located at the headquarters of JBCC. The mainframe contains a database showing which benefits are due to which individuals. A list of the benefits due is printed out weekly and benefits are paid out according to the information on this list. The database is accessed and updated from 10 terminals located in the computer room itself. Staff normally update the database when they return from their visits to individuals requiring benefits.

JBCC has decided to establish a Decision Support System to assist its staff in the application of benefit rules to the situations of individuals. JBCC requires that staff should have access to the Decision Support System at any time during their working day.

Required

(a)   Describe the essential hardware and software necessary to establish the Decision Support System, explaining why each part is relevant in meeting the aims of JBCC.

(12 marks)

(b)   Explain how the new Decision Support System may enable JBCC to improve staff retention.   **(8 marks)**

(Total : 20 marks)

Question 26

WRF Inc

WRF Inc trades in a dynamic environment where it is essential that information is presented quickly and clearly to its staff. The information can come from the company's database or from other staff members. Significant processing of the information is also required on each individual's personal computer (PC) before effective decisions can be made.

WRF Inc intends to upgrade its computer system to improve speed and clarity of information. Each member of staff will have a PC linked to a local area network (LAN). Each PC will run Windows 2000 and a word processor and spreadsheet on its local hard disk. The network will be used for centralised backup, access to a central database, and storage of data files. The LAN will also be used for communication within the office by e-mail.

The systems analyst in charge of the project thinks that users will require a Pentium III processor running at 800 megahertz with 128 megabytes of RAM. The network will incorporate a central file server. He is pleased that the system 'will cost only $US 3,000 per user (about £2,000). The systems analyst is on a fixed-term contract, which terminates when the system installation is complete.

Users have broadly welcomed the move although they have not been formally told of the systems change. The requisitioning department of WRF Inc has now questioned the order for the computer hardware and software because of lack of authorisation from the Board.

Required

Write a report to the Board:

(a)   briefly explaining the systems development life cycle (SDLC); and

(b)   explaining why it is preferred to the situation outlined above as a means of providing a systems changeover for WRF Inc.   **(20 marks)**

Question 27

Library Direct Services (LDS)

Library Direct Services (LDS) is an organisation providing data to central and local government personnel. It maintains a database of

♦   all laws, both statute and case law,

♦   reports of proceedings in central government,

♦   comparative data on the services provided by local government in each region of the country,

♦   and some comparative data on services provided in different countries.

LDS allows access to this database 24 hours a day, 365 days a year. LDS is contractually obliged to provide this information within 30 minutes of receiving a request. All requests are received by telephone or e-mail.

The existing database is accessed primarily via command line input at DOS, which the database administrators can use quickly and efficiently. Any perceived or actual decrease in the usefulness of the database will mean that the administrators are unlikely to accept the system.

Over the years, a number of small, but significant modifications have been made to the original 'off the shelf' database software. It is essential to retain these if the database is to be used, although the programmer who made these changes has left the company and has not been replaced. Program changes are not fully documented.

LDS is now asking for tenders from database suppliers to upgrade the database to Windows functionality. This is likely to involve re-writing the database itself and implementing a new Database Management System. LDS needs to make a decision on which company to choose to make this change for them. For budgetary reasons, any proposed change must be completed within the next six months.

Required

Provide six questions that LDS can use to help evaluate potential suppliers for the systems change contract explained above.

Explain why each of these questions is relevant to the specific circumstances of LDS. **(20 marks)**

Question 28

Homeworking (May 97)

CP Ltd is a small but successful company, which specialises in selling car and home insurance to individuals. All sales are made over the telephone, and there are no personal callers to the company's offices. The company employs 25 staff, 22 in the telephone sales department and the remaining 3 running all the accounts and administration functions. As a consequence of its recent success in the market, CP Ltd is planning to expand its operations.

The company has been evaluating its cost structure and has discovered that the cost of providing office space for each worker is £3,500 per annum. New workers would require office space with a cost per worker of £4,000 per annum. This amounts to a significant cost in the company's operating budget. The Management Accountant has calculated that 90% of office costs can be avoided if the telephone sales staff worked from their homes. This idea has, so far, been discussed only at board level.

At present, employees appear to enjoy working in the office, where they spend most of their time using the telephone and computer system to sell insurance. Coffee and lunch breaks are normally spent in the rest area where staff also compare some notes and queries concerning their jobs. All the data that they need to perform their job is otherwise available on the computer system. This data includes:

♦ records on each customer,

♦ access to a value added network (VAN) providing costs of insurance from other companies which sell insurance,

♦ word-processing and other systems for producing letters and insurance quotes to customers.

The proposal to work from home was put to staff last week and this has met with some initial resistance although the Management Accountant stressed that this proposal was only a possibility.

Required

Write a report to the Managing Director explaining:

(a)   from the viewpoint of the staff, the potential benefits that will be gained by homeworking. Explain the concerns that staff may have over homeworking and whether the IT infrastructure can help alleviate these concerns;   **(12 marks)**

(b)   what can be done to encourage staff to accept the proposed change.   **(8 marks)**

(Total : 20 marks)

Question 29

Intranet (Nov 99)

CC plc is a company employing 2,560 staff in 20 different offices within one country. The company offers a wide range of specialist consultancy advice to the building and construction industry. This includes advice on materials to be used, relevant legislation (including planning applications) and appropriate sources of finance.

The information to meet client requirements is held within each office of the company. Although most clients are serviced by a single office, a lot of the information used is duplicated between the different offices. This is not surprising given that legislation and other standard information such as details of materials used are the same for the whole country.

In the past there has been no attempt to share data because of the cost of transferring information and the lack of trust on the part of staff in other offices. Some senior managers tend to keep part of client data confidential to themselves.

The company has recently provided all employees with e-mail for communications within CC plc and to clients. Software with Internet access is also available so that staff can obtain updated planning information from appropriate websites. The hardware in the company is quite old and only just meets the minimum specification for these purposes.

The Marketing Director has suggested that an Intranet should be established in the company so that common information can be shared rather than each office maintaining its own data. This suggestion is meeting with some resistance from all grades of staff.

Required

(a)   Explain the objectives of an Intranet and show how the provision of an Intranet within CC plc should result in better provision of information.   **(6 marks)**

(b)   Comment on the organisational and human reasons why information may not become more widely available in CC plc, and suggest methods for overcoming these problems.
                                                                                        (14 marks)

                                                                          (Total : 20 marks)

Question 30

Information Overload (May 00)

The JB Company provides specialist information services to organisations which do not have either the staff expertise or financial resources to maintain an information services department.

Information provided ranges from weather forecasts (both regional and national) to railways and airlines, stock market information to stockbrokers and general news bulletins to major TV and radio stations.

Information is collected by the JB Company through a variety of systems including Internet monitoring, reports from employees from any of the 129 offices worldwide, on-line links to stock markets, reviews of newspapers from around the world and monitoring of news reports on TV and radio. Most information is reviewed and summarised by a team of specialist information analysts, so only the appropriate highlights are sent to clients.

Mr A is one of the senior account managers in the JB Company. It is his responsibility to ensure that his clients receive appropriate information, and that he is up-to-date with information supplied to those clients should queries arise. Mr A therefore receives information from a variety of sources including:

♦   e-mail messages from staff and clients. Between 30 and 40 e-mails are received on a typical day.

♦   telephone calls from information analysts and clients. The information analysts require strategic decisions regarding the information to provide to clients, while clients may telephone to request clarification on information received.

- ♦ detailed information from the company's databases and Intranet connections.

- ♦ detailed information from Internet sites which Mr A reviews every hour or so during the day.

- ♦ verbal reports from staff who prefer to see Mr A face-to-face rather than use the telephone or

- ♦ e-mail systems.

Mr A believes that he is suffering from information overload.

Required

(a)   Explain what is meant by information overload, and how this could affect the working efficiency of Mr A.   **(10 marks)**

(b)   Describe the IT and manual procedures that could be used to reduce the information overload on Mr A.   **(10 marks)**

(Total : 20 marks)

Question 31

Implementation Problems (May 00)

Q Ltd is a successful company that sells computers to personal and business purchasers.

The company used to operate a structure where each sales representative was responsible for his or her own customers, with commission being paid on all sales made. Representatives maintained their own database of information to which only they had access. The system worked well; the only complaint from customers was that when their sales representative was not available, information about their particular requirements could not be obtained. About a year ago, it was found that some orders were being lost to a major competitor because customers were refusing to wait for their sales representative to be available to provide information before an order could be placed.

Six months ago, Q Ltd implemented a new Information System based on a company-wide Intranet. The system was designed to enable all sales representatives to share information on customers; the main aim of the system was to enable any representative to access any customer details and so limit loss of orders.

The system was implemented after obtaining user input to try and ensure that the system was appropriate to the needs of those users. However, the system was implemented in some hurry, so final user acceptance and validation was not possible. In fact, some last-minute changes were made by the programmers who made the programs run faster on the computer at the expense of some of the user-friendly interfaces. Because of scheduling problems with annual holidays, most users also missed being trained on the new system.

Unfortunately, the system was not particularly well received by staff. In fact, six months after implementation, it is rarely used and most representatives have reverted to using their own individual databases.

Required

(a)   Explain the reasons why representatives may have stopped using the new system.

(8 marks)

(b)   Explain the actions that can now be taken to try and persuade representatives to use the new system.   (12 marks)

(Total : 20 marks)

Question 32

Human Problems (May 98)

M O'B is the Management Accountant of a small company. He is responsible for:

♦   the preparation of the monthly management accounts and annual budgets for the company,

♦   the preparation of the year-end financial statements,

♦   maintenance of the company's Executive Information System (EIS) and transaction processing systems,

♦   the hiring of staff and negotiation of pay and working conditions with each member of staff, and

♦   preparing and agreeing the company's taxation returns with the relevant authorities (this includes VAT, income and corporation taxes).

The Board of Directors requires a monthly report from M O'B on all of the above matters. M O'B has a staff of two junior accountants to assist him; they are currently studying for their examination. Although they work hard, M O'B finds that they do not always have the detailed knowledge to assist him sufficiently in all of his areas of responsibility.

The company's computer system is used to maintain the transaction processing systems, which form part of the statutory books of account. The separate computerised EIS does provide some useful information, but it is not always up-to-date. The systems are well maintained with the hardware supplier providing on-site maintenance on a regular basis.

M O'B is now working excessive amounts of overtime and has not taken a holiday in the last 18 months. The Board is concerned because recent Board reports have contained a number of minor errors, some purely arithmetical, but others where incorrect or out-of-date information has been used. The junior accountants are demotivated because they do not consider they are receiving sufficient responsibility for their level of knowledge or time spent within the company.

Required

Explain the human problems that the Management Accountant is facing.

Describe what human and IT solutions might help alleviate these problems.   (Total : 20 marks)

Questions 33 to 35 - TEP plc (May 98)

Read the scenario before answering the questions.

Background

TEP plc runs a theme park offering a wide range of activities including rides, shows and parades. The rides vary from 'thrill' rides, where visitors sit in vehicles, which travel around a hilly track at high speed, to slow electric-powered cars in which children can drive around. Visitors pay an entrance fee, which gives them unlimited access for one day to the park's activities. The average entry price is £16 and the park received 2.6 million visitors in 1999. It employs about 6,000 staff for about 9 months of the year: the park closes during a season of poor weather.

It is considered to be the most popular park in the country in which it operates, although in recent years it has tended to attract more young adults and fewer families with younger children. Market research undertaken by TEP plc indicates that families tend to avoid the park because there are very few attractions for children below the age of 10. Many of the technologically advanced rides built by TEP plc have age and height restrictions, making them unsuitable for young children.

The objectives of TEP plc are to

♦   maintain net profit margins at 10%; and

♦   offer the most technologically up-to-date rides.

The company has met these objectives during its last seven years of operation. However, a number of other parks have opened in recent years, offering similar state-of-the-art attractions and rides. These parks have placed considerable competitive pressure on TEP plc. The main area of competition between the parks is in providing the most technologically advanced ride possible, whilst at the same time making the ride sufficiently attractive for customers to want to return to the park to go on the ride again. As a result of this competition, the average cost of providing a new ride is £6 million with annual maintenance costs running at 10% of this amount.

Current information systems

The theme park's information system was installed seven years ago and has received only minor modifications since then. It concentrates on collecting information concerning:

♦   customers entering the park, including cash collection and banking (payment is accepted by cash and credit cards),

♦   stock and sales control of the retail outlets, and

♦   the numbers of customers using each ride.

The Directors' Executive Information System was also installed seven years ago. The EIS is linked to the park's information system, providing the ability to view the daily totals from this system. In the early 1990s, this was considered to be the only data that the Directors required from the computer systems. The Directors now hardly ever use the EIS.

Both the EIS and the park information system are backed up daily with the backup disks being kept in a fireproof safe in the ticket office on site.

Although there are plans to advertise the park on the World Wide Web, the project has been delayed.

Investment decision in 2000

After a substantial review of the theme park market, TEP plc has identified what it considers to be a new area where competitive advantage can be obtained. At present, all the theme parks in the country only offer facilities at the park itself. The board of TEP plc believes that the company should:

♦ build a modern hotel within the park offering accommodation for families with children,

♦ offer a complete holiday package to customers including travel arrangements, accommodation at the hotel, special offers like early entry to the park and souvenirs such as special mugs,

♦ provide more shows and rides suitable for younger children to encourage more families to visit the park, and

♦ purchase a specialist travel agency to provide the holiday package service.

The cost of this investment would be in the region of £6 million, although the hotel would not be operational until the 2001 season.

If the investment is undertaken, it is expected that the travel agency will be able to

♦ access the new hotel's computer system to book accommodation via an Internet connection

♦ provide details of special events directly from TEP plc's theme park Web Site, and

♦ provide an on-line booking and payments system through its own Web Site for customers who prefer using the Internet to book their holiday.

If the hotel investment is made, then no new ride would be produced in 2000. The policy of building one new ride per year would be re-introduced in 2001.

As an alternative, TEP plc could continue its present policy of investing in one major new ride each year. This would help it maintain its position of being the most technologically advanced park in the country. The ride under consideration is a virtual reality simulator of a spaceship crashing into one of Saturn's moons. It will cost £6.2 million to develop and build. So far, no other theme park has considered using Virtual Reality on such a large scale.

The Board must choose between these two investment decisions by the end of June this year.

Question 33
Sources of Information

Identify possible sources of internal and external information that could be used to assist the directors of TEP plc in choosing between the two investment decisions.

Explain why each source of information is relevant to the decision-making process.

(Total : 20 marks)

Question 34

Executive Information System

Assuming that the first investment alternative is taken up, ie including the building of the hotel and the purchase of the travel agency:

Required

Explain the changes that need to be made to the EIS and the information it provides, to enable the Directors of TEP plc to receive the information needed to evaluate the success of this investment. **(Total : 15 marks)**

Question 35

Communicating via the Internet

Comment on the effect on society and on working practices within the organisation of the decision of many companies to concentrate their advertising and booking systems on the Internet. 'Booking' in this context means customers being able to access TEP plc's computer system via an Internet connection, and then choosing and paying for their park visit using only the computer system. **(Total : 15 marks)**

(Total : 50 marks)

Questions 36 to 39 - LT plc (Nov 99)

Brief Organisation History

LT plc provides telecommunication services ranging from residential telephones to large corporate Intranets. The organisation has 20 million customers and a turnover of several billion pounds. Most customers are satisfied with the level of service received. The main area of concern for customers has been that pricing structures are not always clear and appear to favour individual corporate customer needs rather than residential markets.

Over the past few years, LT plc has built up an unparalleled analogue telephone communication network, which it owns and maintains itself. Most other telecommunication companies, including new entrants into the market, lease or rent at least part of their communication network. LT plc has been able to offer more reliable services and fault-fixing times than any other company.

In recent years, LT plc has also been the dominant market leader with over 90% market share in all of its business sectors. However, deregulation of the telecommunications market from 1 January 1998 has meant that its monopolistic power has been significantly weakened in many areas. The Board of LT plc has tended to see this as a threat rather than an opportunity. The view arose partly from a fear of losing market share and partly because information systems were internally focused and so could not provide the necessary competitor information.

One way the Board of LT plc sought to maintain market share has been by forming strategic alliances with similar telecommunications companies in other countries. This strategy has been largely successful, with profits being maintained from these international ventures. However, as a result of IT strategy and information systems being focused on overseas markets, very little attention was paid to the domestic competition or investment during 1998 or the earlier part of 1999.

Other competitive challenges

LT plc is now facing intense competition in its home market from a small number of new companies, which will be able to offer new services including:

♦ digital television,

♦ Internet on TV, and

♦ films on demand.

All these services are being provided over new fibre-optic telephone lines, which LT plc has not invested in significantly. However, no one organisation currently offers all services as a comprehensive package and LT plc currently is considering providing this service.

LT plc is also finding it difficult to obtain information on the home market. The development of its Executive Information Systems (EIS) has followed the strategy of the company, providing summary and detailed information about overseas competitors. This has had the effect of losing focus on the home market.

LT plc is facing competitive challenges not only from additional services that are being offered, but also from a significant amount of cross selling of services. For example, a competing company recently offered a telephone service including access to the five main satellite television channels for the price of LT plc's domestic telephone service. LT plc's market share is now being eroded in all areas partly because the company cannot match the offers on price terms and partly because of the time taken to make strategic decisions to offer competing services.

Integrated digital service

In the near future it is expected that telecommunications companies will be able to provide a fully integrated service of traditional telephone, digital cable TV, Internet access and home shopping. This service should be available by 2001. The system effectively means that consumers, in the domestic and overseas markets, could order their shopping, browse the Internet, view films on demand and make telephone calls, possibly with integrated video, from their living room.

LT plc's response to the competitive challenge

In an attempt to provide more timely decisions and meet the expected demand for new services, in August 1999 the Board of LT plc set up 4 autonomous business units within the organisation. Each unit was to focus on a specific market such as large corporate organisations, domestic users etc. Each unit was to report back to the Board by December 1999 with an indication of the problems faced by that unit and recommendations for resolving those problems. Early indications are that there are common problems facing all units. These problems include:

♦ A lack of information on how to set prices for new services.

♦ Lack of understanding on how to use the existing IT system to stop the fall in market share.

♦ Lack of available capacity in the existing IT infrastructure (bandwidth) to provide enhanced services to domestic customers.

♦ Lack of key critical success factors for each business unit.

♦ Lack of understanding on the social and economic impact of the enhanced services on society.

The Board of LT plc is starting to consider these issues and has requested more information.

Question 36

Information Sources Required

Explain the sources of information that can be used to assist in the setting of prices for the future integrated digital service. Show why each source of information is required by LT plc.

(18 marks)

Question 37

Integrated Service

Discuss the possible effects that an Integrated Digital Service, as outlined in the scenario, could have on employment and society. **(16 marks)**

Question 38

Supporting Strategy

Discuss the problems that LT plc is facing because its systems are not sufficiently supporting the business strategy of re-focusing onto the home market. Describe the actions that can be taken to overcome these problems. **(14 marks)**

Question 39

Improved Decision-Making

Explain what type of information an EIS could provide and show how this would improve decision making for the Board of LT plc. **(12 marks)**

(Total : 60 marks)

Questions 40 to 42 - ARG (Nov 96)

ARG is an international airline operator, based in a central European country. It maintains a fleet of approximately 350 aircraft, and its core activity is to provide passenger and freight services to over 200 destinations worldwide.

ARG maintains offices in each country to which its aircraft fly. Each office provides the following services.

♦   Information provision on the airline services offered by ARG, including flight times and destinations serviced by ARG

♦   Access to ARG's passenger and freight booking system for customers who wish to book either passenger or freight carriage services with ARG.

Each office also has access to ARG's confidential internal data systems, which provide information on aircraft location, servicing history and the company's personnel. The latter includes salary details as well as staff locations.

Systems specification - to support its core business activity, ARG recently invested in a high-speed international wide area network (WAN). This system enabled ARG to transfer large volumes of data relating to its operations between its 200 offices world-wide with a minimum of delay. The systems specification for the new ARG system was rigorous.

The specification included the following requirements.

♦ The basic infrastructure of the WAN, including such items as the cabling and communication hardware, had to have an expected life of 10 years.

♦ Computer chips and other similar system elements had to be upgradable as technology improved.

♦ The entire system had to be easily upgradable, with a fixed capital amount being allocated for this upgrade each year. System upgrades were not to exceed this capital amount under any circumstances.

ARG also assumed that its WAN infrastructure and its core business as an international airline operator would remain unchanged for the next 10 years. Very few equipment suppliers were willing to provide this level of commitment to the system. Finally, a small but financially stable company called AP Ltd successfully tendered for the contract, even though some of AP Ltd's systems were not industry standard.

Systems implementation - the actual systems changeover and implementation were performed with few problems. The staff at ARG were able to use the new system efficiently within one week of implementation.

It should be noted that the Board of ARG made the decision to invest in the WAN on the basis that the company must be at the forefront of the use of technology to support its core business activities. This strategy is seen as being essential to produce a sustainable competitive advantage in the airline industry.

Post-implementation review - in the three months since the system was installed ARG has seen significant increases in productivity and levels of customer service. The investment has therefore been judged to be a success.

During the post-implementation review of the system, it was found that the WAN had considerable excess capacity to take additional network traffic. ARG's initial forecast showed that it would use only one third of the capacity of the network in its first two years of operation. Even optimistic forecasts of network traffic growth indicate that this excess capacity would not be used by ARG for at least another seven years. The board of ARG therefore asked the IT Director to consider ways of providing additional revenue to the company from this excess capacity.

After detailed consideration of the problem the IT Director reported back to the board. The main proposal was to make this excess capacity available to other companies which required a WAN but either did not have the money, or the strategy, to build a WAN for themselves. Should the proposal be accepted, then it is expected that these other companies would require:

♦ A guarantee of the level of service that they can expect from ARG, including access rights to the WAN and delivery times of information across the network.

♦ Internet access to transfer data to customers and receive information back from customers.

♦ A guarantee of data security both from non-ARG WAN users and from the staff of ARG itself.

The IT Director considers that ARG could provide this service, whilst at the same time making a positive contribution to profits. The board has therefore decided to accept the IT Director's proposal and make the required investment to provide the additional services noted above. This decision was made against the advice of a minority of Board members who saw potential conflicts between the core business strategy and the IT strategy of ARG.

Question 40

IT Strategy for Large Companies

Required

(a)   Explain why large companies should have an IT strategy. You should make reference to ARG's situation in your explanation.   **(8 marks)**

(b)   Comment on the decision of ARG to diversify away from its core business by making the WAN services available to other users. Explain the potential advantages and disadvantages this will provide for the company.   **(12 marks)**

Question 41

Information Characteristics

Required

Explain the characteristics that information provided across the ARG WAN, to ARG offices, must have. Show why these characteristics are relevant to ARG.   **(10 marks)**

Question 42

Internet Access

(a)   Evaluate the potential dangers and benefits, both to ARG and to its potential WAN users, of providing Internet access.   **(10 marks)**

(b)   Explain how ARG can provide adequate data security to the companies which are paying to use its WAN. You should consider the potential security problems posed by other WAN customers, by ARG's airline customers and by the employees of ARG itself.   **(10 marks)**

(Total : 50 marks)

Question 43

MQS Ltd (May 96)

MQS Ltd produces specialised industrial chemicals to individual customer orders. Each order is treated as a separate project under the control of three distinct management tiers:

(a)   The *Production Managers* who are responsible for the making of the product, although they have no control over the input mix or the quality of input used. Each product is made from a large number of chemicals and is very sensitive to any change in the quality of the inputs. To maintain a high quality of output, frequent adjustments are required to the input product mix. These adjustments alleviate any fall in quality caused by changes in the quality of the inputs.

(b)   The *Senior Managers* who work in the company's main office. The senior managers collate and produce weekly management reports on the progress of projects for which they are responsible. The reports recommend actions to the Chief Accountant although he must authorise these decisions before they can be implemented.

(c)   The *Chief Accountant* who approves changes to the costing of projects, and the quality of inputs and the input mix used.

Order and production process

Each customer order takes four months to complete from the initial receipt of the order at MQS Ltd. The order and production process involves four stages, each stage taking approximately one month. Each stage is followed in sequential order with, no time overlap.

(a)   *Quotation:* Drafting of a detailed quotation and input requirements listing for agreement with the customer. Only 1% of orders are cancelled during this time, and an initial input requirement can be available in as little as two days, including pricing from standard price lists issued by suppliers.

(b)   *Material ordering:* A price enquiry is sent to three suppliers, who each return a firm quote including quantity discounts not available on standard price lists. A quote has to be accepted by the chief accountant before the approved purchase order can be raised, and goods delivered from the supplier. Goods are ordered from one of three competing suppliers. The order is given to the supplier with the lowest quote. Goods are then available ex-stock. MQS Ltd employs a staff of 10 to negotiate prices and saves on average £25,000 per annum in the process, compared to the standard price offered on trade price lists.

(c)   *Production:* Production itself takes about one week. Quality control checks take about three weeks.

(d)   *Packaging and shipping:* Specialised containers for the delivery of the goods are ordered. Two weeks later these containers are delivered, and the goods are checked into the container. Another week is taken up in organising a specialist courier firm to collect and deliver the goods.

Information for Senior Manager report production

The main weekly report available to senior managers from the computer system includes the following information:

MQS Ltd					
Production report - Week to 30 April 2001					
Report date: 19 May 2001					
Project	*Production cost per batch*	*Profit for week*	*Manufacturing cost*	*Cost to date*	*Sales value*
A	453.98	2,563.98	10,002.43	777,734.90	1,000,000
B	664.23	655.83	8,444.93	76,339	500,000
C	6.34	27,736.9	57,223.94	299,433.93	750,000
D	266.87	17,117.28	38,339	89,222.9	350,000

Project A - input mix		Cost	Stock at 30 April
Material X	453 tonnes	4.53	34
Material Y	65 tonnes	877.30	233
Material Z	477 tonnes	500.00	78

Each report has a separate line for each project that the *Senior Manager* controls. The input mix information is repeated for each product.

Additional information concerning the printout above:

(a)   Information on the reports is manually transferred by *senior managers* onto their own summary reports.

(b)   Reports are regularly sent by the company's electronic mail (e-mail) system. Many *senior managers* see e-mail as a hindrance, forcing them to review reports on-screen and waste time as the reports are printed out. As a result, their e-mail is not regularly reviewed. When they do review reports on e-mail, the senior managers tend to be in a hostile frame of mind, resulting from their dissatisfaction with the system.

Senior managers must produce a report for the *chief accountant* on a weekly basis, which shows the progress on each of their projects to a high level of detail. The reports recommend actions to the *chief accountant,* including those relating to input mix and quality of inputs. The *chief accountant* then approves changes to the costing of projects and authorises decisions on input mix and quality before they are implemented.

Additional information on senior managers' reports

To assist them in their report writing, senior managers also collect information from the following sources:

(a)   verbal reports from production managers who produce the chemicals;

(b)   technical journals providing details of chemical formulae and tolerances for manufacture of those chemicals *(senior managers* normally purchase these journals themselves); and

(c)   a weekly production meeting.

The company's own technical database is used infrequently due to poor access for *senior managers* and the confusing presentation of information.

Office environment

All the *senior managers* work in a large open-plan office of 50 people. Printers are not sound-proof and the main form of communication is by telephone. Each *senior manager* is involved with a large number of projects requiring daily managerial input.

MQS Ltd is considering whether to implement a business change (business process re-engineering project) for its ordering and production process.

Required

(a)   Assess how effective the production report is in assisting *senior managers* with their decision-making. Explain the weaknesses you identify in the format and method of transmission of the report, AND propose amendments to overcome these weaknesses.

You are NOT required to re-draft the report.   **(12 marks)**

(b)   Identify the weaknesses in the company's current provision of information to *senior managers* explaining how these weaknesses affect their decision-making ability.

Suggest how these weaknesses may be overcome.   **(20 marks)**

(c)   Assume that MQS Ltd will change its ordering and production process.

(i)   Describe two critical success factors that can be used to judge the success of the change.   **(6 marks)**

(ii)   Explain the potential benefits of the change to MQS Ltd as a company, and to the staff employed by MQS Ltd.   **(14 marks)**

(iii) Explain how time could be saved within the order and production process.

Provide a detailed estimate of the new production time from the receipt of the order from the customer to the delivery of the finished goods.   **(8 marks)**

(Total : 60 marks)

Question 44

SF Group (May 97)

Company background

The SF Group is in the food processing and production business. The group comprises 42 companies, each of which specialises in a particular food. For example, some companies manufacture sweets and confectionery whilst others produce bread, drinks or other basic consumer foods.

One of the companies in the group, JTK Ltd, produces bread, cakes and similar products. It produces 3 million loaves of bread each day and supplies 15% of the total bread demand for the country in which it operates. JTK Ltd's strategy is to sell as much bread as possible, making only a small margin on each loaf sold. This strategy has worked well in the past because most customers base their decision to purchase bread more on the price than the quality of the product.

Over the past 20 years, JTK Ltd has had two instances of adverse publicity about the quality of its bread. As a result of these, JTK Ltd ensured that the quality of the product was improved and quickly regained its market share.

Production process

The bread manufacturing system is based on the feedback model. This is shown on the diagram below:

```
                                                    ┌─────────────────────────┐
                                                    │ Quality control         │
                                                    │ information inputs       │
                          ┌──────────────────────┐  │ - Historical information │
                          │ Input mix standards   │◄─┤   from JTK Ltd           │
                          │                       │  │ - Professional knowledge │
                          │ Set by the company    │  │   from staff employed in │
                          │ Amended on a monthly  │  │   the quality control    │
                          │ basis                 │  │   dept.                  │
                          └──────────────────────┘  └─────────────────────────┘
```

Input mix standards — Set by the company. Amended on a monthly basis

Quality control information inputs
- Historical information from JTK Ltd
- Professional knowledge from staff employed in the quality control dept.

Company standards

Raw material purchases

Raw materials purchased when stock falls below EOQ.

EOQs have remained unchanged for 15 years

Standard information

Quality control department

Compares the samples of bread to the company standards which ensures ingredients meet legal requirements for artificial additives

Hours of work: 12 noon to 10.00pm

'Control' loaves

Quality control

10 loaves are taken from the start of the production run

'Control' loaves

Raw materials from store

Inputs

The main inputs are: flour, yeast, salt and various artificial additives and flavours

Transfer to production

Production

All raw materials are combined in a set formula to produce the bread.

Production takes place overnight and is complete by 4am. Old machinery makes quantity of input difficult to manage towards the end of the production run.

Bread

Finished goods

All goods are despatched and sold on the day after production due to the perishable nature of the product

Goods sold

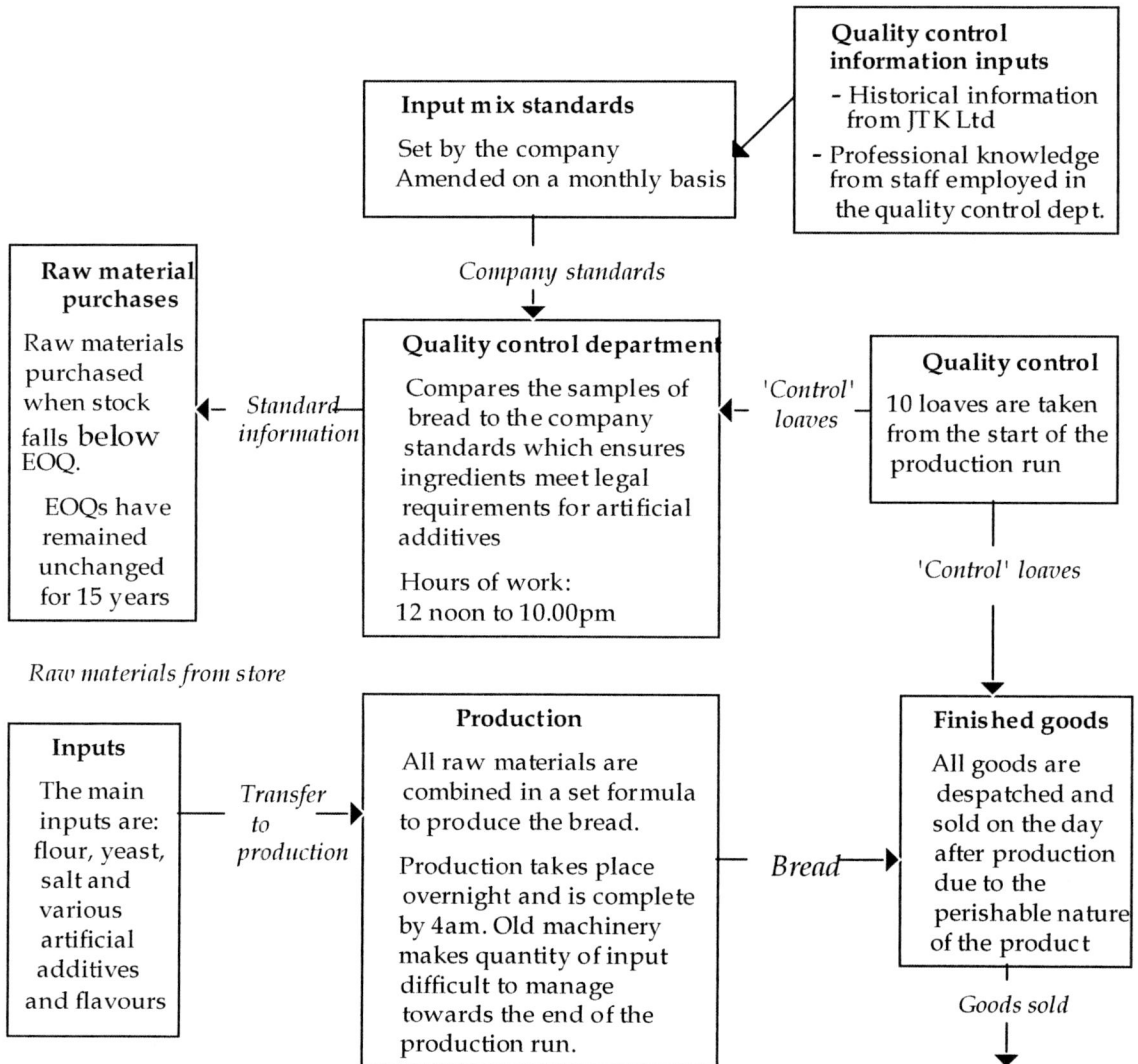

Average raw material stocks have shown a small but marked increase over the last five years although suppliers have improved the efficiency of their delivery systems.

The production process is operating at full capacity.

Different staff work in the quality control department each day, on a rotation basis. Results from the day's quality control checks are pinned to a notice board along with summaries of changes to input mixes and any problems. This attempts to ensure that information concerning each day's quality control checks reaches the staff working on the next day.

Board opinions and market trends

Janice, a recently qualified and newly appointed Management Accountant, has obtained a copy of a market survey into the bread market. The survey predicts that:

♦ the demand for basic cheap bread will change in the next three years in line with the following information:

Probability	Demand
0.1	Increase by 10%
0.3	Decrease by 10%
0.3	Decrease by 15%
0.2	Decrease by 25%
0.1	Decrease by 35%

♦ over the same timescale, it is certain that demand will increase for breads containing fewer artificial additives and for speciality breads (like bread with fruit or honey in it) although the extent of the increase in demand cannot be quantified.

JTK Ltd cannot make any of these breads with its current production system. To make these breads, JTK Ltd would need to invest in new capital equipment and computer-controlled monitoring systems for this equipment. This investment would replace the existing capital equipment and provide some additional production capacity.

Janice took this information to a Board meeting and presented it in a fairly forceful manner in support of her recommendation for investment in new specialised capital equipment. The other Board members were very sceptical of it. They are of the opinion that the company has made profits over the last 20 years and will continue to do so in the future. They consider that the market research information is incorrect and plan to invest a significant amount of money in new capital equipment to continue production in its present form. Janice believes that the capital investment must be directed towards new computer systems and specialised capital equipment that will enable JTK Ltd to produce the breads that are increasing in demand.

NOTE: *No knowledge of actual bread production processes is required to answer this question.*

Required

(a) State and discuss the different sources of information that could be referred to by the management of JTK Ltd in order to monitor the quality of bread that is being supplied. Give examples of the information, which each source might provide. **(14 marks)**

(b) Explain the limitations of controlling the production process as a 'closed loop' system. Clearly explain any weaknesses that are inherent in JTK Ltd's system. **(18 marks)**

(c) Explain the limitations of using the information concerning future demand contained in the market research survey. **(8 marks)**

(d) Comment on the financial Critical Success Factors and Performance Indicators that JTK Ltd can use to justify expenditure on its capital equipment as proposed by the new Management Accountant. Comment on any problems that might arise with using these CSFs and PIs. **(12 marks)**

(e) Comment on the problems that quality control staff may find with using a notice board to display quality control information, and explain how a computerised bulletin board system could help to alleviate these problems. **(8 marks)**

(Total : 60 marks)

Question 45

SPK plc (Nov 97)

Company background

SPK plc manufactures motor vehicles, with annual sales of £560 million. This represents about 50,000 cars sold per annum.

Five years ago, the company formed a strategic planning unit to review the market for motor vehicles. Its remit was to report back to the Board on a regular basis concerning potential changes to the market, and make recommendations concerning the future production of motor vehicles within the company.

The most recent report from the unit identified a growing customer preference for motor vehicles which are highly tailored to customers' individual requirements. Customers are starting to express preferences, not only for the colour of the vehicle being purchased, but also more fundamental features like the size of doors and the ability to add, on demand, extras like air conditioning. The unit has recommended that SPK plc should establish a new production line, which can produce motor vehicles to individual customer orders. In the past, catering to customer requirements to this extent has been possible only in expensive, non-automated, factories.

If the unit's proposal is accepted, the new production line will provide a similar product, but at a reduced cost because of increased use of industrial robots. The customer will, in effect, be able to design the motor vehicle that they require, using a computer terminal in the car showroom, and then have this built by the new production line. It is recognised that many customers in the showroom will not be computer-literate. While customers might therefore expect that the designing of their own car will be fun, it is also likely that they will require some guidance from the system to explain how it should be used.

Decision on new production line

On 14 November, the Board agreed in principle to the proposal to establish a new production line, although more information was requested. Three separate requests for information were sent on behalf of the Board to different sections of the company: to the Chief Executive Officer, the Production Manager and the Operational Manager. Extracts from the responses to these requests are shown below.

MEMORANDUM

From: Chief Executive of SPK plc   **To: The Board of SPK plc**

Private and Confidential   14 November 200X

Proposal to build new production line

The proposal to build a new production line will involve the following:

♦   Increase in factory space. This will cost between £5 million and £20 million.

♦   Use of *CAD/CAM* production processes.

♦   The assumption is that the market will expand by 20% per annum over the next five years.

Board authority will be required for

♦ the total cost of new proposal including factory, investment in automation and additional annual costs of employees, and

♦ the design and build of *CAD/CAM* system including customer interfaces at car showrooms.

The Critical Success Factor for the investment will be the raw material cost per tonne of steel used in the production process.

MEMORANDUM

To: Chief Executive of SPK plc   From: Production Manager

Private and Confidential   20 November 200X

Proposal to build new production line

Information requested in your memo of 14 November:

Budget for production line - assumption 15,000 units produced per annum:

	£000
Materials	51,326.94
Labour	32,223.90
Automation expenditure	19,294.96
Sales forecast (at average selling price)	180,008.08
Additional staff required	1,702

Detailed budgets are on the enclosed disk because it would take too long to print out all the information. The budgets should be reviewed to ensure that a complete picture of the proposals is obtained. The program used is the new spreadsheet purchased by the department last month.

MEMORANDUM

To: Chief Executive of SPK plc

From: Operational Manager's Assistant: Personnel and Requisitioning Department

16 November 200X

Private and Confidential

Proposal to build new production line

Information requested by your memo of 14 November. Unfortunately, the Operations Manager is on long-term sick leave. I have therefore produced this information to show my best guess of the future figures. A more detailed report will be available when the Manager returns.

Personnel

Additional staff can be hired at £325 per week. The labour market is generally buoyant at present and it is unlikely that more than 1,200 workers can be found in the local area. Increasing wages to £350 per week should provide up to 1,500 workers. A recruitment company can help find the required staff at a fee of 15% of wages, although there is a 20% chance that 35% of these workers will still need £365 per week. This means that 20% of them will leave in the first six months with a probability of 0.1.

Absenteeism rates are currently at industry standard of 5 days per annum. In fact we are doing about the same here compared to other similar industries as well.

Materials

The average material costs are:

	£
Body	1,252.89
Car interior	483.32
Engine and accessories	739.16
'Extras' requested by customer	328.24

Each car produced could vary by a further £387 from the above depending on the complexity of the specification received from the customer.

Factory cost

The factory cost will be in the region of £5 million to £20 million.

Finish reading the scenario before attempting this question.

NOTE:

No knowledge of the car manufacturing process is required to answer this question.

Required

(a) (i)   Explain briefly the characteristics of information that will be used at each of the strategic, tactical and operational levels of management in SPK plc.

(6 marks)

(ii)   Critically assess the information provided in the three reports. Your answer should show whether or not this information meets the required characteristics for information at that management level. **(18 marks)**

(b)   Appraise the importance of information technology in SPK plc's new system. In particular, suggest which parts of the new system could not work without the use of information technology. **(10 marks)**

(c)   Explain the responsibilities for, and actions that should be taken in respect of, data security for each of the strategic, tactical and operational levels of management in SPK plc.

You may refer to appropriate Data Protection legislation when answering this question. **(12 marks)**

(d)   Explain the different hardware and software elements of the human computer interface, which will be used in the showroom where the customers design their own cars. Show how these elements can be made to help the customer make a complete and accurate input into the computer system.   **(14 marks)**

(Total : 60 marks)

Question 46

KJ plc (Nov 98)

Introduction

KJ plc supplies office and stationery products by mail order to a wide range of companies and individuals. Customers telephone or fax their orders to KJ plc's sales department which takes the order details, checks the stock in real-time to ensure that the order can be fulfilled and then transfers the order to a central warehouse for packing the stock ready to deliver to the customer. All orders received before 5.00 pm are delivered on the next working day.

Because KJ plc is in a service industry, it has always tried to maintain a good standard of customer service. On the whole, this objective has been met. A recent survey of 100 customers, which asked them to rank the importance of various aspects of the business, produced the information shown below:

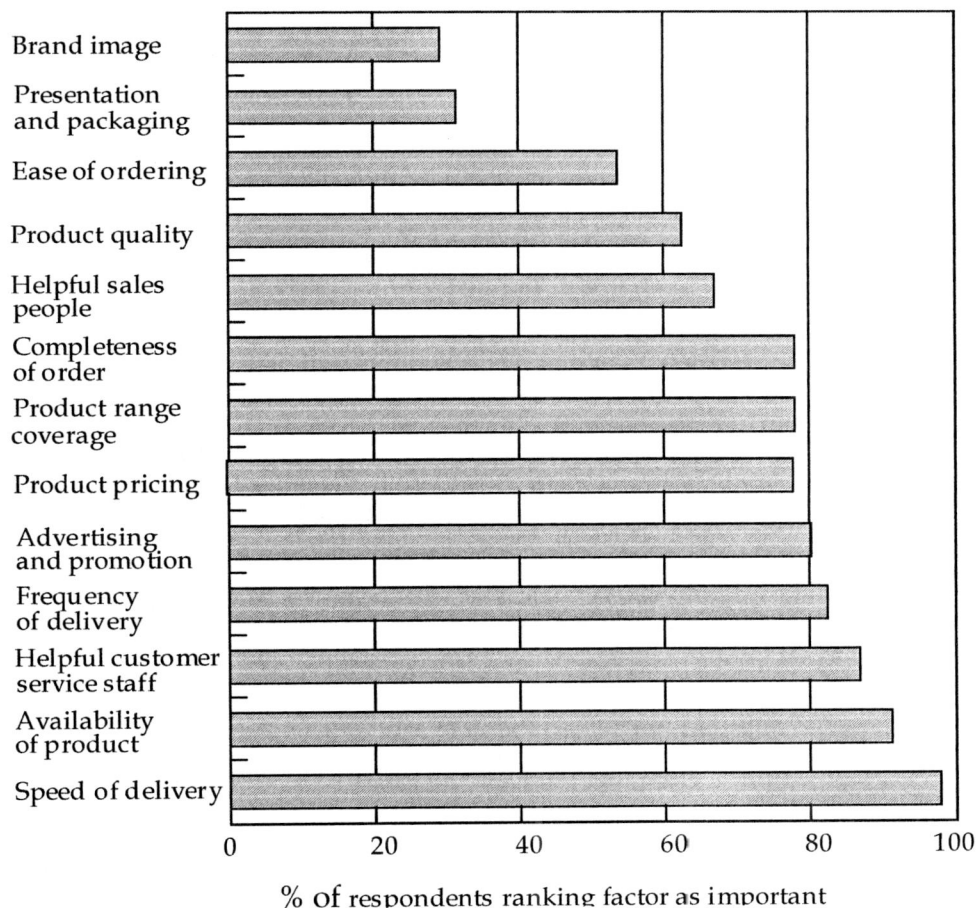

% of respondents ranking factor as important

Existing computer systems

KJ plc's Transaction Processing System provides a vast amount of information, which is used by managers at all levels in the organisation. Very few complaints have been received concerning the information that is normally supplied. The DP department has therefore concentrated on maintaining the system and fine-tuning this to requests of employees, where the Managing Director would allow this. Significant change was not allowed because of the authoritarian approach of the MD.

IT strategy

The main objectives of the IT strategy have been to

♦   ensure goal congruence between the different sections of the company (such as sales, warehouse despatch and stock control) so that they are all working together to provide good customer service,

♦   ensure that good service has been provided to customers, from the point of view of the customer, and

♦   maintain an acceptable Transaction Processing System.

This strategy has been successfully implemented in recent years. However, there is now evidence of potential problems: a meeting of managers has revealed that some managers are uncomfortable with the MD's authoritarian style of management, and the latest customer survey indicates revised customer priorities.

Management structure

The MD takes most tactical and strategic decisions. This limits the decision-making ability of managers and has resulted in a fairly high staff turnover in middle management positions.

Middle management now consists of two distinct groups: a minority of long-serving managers who are satisfied that the MD should continue to make most of the strategic/tactical decisions, and a majority who have been recently appointed and would like to take a more active role in decision-making. The concerns of the majority were expressed to the MD in a recent meeting. One manager from this group resigned following the lack of any definite action plan from the MD. Also, as a result of this meeting, some long-serving managers have been expressing dissatisfaction with the amount of control exercised by the MD.

The MD has finally recognised the need to enhance the decision-making opportunities of his managers, although he does not know how to implement an acceptable solution.

Systems change information

Because the computer systems are now approximately 5 years old and maintenance and other costs are increasing, the board of KJ plc has decided to replace the Transaction Processing System. Two alternative systems are currently under review, details of which are given in the table below. The company could pay for either alternative by outright cash purchase or an operating lease agreement.

	Alternative 1	**Alternative 2**
Supplier	KJ plc's current supplier (well-established but not industry-standard)	Y plc, an established supplier specialising in IBM-compatible equipment.
System structure	Centralised, with one large mainframe computer being maintained by a specialist department. All staff would have access to a common database, which would keep information concerning all of the company's activities The MD would retain control of major decisions regarding the computer system.	De-centralised, with each department maintaining its own computer systems and making its own decisions regarding the use of those systems. Managers would be given responsibility to make the tactical operational decisions necessary to run their own departments and computer systems. Essential information, like store transactions would still be shared, but via an internal Intranet system, not by all individuals having access to a shared database.
New features	Delivery times decreased to allow same-day deliveries in major cities for orders placed before 11.00 am. A fully integrated system will mean that stock-outs can be rectified within 24 hours, not 72 which is the fastest time under the existing system.	E-mail for all employees and Internet access for some employees. Ease of upgrade due to purchase of industry-standard equipment. Customer orders will be taken by telephone, fax, e-mail or Internet, with the company's own branded products being offered as a first choice in all ordering methods. Speed of delivery is likely to be adversely affected because of the increased time required to transfer information between the company's new computer systems.
Information to be provided	The same as KJ plc's existing system with the addition of a strategic planning module for use by the MD. Historical data from the old system would not be transferred, although access to this would continue to be available up to six months after the system changeover.	A full range of strategic to operational information to meet all managers' information needs, including some powerful database query tools designed for analysis of old databases. Key historical information would be available on the new system changeover, if managers can afford to make the transfer from their own department budgets.

First read the scenario and then answer this question

Required

(a)   Compare the two new systems to show whether either of them would provide an acceptable basis for the three key areas of IT strategy for KJ plc.   **(22 marks)**

(b)   Explain to what extent KJ plc's current system meets the information requirements of managers in the company, and whether you consider Alternatives One and Two would provide any improvement in the information provided.   **(14 marks)**

(c)   KJ plc is considering obtaining new computer equipment either by outright cash purchase or by an operating lease.

Contrast the strategic and operational advantages to KJ plc of these two alternatives.

          (8 marks)

(d)   Assume that Alternative Two is adopted by the company.

(i)   Discuss how the motivation of all managers can be improved by implementing this system.   **(10 marks)**

(ii)   Comment on the actions that can be taken with the introduction of Alternative Two that might lead managers to accept more responsibility.   **(6 marks)**

          (Total : 60 marks)

Question 47

Criminal Justice System

Introduction

The criminal justice system in a country is based on a trial by jury. Defendants are examined before a judge and a 12-person jury in one of 42 Regional Courts, which are located in many of the major towns and cities of the country. Each Regional Court has up to six Courtrooms, which are used to review individual cases. A larger Central Court in the country's capital city reviews appeals from people who believe that they have been wrongly convicted of a crime, and also makes judgements on cases that the Regional Courts cannot resolve.

Court Service Information Systems

Information systems are available within each Court, providing details on:

♦   *Statute and case law* - these databases are updated each week as the country's government enacts new laws and the decisions in cases from all other Courts are received.

♦   *Court organisation schedules* - these include lists of judges, jurors and Court officials who will be present in Court on any given day, along with details of the cases that will be heard in each Courtroom.

♦   *Fixed asset register* - this contains details of the assets under the control and ownership of the Court.

♦   *Salary information relating to Court officials.*

Note that the Central Court pays all judges.

While the information systems in each Regional Court provide similar information, the actual method of processing is very different from Court to Court. Existing systems vary from complex manual systems to various types of database and Management Information Systems. Any revisions to the system are likely to be expensive because the vast majority of Courts do not have computers with a sufficiently high specification to run the latest software. The system is run by an Administrator in each Regional Court.

Government requirement for efficiency gains

Although there are no problems identified with the information systems in any Court, recent political decisions require the Court Service as a whole to make some efficiency gains. The government has indicated that these gains may be achieved in various ways, ranging from the implementation of new information systems to the amalgamation of some Regional Courts. A management committee has been established to review what changes are feasible. Employees in the Courts will welcome any review of the systems, because the implementation of common systems will enhance job mobility and sharing.

In an attempt to improve efficiency, two alternative information systems are actively being considered by the management committee of the Court Service. These two systems are:

Information System Alpha	*Information System Beta*
Decentralised configuration with all information required by each Regional Court being available from computer systems maintained within the Court building.	Centralised configuration for common data required by all Courts such as databases of case law, but each Regional Court maintaining its own information system regarding salaries and Court scheduling.
Common information distributed via CD-ROM from the Central Court each week. Distribution will be by the standard postal service. A courier will transfer any urgent information from the Central Court between the weekly updates.	Information on common databases accessed via telephone lines from each Regional Court to a central server. Dial-in access is provided for each Court.
The Court Administrator to remain in charge of running the information system in each Court.	Responsibility for information systems split between the Head of Court Data Services for centralised information and the Court Administrator for local information. Court Administrators are likely to be averse to this move because of the reduction in their control over the databases.
Both systems will have a new Management Information System that will collate the operational information in each Court and provide a summary of this information to the Court Administrator.	

A further alternative information system (called Gamma) had been considered by the management committee. This system was to have held all information centrally. The data would have been accessed via a secure Virtual Private Network (VPN) using spare capacity on the Wide Area Network of the national rail company. Each Court would have been able to access the central database using a dedicated leased line to the nearest access point to the VPN. This alternative was dismissed as being too expensive.

A Cost Benefit Analysis is due to be carried out on systems Alpha and Beta to try and determine which system will be more cost-effective for the Court Service. It is hoped that this analysis will identify costs and benefits, both tangible and intangible, in areas like hardware and software requirements as well as systems development and usage within the Court Service.

Critical Success Factors (CSFs)

Efficiency in the Court Service is currently measured in terms of

♦ whether the annual budget has been spent (the Court Service receives a grant each year from the government which has to be accounted for on a cash basis - any cash not spent is deducted from next year's budget), and

♦ percentage utilisation of each Courtroom.

The management committee of the Courts has recognised that these measures may not be appropriate when the efficiency and economy of the Service is being investigated.

New CSFs have therefore been recently agreed:

♦ Internal CSF:

To ensure efficient allocation and use of the public resources that the government commits to Courts.

♦ External CSF:

To minimise the time for cases to be taken through the Court system.

These new CSFs have met with broad approval from government, although all Court employees have not yet accepted them.

Finish reading the scenario before answering this question

Required

(a) Explain the likely costs and benefits (tangible and intangible) of each of information systems Alpha and Beta. **(20 marks)**

(b) (i) Explain the need for Critical Success Factors (CSFs) and Performance Indicators (PIs) in a public service organisation such as a Court Service.
(8 marks)

(ii) Suggest PIs that can be used to support the new CSFs of the Court Service. Explain why the PIs that you have suggested are appropriate in this situation.
(10 marks)

(c) Describe the data that will have to be input to the different sections of the new Court Service Information System and explain why this data is needed in the Information System. **(12 marks)**

Note: Your answer to part (c) should ignore case and statute law.

(d) Discuss the risks and benefits of database access and update if all relevant Court information were to be placed on a secure Virtual Private Network with remote access being available from all Courts. **(10 marks)**

(Total : 60 marks)

PILOT PAPER

FINAL LEVEL

MANAGEMENT ACCOUNTING – INFORMATION STRATEGY

Instructions to candidates

Read the scenario and answer the **one** question in Section A. Section B contains **four** questions: candidates should answer **two** of these.

Time allowed: **3 hours**

This is a **Pilot Paper** and is intended to be indicative of the style of questions that will appear in the future. It does not purport to cover the range of the syllabus learning outcomes.

The mark allocations for particular topics within the paper are subject to change in the future, as is the range of topics covered. The layout of the printed paper may be subject to slight variation in the future.

PILOT PAPER QUESTIONS

Section A: 50 marks

Read the scenario and answer the question

Question 48 (Question 1 of Pilot Paper)

Q.NET sells books on the Internet. It has a turnover of (euro) €50 million with gross profits of €5 million. Operating costs are relatively low because most transactions are carried out electronically by the computer system with little or no manual intervention. Q.NET's main expense is interest on bank loans which were used to purchase initial hardware and software and provide some working capital for the new business. Over €20 million was invested in computer hardware, software, stocks of books and warehousing space when the organisation commenced business last year. Interest repayments alone mean that Q.NET is unlikely to see any net profit being made in the next three years.

Business strategy and vision

The overall vision of Q.NET is to obtain 10% of the retail book market within three years with a positive net profit. The underlying business strategy of Q.NET supports this vision by providing:

♦ appropriate information to, and ordering facilities for, customers;

♦ basic financial information for management; and

♦ suppliers with appropriate information on book sales.

Information systems – ordering and sales

Expenditure on hardware and software for transaction processing included mainframes linked to the Internet to receive orders from customers, maintenance of a large database of books in print and sophisticated encryption technology to ensure that payments on the Internet are secure. Some sections of the hardware configuration were below the recommended specification when they were implemented.

Q.NET, along with the other major bookshops on the Internet, offers information on up to four million books in print. Books are ordered over the Internet using a secure landline and credit card facility. Despatch of popular titles is normally within 48 hours; rarer books in four to six weeks. All Internet booksellers offer a similar lead time for orders. Payment is made with the customer's authorisation for a credit card transaction on despatch of the order. Payments are made to suppliers within the standard credit period of 30 days.

Customers purchase books after identifying their book requirements by author or book title from the database of books maintained by Q.NET. Information provided about each book includes price and shipping time; popular books also have a scanned image of the cover. Additional information on each book is available on Q.NET's database, although the lack of bandwidth from the database to the Internet server means that this information cannot be displayed to the customer.

Details of customer orders are maintained on the system for six weeks, or until the order is fulfilled. This information is then removed from the hard disk to save space.

Information systems for sales and support staff

Sales and support staff work from their homes using a Virtual Private Network (VPN) to access the main computer systems at Q.NET's head office. Sales and support staff are required to:

♦ answer customer queries via e-mail;

♦ check stock movements and order additional copies of popular books, which would normally be in excess of normal forecast sales;

♦ review new books from publishers so that Q.NET's website can be updated with details of each book prior to publication; and

♦ write amendments to the website to add new books and remove discontinued books.

Each member of staff focuses on one of the main activities outlined above. Staff work from home, partly as a result of the security of the VPN, but mainly to minimise the use of expensive office space. Q.NET provided all the hardware and software required and had no difficulty in recruiting the 25 staff required. However, six months after initial recruitment, more than half of the staff have resigned and Q.NET is facing increasing charges from having to reallocate computer hardware to new support staff as well as, in some situations, providing appropriate ISDN telephone connections to the VPN.

Future activities

The board of Q.NET is concerned that the organisation is not using technology effectively to gain any competitive advantage over its rivals.

One proposition is to have additional EDI links to major book publishers to order books that Q.NET currently does not have in stock. However, the publishers are unwilling to be locked into this type of agreement in case they are seen to be favouring one bookshop over another.

Required

(a)   Evaluate how Q.NET can use IT to gain competitive advantage using Porter's Five Forces Model as a framework for your answer.   36   **(20 marks)**

(b)   Discuss the reasons why sales and support staff turnover is so high. Explain methods for improving the retention of these staff.   27   **(15 marks)**

(c)   Explain the purpose of an information strategy in a commercial organisation. **(5 marks)**
9

(d)   Evaluate how effective the IT system at Q.NET is in supporting the business strategy.
18   **(10 marks)**

(Total : 50 marks)
90

2 PM.

Section B: 50 marks

Answer two questions only

Question 49 (Question 2 of Pilot Paper)

HB Ltd manufactures cement from a range of raw materials. The basic product is used in many different applications from building sites to road construction. Competition within the cement market has been increasing in recent years, with a significant number of new manufacturers commencing production in the last year. There are few barriers to entry; the main factor limiting competition is the availability of mining sites from which the raw materials are obtained to make the product.

Like most manufacturers, the production system at HB Ltd uses very few computers and relies extensively on the skill and judgement of the production staff to make an acceptable product. For example, raw materials can only be weighed to the nearest 100 kg because of a lack of accurate weighing equipment. There is very little quality control, with the skill of the production supervisor being the main check on the acceptability of the cement being despatched to customers.

There is a growing market for some specialist cements to be used for a wide range of purposes, including earthquake-proofing on buildings and use in sculptures, as well as coloured cements for identifying special bicycle-only lanes on roads. HB Ltd is attempting to capture a significant share of this market because the margins that can be obtained are higher than for the normal cement applications. However, success has been limited because of poor quality control and delivery times.

In an attempt to improve the company's performance in terms of increasing market share and improving profitability, the board of HB Ltd hired a consultant with a brief to show how the company could meet these objectives. The consultant's report included a graph (Figure A) which was used to explain how HB Ltd could meet its objectives. Two main areas of improvement were noted:

♦   increasing the contribution from each unit of cement sold;

♦   decreasing the fixed costs of the company.

Fixed costs in HB Ltd include staff in all departments, factory overheads and selling and marketing activities.

Figure A   HB Ltd: Shift in breakeven points arising from changes in contribution and fixed costs

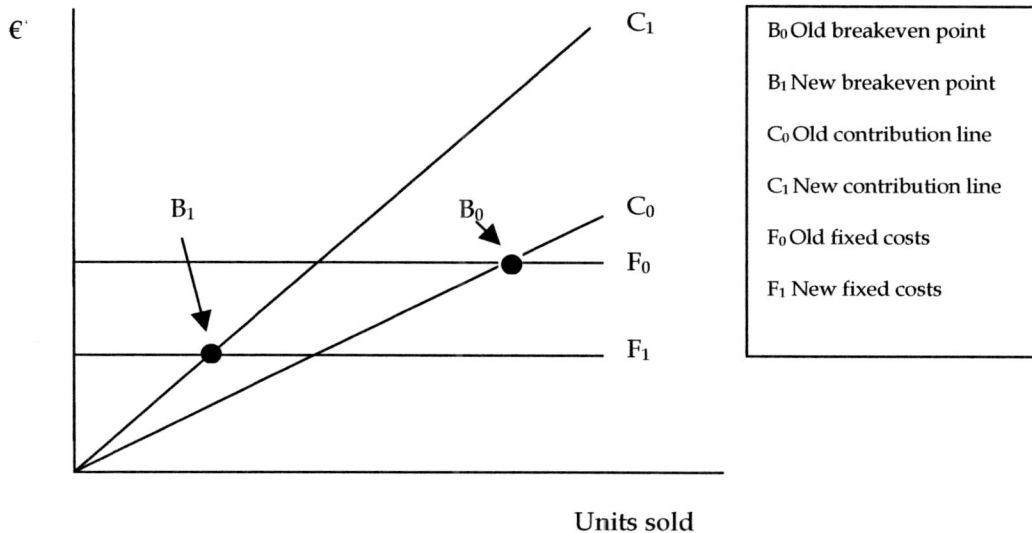

The main recommendation from the report was that investment was needed in a new computer system to monitor the whole production process from purchase of raw material to monitoring of customer orders and delivery schedules. The board of HB Ltd welcomed the suggestion, although some further work on quantifying the benefits of the investment is still required.

Required

As the management accountant of HB Ltd produce a report to:

(a)   Explain how the proposed investment in a new IT system could help to produce the shifts in the contribution and fixed costs lines shown in the consultant's graph.

(18 marks)

(b)   Discuss any other ways in which the new IT system will help HB Ltd to gain competitive advantage over other cement manufacturers in sales and marketing activities.   **(7 marks)**

Your answer should make appropriate references to the computerised production system.

(Total : 25 marks)

You should assume that there are no significant changes to the size of the company in the short term, although existing resources could be diverted into specialist cement manufacture.

Question 50 (Question 3 of Pilot Paper)

The HK Consultancy Company specialises in helping organisations to benefit from the implementation of IT systems. On a typical client project, staff from HK Consultancy will review the use of IT within an organisation, identify how staff should be using the IT systems, obtain information about proposed IT systems and then ensure that the revised IT systems meet the requirements of the users.

As the newly appointed, experienced management accountant, your responsibilities include ensuring that the information systems of the company support its strategic direction, and advising the board on any changes that could be made to the overall company strategy. Prior to your appointment, the board recognised that growth in its existing market was limited, and required some diversification to meet the consultancy's objectives of sales and profit growth.

An intranet has been established utilising a package which provides databases for technical information, bulletin boards, electronic mail and customer contact information. The intranet is used by the management accountant frequently throughout the day, mainly to answer e-mails, but also to check information on the technical databases and bulletin boards. You also receive information from:

- professional staff who visit client organisations, in the form of verbal queries and written reports;

- various journals specialising in IT systems;

- administration staff who produce client proposals for review prior to sending out consultants to potential clients;

- telephone queries directly from clients regarding the status of different projects;

- the Internet, where different client and competitor websites are reviewed on a daily basis by the management accountant.

Your first project is to provide a report to the board summarising the company's current strategic situation compared to its major competitors and suggesting alternative strategies for diversification.

Required

(a)   Explain how you, as the management accountant, would refine or amend the information system in the HK Consultancy to limit the amount of information being delivered to you, so that you can focus on this first project.   **(17 marks)**

(b)   Evaluate the characteristics that should apply to the information being given to the management accountant to ensure that the information is quickly and accurately understood.   **(8 marks)**

(Total : 25 marks)

Question 51 (Question 4 of Pilot Paper)

SN plc provides a large range of insurance services and advice to clients ranging from private individuals to large corporate organisations. The sales staff are supported by a wide range of information systems, which are designed to be user-friendly. The systems are regularly reviewed to ensure that the information requirements of the professional staff are being met by those systems.

The information systems are maintained and upgraded by a team of trainers; sales personnel are not involved in the design of systems because this would result in a loss of chargeable time. The actual process of maintaining the information system is outlined in Figure B.

Figure B   Maintaining SN plc's information systems

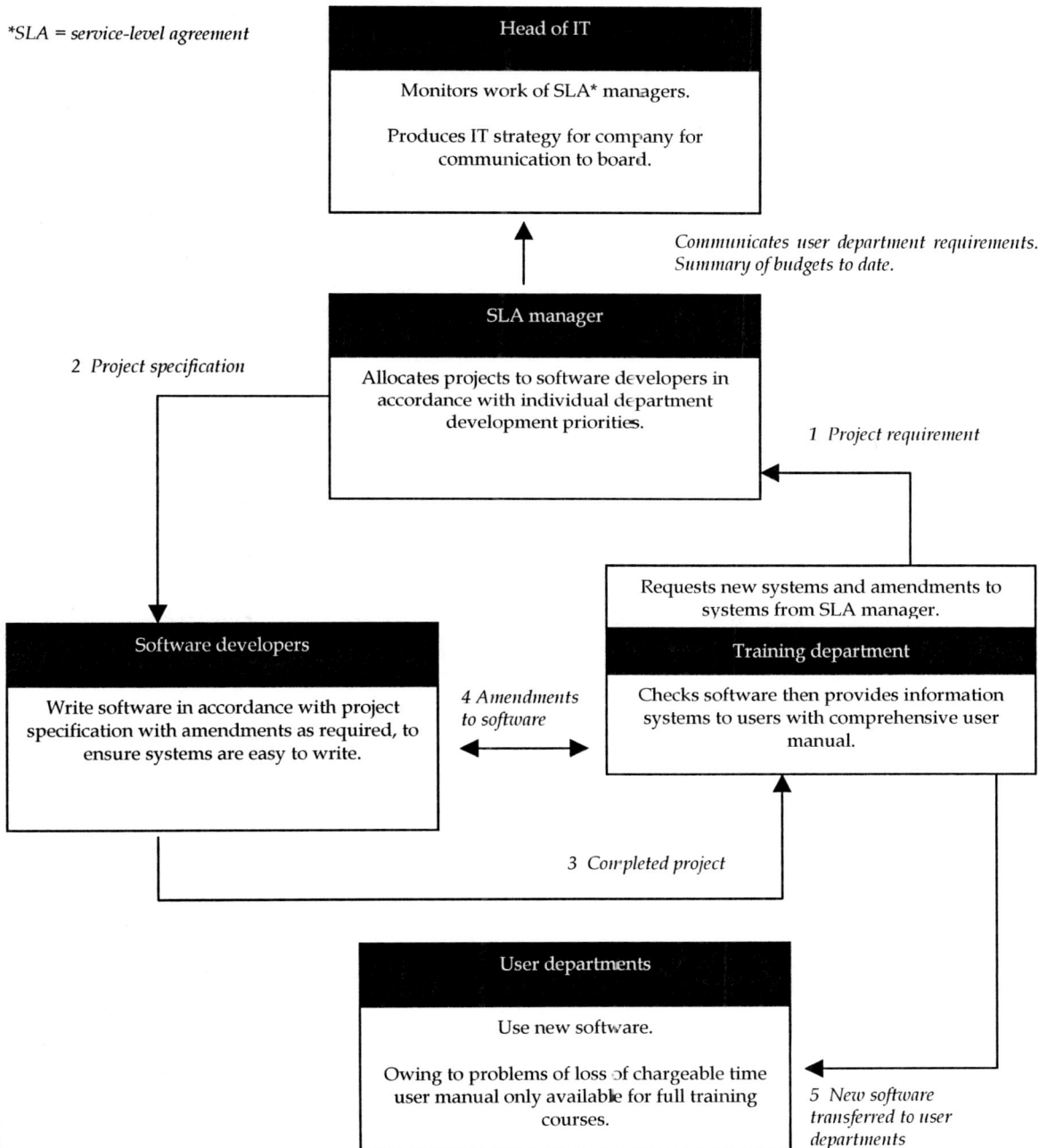

Other relevant information

♦ Costs of training and IT department are allocated to the different user departments in accordance with staff numbers in those departments. The costs of the IT department include software development and all costs relating to the SLA managers.

♦ The IT staff work in the main development centre, which is located on a university campus for reasons of cost and accessibility to a supply of trained programmers.

♦ The IT department has a reputation within the company for not meeting user requirements in a timely manner.

Required

As the management accountant of SN plc write a report to the board which:

♦ explains the weaknesses in SN plc's infrastructure for maintaining the information systems for sales staff, and

♦ produces specific recommendations to alleviate those weaknesses.

(Total : 25 marks)

Marks are allocated evenly across the two requirements.

Question 52 (Question 5 of Pilot Paper)

Compare and contrast the organisations specified below in terms of:

(a) whether e-commerce should be adopted as part of the business strategy; and **(20 marks)**

(b) showing which organisation will benefit more from the use of e-commerce. **(5 marks)**

The two types of organisation to be considered in this question are:

♦ a local independent supplier of garden plants, fences, sheds and other garden accessories selling within 20 kilometres of its main site; and

♦ an international consultancy supplying financial advice to private individuals and large multinational organisations.

(Total : 25 marks)

RATIONALE

General

♦ The examination will be unseen. Its duration will be three hours. The examination will include a compulsory scenario question worth 50 marks

♦ *Cognitive skills.* Candidates will need to be able to display understanding of the subject area and apply their knowledge to specific circumstances in the case study.

♦ *Practical proficiency sought.* Candidates will need to be proficient in applying appropriate knowledge to a given situation and be able to communicate that knowledge clearly and effectively in a professional manner.

Question 1

Background

This question is relevant to syllabus areas (ii), (iii) and (iv); in particular: *Evaluate the use of IS/IT to gain competitive advantage* and *identify and evaluate the cultural dimensions of IT acceptance* and *Analyse the contents of elements contained in IS, IT and IM strategies.*

This question is based on an Internet bookstore similar to Amazon or Waterstones. At the time of writing, very few Internet "shops" are making a profit, and the case study identifies this as an issue resulting from the large capital investment required to establish the website in the first place. The question investigates two key areas:

♦ direct application of knowledge to a given situation, in this case Porter's Five Forces Model; and

♦ the cultural problems of establishing a workforce with no office base.

Candidates will be expected to provide practical and relevant comments on these two areas, with sufficient explanation to show why the points made are appropriate to the case study.

Knowledge required

Knowledge of Porter's Five Forces Model is essential to answering section (a). More general knowledge of the cultural problems of homeworking and the disbenefits this can bring for employees and the company are needed for part (b).

Question 2

Background

This question is relevant to syllabus area (ii), and in particular: *Evaluate the importance of process innovation and re-engineering.*

This question is based on a cement manufacturing company. The logic is to show that IT, and the information produced by IT systems, can make a significant difference in a wide range of industries, even those where the information content of the product is relatively low.

Knowledge required

Candidates will have studied economics at an earlier level. The inclusion of the breakeven point graph provides a link to that level and helps the candidate to focus on the specific aspects of the system that must be mentioned in the answer. However, it is expected that candidates will focus answers on the scenario information contained in the question, rather than listing their knowledge of economics or breakeven points. The inclusion of part (b) in the requirement allows the candidate to use more general knowledge to show how IT can assist the company in gaining competitive advantage in other ways, rather than just focusing on cost and revenue control.

Question 3

Background

This question is relevant to syllabus area (i), and in particular: *Evaluate the use of information as a key resource in different organisational contexts.*

The principle of discarding information is important in almost every work situation. Management accountants, in particular, must understand and identify the information that they require and, therefore, be able to filter out or discard any less relevant information. The scenario for this question is focused on a management accountant who could be suffering from information overload. The candidate is required to show how to limit the information being given to the management accountant, while at the same time ensuring that important information still reaches him. The management accountant must, therefore, be happy that the filters used are both effective in decreasing the volume of information, and provide sufficient discrimination, in that important information is not filtered out.

Knowledge required

Knowledge of different information filtering techniques from delegation through to the use of intelligent agents on the Internet will help the candidate to produce a sufficiently wide ranging and relevant answer.

Question 4

Background

This question is relevant to syllabus area (iii), and in particular: *Recommend strategies for achieving the integration of technical and business staff.*

The question is based on a financial services company. The scenario concerns professional staff being too involved with sales to be involved in systems specification or receive appropriate training. The issue of having the IT department in a separate building has been discovered in practice to be a disadvantage.

Candidates will be expected to identify the weaknesses in the software development system outlined in the scenario, and then to show how those weaknesses can be overcome. Marks will be awarded specifically for relating to issues raised by the scenario and for providing practical and workable solutions to those problems.

Knowledge required

Candidates will require knowledge of the development of software and training solutions, including best practice for involving users and other interested parties in the software development. Any practical knowledge acquired from being involved in software implementation in the workplace will also be beneficial, although this is not essential to achieve a good pass standard for this question.

Question 5

Background

This question is directly relevant to syllabus area (ii), and in particular: *Evaluate the use of IS/IT to gain competitive advantage.*

The question is deliberately short – partly so that candidates can make their own assumptions about the organisations, but also to send the message that this paper includes discussion questions in respect of which candidates will have to apply their knowledge to more theoretical situations. It is hoped that candidates will not simply dismiss the garden centre as not being interested in e-commerce. Almost all of the literature on this subject is now suggesting that the Internet lowers barriers to competition and allows even a small firm to trade to a much wider market.

Knowledge required

Candidates will require knowledge of the World Wide Web and how this can be used for international and local trade. An ability to relate the business aims of an organisation to the use of e-commerce will also be necessary. Finally, owing to the lack of a scenario, candidates will have to show that they can plan a discussion answer adequately, without reference to any predetermined "hints" in the question.

May 2001 Exam Questions

Question 53 (Question 1 of Exam Paper)

Overview of MB Ltd

MB Ltd manufactures high-quality hand-built motor vehicles, customised to individual customer requirements. The company has been manufacturing cars for 42 years and has remained independent, resisting offers of purchase from other larger car manufacturers.

Each car sells for around $120,000 and MB Ltd produces around 8,000 cars each year. It employs a total workforce of 1,800 people. The price represents a premium of about $30,000 on similar mass-produced cars; MB Ltd is able to maintain this price difference as a result of excellent customer service, short delivery times and the high resale value of cars made. The amount of warranty and repair work on cars after delivery is negligible.

Ordering and manufacturing process

The current ordering and manufacturing process was implemented one year ago, to try and provide a competitive advantage for MB Ltd.

Cars are ordered by customers directly from MB Ltd's Internet site or by visiting one of the company's four showrooms. Basic details of the type of car are obtained at this stage, such as the engine size and overall body design (for example, 2 or 4 door, saloon or sports car). The customer is then issued with a Wireless Application Protocol (WAP) Personal Organiser. This device works in a similar way to a WAP mobile telephone that can access the Internet. However, in this case, the Personal Organiser can send and receive text and picture messages between MB Ltd and its customers and suppliers. The production process for the car is illustrated in the diagram below.

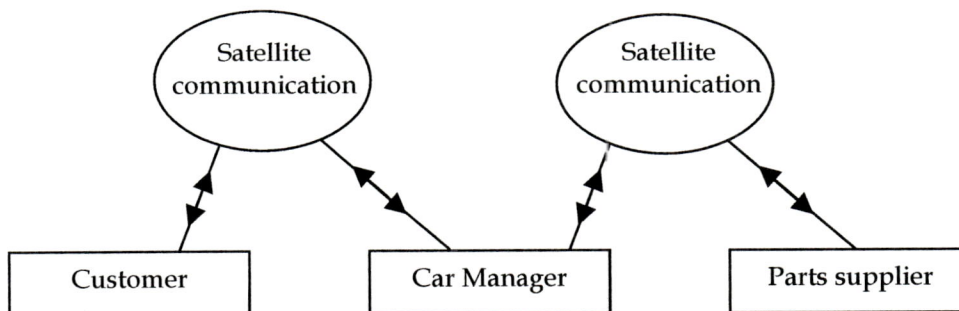

Each car is allocated to a Car Manager (CM). The CM oversees the entire production of the car in MB Ltd's factory, organising production staff and ordering parts, checking the order is complete and finally driving the finished car to ensure that it has been built correctly. Information on the stage of production is updated hourly so that the exact stage of production is always known.

Daily reports on the car's manufacture, including pictures, are sent to the customer's Personal Organiser. The report includes queries regarding the design of the car, ranging from colour and type of seats required to the location of the digital display for satellite navigation and positioning of drink holders. The customer can effectively see the car being made and can send back answers to the CM's questions on a daily basis.

Stock ordering system

As MB Ltd holds minimal amounts of stock, the CM orders car parts from suppliers using a similar WAP Personal Organiser.

Goods are received next day, with manufacture being complete within 8 working days. Although contacting the customer seems to be cumbersome, market research has shown that customers appreciate involvement in the manufacturing process.

Purchase history information is maintained on a database in the main factory. The CMs use this to check the progress on individual cars and forecast likely completion dates for the customer where necessary. The database is linked directly to the main financial and data storage systems in the company for ease of update of the suppliers' ledger and historical records such as customer histories. Reports regarding the location of any car part or a full listing of all parts being used are available from the database at any time.

New systems development – IT department

The IT department in MB Ltd is investigating amending the ordering system for parts, although this project has not been discussed with the CMs. In an alliance with three other much larger car manufacturers, MB Ltd is taking part in a trial of a central purchasing system. All requirements for parts are placed into an electronic trading room with suppliers making bids to provide the parts. After three days, the most suitable bids are accepted by the purchasing manager at MB Ltd and the parts delivered on the next working day.

All purchase information will be maintained on a separate secure database in the accounts department. Because of concerns over security, this database is not accessible either by the main database storage systems in MB Ltd or by the CMs.

Until recently, amending the ordering system was being investigated without the knowledge of the Board or the CMs in MB Ltd. The IT Director only found out about the IT Manager's involvement when a purchase requisition in respect of a file server to provide a fast Internet connection was queried.

Required

(a)   As the management accountant of MB Ltd, produce a report advising the Board on whether or not to implement the new stock ordering system.   **(20 marks)**

(b)   In the context of the development of the IT strategy for MB Ltd, discuss the investigation into amending the ordering system for parts.   **(15 marks)**

(c)   Discuss the information requirements of the Car Manager in order to monitor the progress of car production and contrast this with the information required by the Board of MB Ltd to help them to run the company more effectively.   **(15 marks)**
(Total = 50 marks)

Question 54 (Question 2 of Exam Paper)

Required

(a)   Discuss the benefits and limitations of using cost benefit analysis to assess the value of information.   **(10 marks)**

(b)   Eagle Inc manufactures sports shoes used for playing sports such as tennis, squash, and badminton and for running. It has a unique brand name and logo, and promotes its shoes with the slogan 'Wear Eagles to Win'. The company successfully sold 3.5 million pairs of shoes worldwide last year with a net profit of $20 million.

Although the company is successful, the Board of Eagle Inc is always looking for methods of gaining additional competitive advantage. The market research department has identified a small but growing demand for sports shoes which are personalised to the individual wearer. Customers would like the facility to change certain aspects of the shoes such as sole and trim colour, depth of the sole and pattern on the top of the shoe.

The manufacturing system at Eagle Inc can be amended relatively easily to provide this degree of tailoring to individual shoes. The Board has therefore decided to conduct a trial to determine whether or not the facility for customers to order shoes via the company's existing web site should be introduced. This trial will initially be limited to a central European country of 20 million people, and will offer both standard and personalised shoes. 275,000 pairs of Eagle Inc shoes are currently sold in that country each year.

Required

Discuss the information that will be required to determine the success, or otherwise, of the new web-based ordering system. **(15 marks)**

(Total = 25 marks)

Question 55 (Question 3 of Exam Paper)

Porter identified various strategies that can be used by organisations in order to avoid competition based solely on price.

However, many products, such as holidays, are now purchased on the Internet where it is easier to compare the prices of products rather than the products themselves.

Required

(a) Explain the strategies identified by Porter for dealing with competitive forces, and discuss whether these have any relevance to the Internet. **(15 marks)**

(b) Advise a company providing holidays how value may still be added to its product by provision of information or other features on the Internet site. **(10 marks)**

(Total = 25 marks)

Question 56 (Question 4 of Exam Paper)

The SH Company provides banking services to over 2 million personal customers within one country. Two months ago, SH introduced a new banking service, and customers are now able to access all their normal banking services via mobile telephone. In effect, customers can do such things as check their bank balances, pay bills, transfer money between their accounts, from any location (so long as there is mobile telephone reception).

There are currently only two specific models of mobile telephones that meet the WAP (Wireless Application Protocol) standard for display of text and graphics necessary for mobile telephone banking. However, the use of the mobiles is also limited by the need for a CSSS (Country Specific Security Standard) necessary to transmit information on encrypted frequencies to provide security for the transfer of banking transactions via the mobile telephone network within that individual country. Both WAP mobile telephones meet this requirement. A generic security system which works anywhere in the world should be available in the next two years.

The new mobile telephones are expensive to produce and purchase. Recent production forecasts for the mobile phones indicate that 15,000 units each month for each phone will be available for sale.

The telephone network to support the SH Company's mobile telephone banking is provided by the ADO Company. This has been on a trial basis and SH will be reviewing ADO's contract with a view to signing a three year agreement in the very near future. The major issue at the moment is network coverage; ADO can only offer an 85% coverage of land area in the country while other network providers can reach 98%.

The initial economic plan produced three months ago for the SH Company for the 12 months to June 2002 forecasts that 500,000 customers (of which about 20% are new customers) are expected to want to use mobile telephone banking. This plan stated that planned production levels were unknown. As a result of this forecast, SH expects to close half of its branches (at locations in cities where customers can obtain banking services).

Required

(a) Identify and discuss the social and technological issues that may prevent the SH Company reaching its mobile telephone customer target in 2001/02. **(15 marks)**

(b) Discuss the issues that the SH Company must take into account when discussing the network contract with ADO. **(10 marks)**

(Total = 25 marks)

Question 57 (Question 5 of Exam Paper)

SID plc is a large manufacturer of clothes and supplies many of the main retailers in a medium-sized country. It consists of a holding company with six subsidiaries, with each subsidiary focusing on the manufacture of clothes for a particular target market such as ladies' coats and jackets or children's clothes.

Within each subsidiary, a Junior Management Accountant (normally a part-qualified CIMA student or a recently-qualified CIMA member) is responsible for producing the monthly management accounts. Information for these accounts is obtained from the various information systems located in each subsidiary, such as the stock and work-in-progress system and the finished goods system, along with explanations for significant variances from the managers of each system. The monthly report provides a summary of these results, along with narrative explanations of any significant variances. The timetable for the production of the report is strict, and deadlines cannot be missed.

In the holding company, the Financial Director (FD) is responsible for presenting financial information to the Board of SID plc. The report contains a financial summary of the results of each of the subsidiaries, as well as forecast sales and profit projections for the year and occasional reporting on cash investments, new projects and financial analysis of competitors. The FD may also be asked to provide verbal commentary on the report in the Board meeting. The information for this report is obtained from various locations including the Junior Management Accountants in each subsidiary. These Junior Management Accountants report directly to the FD. Other information sources include newspapers and business information from a new company providing information on the Internet. The FD receives and presents information in a variety of formats including numeric, text and graphics.

Required

(a) Explain the steps involved in processing information as it relates to Human Information Processors (HIPs). Discuss the advantages of human information processing in the input and processing of data compared to computers, providing appropriate examples. **(15 marks)**

(b) Compare and contrast the HIP problems facing the Finance Director and the Junior Management Accountants, clearly explaining possible causes for errors in the work of each person. **(10 marks)**

(Total = 25 marks)

November 2001 Exam Questions

Question 58 (Question 1 of Exam Paper)

Company overview

CLB is a profitable manufacturer of clothes with an annual turnover of $650 million. The organisation sells by mail order from a paper catalogue sent out to customers and via a web site. There are approximately 2.5 million customers on the sales database. Customers spend on average $110 per order.

Clothes are manufactured in ten different factories, with finished goods being transferred to a central warehouse, where they are placed onto the computerised stock system for Internet and catalogue sales. All customer orders are routed to the central warehouse; the factories do not have any sales facilities.

The clothes produced by CLB are fashionable, with most customers being satisfied by the range available. A recent move to sourcing more supplies from overseas has helped to cut costs, although there is increasing competition from some low cost imports.

Company aims and mission

The mission of the organisation is '*to produce a wide range of reasonably priced clothes that appeal to the majority of the population*'. To meet this objective, CLB has three main critical success factors (CSFs):

♦ Maintain overall gross profit at 40% of sales;

♦ Increase customer satisfaction each year; and

♦ Minimise raw material inventory cost.

A 40% gross profit percentage is slightly above the industry standard, but thought to be achievable by the Board of CLB. The organisation needs to sell $600 million of clothes each year to break even.

Maintenance of customer satisfaction is essential to selling clothes. However, the Directors have had some difficulty in establishing appropriate performance indicators (PIs) to measure the CSFs.

Maintaining control over inventory is essential; not only does raw material stock tie up working capital, but any unused raw materials are difficult to dispose of. Changes in fashion mean that raw material stock becomes obsolete very quickly. Finished goods stocks are easier to dispose of – completed garments can normally be sold at cost price or slightly above ensuring that some contribution is made.

Trends in sales

For a number of years, the Board of CLB has been concerned that the brand awareness of the company's products has been falling. Sales of new product lines have also been less than budgeted, both in absolute terms and in comparison to similar clothes produced by competitors. (Information on competitor sales is obtained from their published accounts and for some products from the *Clothing Gazette*, a trade journal.) The fall in brand awareness and sales has provided a decision trigger to the Directors that some amendments may be required to the information systems in CLB. However, they are unclear regarding the information to be obtained to help them make this decision.

CLB information system

At present, each of the ten factories of CLB maintains its own information system to provide detail on raw material stocks, production and finished goods ready to transfer to the central warehouse. While this means that there is no overall picture of stocks, the benefit of maintaining decentralised control is thought to outweigh this problem. The Director of Human Resources is keen to maintain motivation of individual factory managers by retaining the existing systems. This strategy has again been queried at Board level in the last few months, particularly as manufacturing operations mean that each factory is using similar raw materials.

Implementation of a centralised system has been rejected by the HR and IT directors.

Required

(a)   (i)   Recommend performance indicators (PIs) that can be used to support the critical success factors (CSFs) of CLB, discussing why these PIs are appropriate to the company. **(8 marks)**

         (ii)   Explain the information systems that will be required in order to determine whether the PIs suggested in your answer to (a)(i) have been achieved. **(12 marks)**

(b)   With reference to the falling brand awareness, advise the Directors on a suitable decision making process when considering the update of the information systems within CLB. Include relevant examples from the situation in CLB where possible. **(15 marks)**

(c)   Describe an information system that can be used to coordinate information transfer between the different production factories and between the factories and the central sales warehouse.

         Explain the business benefits to CLB of such a system and any disadvantages of it. **(15 marks)**

(Total = 50 marks)

Question 59 (Question 2 of Exam Paper)

The MSV Company owns and operates six forests in different locations in a large country. Trees are grown to be sold to lumberyards (also called wood processing factories). These lumberyards cut and prepare the wood and then produce:

♦   timber for making furniture or for resale to the public; and

♦   wood pulp for paper.

Trees take between 30 and 60 years to mature, depending on the variety of tree and the location that the tree is grown in. In cooler areas of the country, trees grow more slowly and softwood trees are normally planted. However, in warmer regions of the country, hardwood trees are normally grown. The organisation has a strict environmental policy: for every tree that is felled, at least one new tree is planted.

The MSV Company has been in business for 152 years. Over this time, various centralised information systems have been devised and implemented by various directors to try and record details of trees planted and sold. At first, the systems were manual but some have since been computerised: both types of system have tended to be amended as required. For the last ten years, each forest office has also kept a local record of the actual trees planted each year. Up to a few years ago, these systems provided fairly accurate information on the number and type of tree that can be sold each year. Because trees take such a long time to mature, the actual supply of trees can be forecasted each year, with a high degree of accuracy.

Detailed records of tree planting are also maintained, although loss of all data 45 years ago in a fire means there is some uncertainty about the age of older trees in each forest.

The only external information system available to the directors shows the number and price of trees to be taken by lumberyards each year from the MSV Company's forests. These figures are generally agreed up to five years in advance.

In the last few years, the Board of the MSV Company has found estimates of demand and supply of trees to be incorrect, by increasingly large percentages. The reasons for these inaccuracies appear to be:

♦   climate change altering the rate of growth of trees; and

♦   decreased demand for some varieties of tree caused by plastic substitutes being used for furniture.

The decrease in demand is the more significant of these two factors. Lumberyards are now revising downwards the number of trees that they wish to purchase each year. Given that the supply of trees will not vary significantly for the next 30 years, the Board of the MSV Company is uncertain on how to respond to this situation, or whether the Company has appropriate IT knowledge available to make any appropriate decisions.

Required

(a)   Analyse the deficiencies in the information system of the MSV Company, showing the effect of those deficiencies on the decision-making ability of the Board of the company.
(15 marks)

(b)   Explain why implementation of any new information system will be difficult, taking into account the specific situation in the MSV Company.   **(10 marks)**

(Total = 25 marks)

Question 60 (Question 3 of Exam Paper)

(a)   Evaluate the use of Intelligent Agents with specific reference to their benefits and limitations in data mining.   **(10 marks)**

(b)   The government of Xanadu, a country with an extensive road network, has recently introduced a road-pricing scheme. This means that car drivers are charged for using certain main roads and bridges in the country. Roadside scanners collect information on road usage, by 'reading' the number plate of each car as it passes a scanner. Scanners have been placed on all roads and bridges where a charge is to be made. As car number plates are unique, and the scanning system is extremely accurate, use of roads can be accurately determined. Information collected from the scanners is stored on a central database.

The system has been operational for eight weeks. Car owners are expressing significant concern about the system. They now realise that the central database contains details of their exact locations and times they were at those locations.

As well as using the database for charging car owners for use of the roads, citizens suspect that the government might use this data for purposes other than road pricing (scanners have been placed on approaches to the country's three main assembly and concert halls).

Required

Discuss the strategic benefits to the government of collecting data on vehicle movements and explain the limitations of the data being collected. **(15 marks)**

(Total = 25 marks)

Question 61 (Question 4 of Exam Paper)

ZX is a pharmaceutical company which specialises in the development and marketing of new drugs. On average, the company spends $100 million each year (about 10% of turnover) on research and brings five new drugs to the market each year.

Before any drug can be licensed for use, the country's Drug Administration Unit (DAU) undertakes a detailed review. This review takes up to 15 months, with several thousand pages of material on the drug being submitted to the DAU by ZX. Most of the time for the review is taken up by DAU employees finding specific information in the paper documentation supplied by ZX, and occasionally requesting duplicate copies of missing or mislaid documents.

Prior to the review, and to comply with DAU requirements, information on each drug has to be prepared and checked through a quality control process at ZX. The process involves preparation and the checking of drugs and review material in four separate stages in offices in different geographical locations. Each group of employees reports to a central manager in the company's Head Office. To ensure completeness of processing of information on each drug, tasks are arranged and completed in a strict order. Although some tasks could be run in parallel, this does not happen. Processing of this information is slow. Further delays result from teams occasionally duplicating work or waiting for reports, which are subsequently found to be lost in the internal mail at ZX.

Work may also be duplicated between ZX and other pharmaceutical companies in the market. Sharing information between different pharmaceutical companies might avoid duplication of work and save money.

There is considerable pressure on ZX to decrease the overall time taken to place new drugs on the market. The pressure comes from two sources:

♦ the Board of ZX which recognises that every week saved in the R&D process and review will generate up to $1 million each year in extra revenue for the organisation; and

♦ customers – particularly for new HIV and cancer drugs.

Required

(a) Evaluate the current system at ZX showing where the use of an Intranet would help to meet the expectations of customers and the Board. **(15 marks)**

(b) Discuss the limitations of using an Extranet to share information between different pharmaceutical companies. **(10 marks)**

(Total = 25 marks)

Question 62 (Question 5 of Exam Paper)

The SPV bank was established in 1750 to provide general banking services to organisations and individuals. The bank has been successful and profitable since this time, although the overall impression given is of a slow-moving institution, which has not kept up to date with recent changes in technology.

The bank has a web site to promote its services, but on-line banking using the Internet is not yet available to its customers. The Board of SPV recognises that Internet banking must be provided in the near future if the bank is to remain competitive.

You have been appointed as a special project accountant with specific responsibility to oversee the upgrade of the bank's Internet strategy.

Required

(a)   Advise the Board of SPV on how to develop and implement an Internet banking strategy.   **(13 marks)**

(b)   Discuss the advantages and disadvantages of outsourcing the writing and maintaining of the web site for SPV's Internet banking operations.   **(12 marks)**

(Total = 25 marks)

May 2002 Exam Questions

Question 63 (Question 1 of Exam Paper)

Introduction

The Law and Consumer Agency (LC) is a government body established five years ago with the aim of providing advice on all aspects of the purchase of goods and services to citizens in the country of Xanadu.

LC has established a database on over 15,000 specific products including selling prices, common faults, details of manufacturers and suppliers etc, as well as information on about 115 statutes governing the sale of goods and services. These statutes range from the Sales of Goods Act and the Unfair Contract Terms Act to more detailed statutes such as Health and Hygiene regulations for hotels and shop opening hours on specific national holidays. The information is maintained on a purely factual basis. No opinions regarding the service offered by suppliers, or the suitability of products for different tasks, are recorded. This is necessary to ensure that the country's Data Protection legislation is not broken.

At present, this database is only available to LC staff: public access is not permitted.

Current access and maintenance information

LC maintains a telephone call centre in a small town employing over 300 trained staff. Citizens of Xanadu can telephone these staff with specific queries. The staff access the database and provide the relevant information to the citizen.

An analysis of callers to the agency shows the following characteristics:

♦ 10% of callers are aged between 18 and 22 and 65% between 45 and 75.
♦ 60% of callers work in manual or associated jobs.
♦ 90% of callers have a basic qualification in English.
♦ 5% of callers have undertaken some form of computer programming.
♦ 45% of callers have access to the Internet.

The Information Technology systems of LC are maintained by DD, an outsourcing company. For an annual fee, DD maintains and services LC hardware and software and implements new releases of software including the database used by LC. Although the standard of service has generally been good, the senior staff at LC feel that they have a lack of control over the system. DD tends to make changes according to its own timetables, rather than meeting specific requests from management at LC.

Within LC, outsourcing appeared to have the distinct benefit of allowing senior government employees who run the agency, to focus on the type of information being collected, rather than the more basic issues of delivering that information to in-house users.

Developments over the next 24 weeks

Recent developments in communication technology mean that the LC database could be accessible to any citizen via the Internet. Other government agencies have already established similar systems with varying degrees of success. However, the database will need to be transferred from the existing DOS system into a Windows-based relational database. New search and retrieve software will need to be written to facilitate access by untrained users (namely citizens of Xanadu).

As provision of access and maintenance of the database will be the core activity of LC, management are uncertain whether the outsourcing arrangement with DD should continue. However, it is clear that following the implementation of an Internet site, the telephone support centre will be significantly downsized with the loss of up to 300 jobs.

There are a number of alternative development methods currently under consideration for updating the database and implementing the on-line system. These include:

♦ extending the existing outsourcing arrangement.

♦ establishing a new IT department in LC.

♦ employing PP (another government agency, where a similar system is already in place) to establish the database which DD would maintain in-house.

No development method has yet been chosen, although the new system must be implemented within the next 24 weeks in order that the expenditure can fall into the current fiscal year.

Required

(a)   Evaluate the options for updating the database in LC, justifying your choice of strategy. **(18 marks)**

(b)   Using McFarlan's Application Portfolio Theory, evaluate the need to amend the information systems in LC. Illustrate your arguments with examples from the scenario. **(12 marks)**

(c)   (i)   Evaluate whether the new database and Internet site provide an appropriate communication channel for users of the information provided by LC. **(8 marks)**

        (ii)   Evaluate any problems with the design and implementation of the proposed Internet site. **(12 marks)**

(Total : 50 marks)

Question 64 (Question 1 of Exam Paper)

The XYZ partnership is a firm of surveyors operating from seven locations in one country. Each of the 72 partners produces detailed plans for new buildings ranging from individual houses through to small factories and large office blocks. There are 250 support and administration staff distributed evenly around the different offices. The partners and staff use a variety of software ranging from basic word processing and spreadsheets through to specialist computer-assisted drawing and project management packages.

The normal work method within each office has been to implement and use software required in that office with little or no regard for the use of common software. Communication between each office has been limited to typed memos.

After gaining some significant contracts in the last few months, partners and staff have found themselves working from more than one office. One specific difficulty that has arisen is the inability to use the different computer systems because of a lack of standard software. Many partners and staff are also using the Internet at home. The senior partners are now realising that there are synergies to be gained from networking all offices using a Wide Area Network and are considering the implementation of this system.

Required

(a)   Explain how knowledge of the Internet may have helped the senior partners identify deficiencies in the IT systems at XYZ.   **(10 marks)**

(b)   Discuss the problems involved in implementing a suitable information sharing system in XYZ.   **(15 marks)**

(Total : 25 marks)

Question 65 (Question 3 of Exam Paper)

The R&G Computer Company manufactures computers and sells them in 44 different countries. The number of computers sold exceeds 50,000 units each day. The company is profitable and maintains good relations with its customers, suppliers and employees.

After-sales support is provided in a variety of ways including telephone hotlines, on-site visits to major clients and e-mail answering. As explained below, the e-mail support system has just been upgraded with intelligent agent software to assist the support staff.

The R&G Computer Company receives about 600 e-mails each day containing questions about its computers. Topics range from possible system errors to minor problems, such as identifying a specific key on the keyboard or how to use specific features of application software. To try and reduce the work pressure on the support staff, the intelligent agent software is now being used to review the content of e-mails. Keywords in the e-mail are matched to references in the R&G technical support database and these are displayed along with the e-mail, ready for the support staff to provide an answer to the query.

The intelligent agent software can also be configured to monitor the activities of support staff including details such as typing speed and number of e-mails answered each hour or day. The support staff were and remain in favour of implementing the intelligent agent system but are currently unaware of this additional functionality of the software.

Required

(a)   Explain the key characteristics of intelligent agent software that allow autonomous working by those agents.   **(10 marks)**

(b)   Evaluate the usefulness of intelligent agents in assisting the work of the support staff at the R&G Computer Company.   **(15 marks)**

(Total : 25 marks)

Question 66 (Question 4 of Exam Paper)

The AHM Company manufactures luxury sports cars in three factories located within one country. Each factory manufactures a specific model of car and maintains its own production, administration, sales and research departments. Although this effectively replicates all the company systems in each factory, the directors consider that the benefits of local control far outweigh the tangible costs of maintaining those systems.

There is very little communication between the three factories and there are no direct computer links.

The research staff at each factory have recently queried the overall policy of the directors regarding the communication infrastructure. At their first joint staff meeting for five years, the research staff found that many of the projects they were working on were duplicated in the company's other factories. They also found that some useful ideas from the directors and workers had been ignored because they had not been brought to the attention of research staff. Finally, the group discussion also identified four separate potential improvements to models that individual research workers had not found.

Required

(a)   Discuss the organisational, social and technological barriers to sharing of knowledge in the AHM Company, commenting on the impact of these on the efficiency of information transfer within the organisation.   **(13 marks)**

(b)   Evaluate the different systems that could be used to facilitate the sharing of knowledge between the three groups of research staff.   **(12 marks)**

(Total : 25 marks)

Question 67 (Question 5 of Exam Paper)

The WOWR organisation produces books and magazines. It employs 560 staff in 7 different locations. The organisation has been using IT in various departments as follows:

◆   **Production** - stock control including real-time stock and finished goods levels.

◆   **Sales** - historical record of books and magazines sold for the last 15 years.

◆   **Finance and administration** - maintenance of all ledgers, cash book and wages details.

◆   **Human resources** - factual information on employees, such as rate of pay, department, home address and date of birth.

In other words, most of the basic transaction systems within the organisation have been computerised. Additional investment in IT has been limited, partly as a result of the success of the organisation's core businesses, and partly from a lack of desire for change on the part of existing managers.

Recent changes in the senior management of the organisation now mean that additional appropriate IT investment is seen as being a key success criterion.

Required

(a)   Explain a framework that can be used by managers to help assess the priority for investment in competing IT systems within the WOWR organisation.   **(10 marks)**

(b)   (i)   Explain the difference between process innovation and business process re-engineering.   **(5 marks)**

        (ii)   Explain the reasons why process innovation and business process re-engineering are important in an organisation, making reference to the situation in the WOWR organisation where appropriate.   **(10 marks)**

(Total : 25 marks)

November 2002 Exam Questions

SECTION A - 50 MARKS ANSWER THIS QUESTION

Question 68 (Question 1 of Exam Paper)

XL

Organisation overview

The XL organisation searches for, drills, extracts and refines oil and sells petrochemical products. It is split into three main divisions:

- *Drilling and extraction* - responsible for locating new oil deposits, assessing their economic viability for drilling, and then extracting oil from viable locations.

- *Refining* - transporting of oil to refineries around the world and refining the oil into various products from plastics through to petrol and diesel products for motor vehicles.

- *Retail* - various sub-divisions responsible for selling oil and petrochemical products obtained in the refining process.

The FB division

One of the Retail sub-divisions is the FB division. It sells petrol from retail outlets (also called 'petrol stations') for all types of road vehicles. The division owns 315 petrol stations in one country, and has retail sales which represent a 23% share of the total market in that country. One of the FB division's objectives is to attain a market share of 30% in that country within the next five years, partly by increasing sales in existing locations and partly by opening another 35 petrol stations.

In the past five years, 27 new petrol stations have been opened by the FB division, mainly on new motorways and major roads. Very little information was needed concerning the economic viability of each of the new locations. Generally, if a new road is opened then cars start using it. The government is unlikely to build a road where one is not required. However, a shift in emphasis by government away from road building and towards improving the railway infrastructure limits possibilities for building new roads.

Petrol station management

Each petrol station sells a range of goods, apart from petrol. Depending on the location of the petrol stations and the profile of customers visiting them, the range of goods sold may include groceries, newspapers and magazines, car-care products, confectionery, and houseplants and flowers.

Each petrol station has a Manager who is responsible for the day-to-day running of the petrol station including the ordering of goods and petrol, maintaining appropriate stock levels, hiring staff and allocating working hours on a rota basis. Each Manager is paid a basic salary and a bonus based on the net profit earned by the petrol station.

Executive information system

The Board of XL has access to an Executive Information System (EIS), which was developed and installed five years ago. The EIS focuses on the provision of internal information, providing summaries of the profits of each petrol station, along with numbers of staff employed and performance against budget for the current year.

The user interface is based on an old version of Windows (Windows 3.1), although the output is mainly text based. Information is, however, provided on a timely basis with detailed performance information made available within three days of the end of each month.

Strategic planning

A recent addition to the EIS was a strategic planning model. This software attempts to analyse the current performance of each division of XL, and by applying external information such as general interest rates and inflation rates, outputs information on the future profitability of the organisation. This software has been well received by the Directors. The ability to forecast three years into the future has assisted their strategic planning discussions considerably.

Overall, the Directors value the current system and see little point in amending it. The IT Director has proposed changes other than the strategic planning model in the past, although these were not implemented. One of the main fears expressed by the Directors regarding any change in systems was the possibility of information overload and consequent lack of focus on the key operational areas of the XL organisation.

Required

(a)   Compare and contrast the characteristics of the information requirements of petrol station Managers with those of the members of the Board of XL.   **(12 marks)**

(b)   Recommend amendments to the EIS which will help the Directors to make more informed decisions regarding the siting of new petrol stations.   **(15 marks)**

(c)   Explain how an information system can be designed to prevent information overload occurring for the members of the Board of XL.   **(13 marks)**

(d)   Discuss the limitations of using the current strategic planning model in the XL organisation.   **(10 marks)**

(Total : 50 marks)

SECTION B - 50 MARKS ANSWER TWO QUESTIONS ONLY

Question 69 (Question 2 of Exam Paper)

Expert Systems

Required

(a)   Discuss the extent to which Expert Systems can be used in the management of strategic information.   **(10 marks)**

The SZ hospital is located in a large city. It employs 300 administrative staff as well as 500 medical staff, including 160 qualified doctors. Over 65,000 patients are treated each year for a wide range of illnesses.

In an attempt to decrease costs and enhance services to customers, the governing body of the hospital has recently introduced two new expert systems.

System A reviews the performance of doctors by monitoring hours worked, success rate of operations, number of patients treated and similar indicators. In other hospitals, monitoring these trends has been found to be a more reliable method of identifying decreases in the operational efficiency of doctors than using reviews performed by human staff. The system cost £1.5m and has an initial cost saving of 7 administrative staff. Doctors and their professional union have rejected the system on the grounds that it causes them unnecessary stress and detailed monitoring of their work is not required.

System B is a diagnostic expert system. It aims to assist junior doctors to make more accurate diagnoses of illnesses. However, use of the program was halted when a patient died after a junior doctor followed a recommendation made by the expert system. Initial investigations, still confidential, disclosed a programming error in the system. A proposed decrease in the number of junior doctors has been postponed while the software supplier carries out a more detailed investigation.

Required

(b) Evaluate the social and employment effects of the expert systems at the SZ hospital.

(15 marks)

(Total : 25 marks)

Question 70 (Question 3 of Exam Paper)

RR University

The RR University provides tuition to degree level to 12,000 students, both on campus and by distance learning courses. The University has 34 different departments, each of which specialises in one specific area, such as economics, geography or astronomy.

Over the past 10 years, information systems have been developed in each department to meet the specific needs of that department. However, the systems are incompatible with each other and use a wide range of software applications.

The information systems are becoming expensive to operate, as well as requiring duplication of input where students study in more than one department. Additional duplication occurs when student details have to be entered into the central University database, which is used for monitoring total student numbers.

The Board of Management of the University has decided that the University should develop and implement an integrated database for future information requirements and place all existing data into a single data warehouse.

Moreover, any new system must meet the information requirements of the central database as well as those of the individual departments.

Required

(a) (i) Evaluate the use of data within the University. **(7 marks)**

(ii) Explain how the Board of Management should use Critical Success Factors (CSFs) in revising the current information system. **(8 marks)**

(b) Discuss the disadvantages of data warehousing with specific reference to the situation at the RR University. **(10 marks)**

(Total : 25 marks)

Question 71 (Question 4 of Exam Paper)

IT strategy

Required

(a)   Evaluate the need for an IT strategy in a business operating in the service sector (such as a large international firm of accountants). Assume that the primary method of customer contact is face-to-face or by telephone.   **(15 marks)**

(b)   Explain the information intensity matrix of Porter and Millar and discuss its relevance to a service sector business such as an accounting firm.   **(10 marks)**

Note: you may refer to any appropriate service sector business in answering this question.

(Total : 25 marks)

Question 72 (Question 5 of Exam Paper)

VNS

The VNS charity monitors and collects information on various diseases affecting the brain. It was established in 1960 to provide hospitals with detailed statistical information concerning the effects of these diseases and provide recommendations for treatments. This information is generally well received by hospitals and has led to a fall in mortality rates. Over the years, the charity has established a large database of information, including numerous case studies from people showing how they have learnt to live with the different diseases.

The charity is now receiving over 250 telephone calls each day from hospital staff and members of the public requesting information. Staff within the charity are becoming over-worked trying to provide this information. Other important activities such as updating the database of cases and supplying statistical information on the diseases to hospitals are also *not* being carried out in a timely fashion. A few members of staff are actually retaining information deliberately because they see power in retaining access to the information rather than sharing the information with colleagues through a database.

To try and alleviate these issues, the management of the charity has decided to implement an Extranet, and allow registered users of the charity full access to the database of information. This solution will involve diverting over 25% of the charity's budget to the production and maintenance of the Extranet and associated hardware. Existing staff will be required to re-input information in specific formats for internal statistics collation and Extranet use. The Extranet database will be updated daily and staff will be responsible for vetting applications for access to the Extranet.

Required

(a)   Evaluate the potential use of an Extranet within the VNS charity.   **(15 marks)**

(b)   Identify and evaluate other information-sharing systems that the VNS charity could implement to provide information to third parties.   **(10 marks)**

(Total : 25 marks)

Answers

Answer 1

Information Systems

Tutorial note:	
Required	- This question is relevant for several areas of the syllabus, especially those which stress the evaluation of information and information systems.
	You must apply your knowledge to the information given in the scenario to answer both parts of this question.
Not required	- General discussion on executive information systems and use of information, without referring to the scenario in parts (a) and (b).

(a)   One of the main reasons why B5 Cars' EIS is becoming expensive to operate is the amount of data which has been, and is being, accumulated. For an EIS to be effective there is a requirement for large amounts of information to be easily accessible: the data should be on-line and as up-to-date as possible. This has disk storage implications, which increase over time as the volume of information increases.

The increased costs do not end with disk storage, however. As the system is required to handle larger volumes of data, there are numerous knock-on costs. The larger the database the more processing power required to conduct straightforward operations. Therefore, another increased expense may be a requirement to invest in hardware, as the original processor proves inadequate to handle the volume of information within acceptable response times.

Data is obtained from various different external sources; this may be causing a requirement for extra disk storage in excess of the amount required as a result of the normal growth of the databank.

The information requirements of the executives using an EIS may change over time. This means that, however carefully the system was set up originally, there will be costs involved in making changes to the way in which the system is set up. The degree with which maintenance and support costs increase will be dependent to some extent on the original design of the programs and database and to what extent the information requirements alter.

The costs of transmission of information could have increased since the EIS was originally installed. Network charges could have increased and, as the volume of data increases, particularly if appropriate hardware investment is not made, it is likely that it will take longer to extract the required information. This will result in greater costs of actually using the line.

The EIS uses data collated from various sources. There are potential costs associated with the capture of this data; large amounts of data may need to be manually keyed in which has implications on staffing costs or the cost of hiring an agency to do the work.

The external information being purchased by B5 Cars might have increased in price, or they might be purchasing more than they originally anticipated. Cost of information could therefore be a factor in increasing the overall cost of the EIS.

Examination tip – Your answer to this question must be directed at the company itself. The examiner is looking for you to interpret the problems faced by B5 Cars.

(b)   Management's decision to concentrate on internally produced information will have serious implications.

Market information - it is important for companies to be aware of the activities of their competitors. By collecting only internally produced information the management are getting a restricted picture of what is really taking place. Management need to know how their products measure up to those of their competitors in terms of quality, design and production.

Without external information the information system can hardly be described as an EIS, but would be providing information at an operational level. It is important for organisations to establish their own indicators as a means of measuring their performance, but it is at least as important to set these in context. For example, if a production unit is performing well against its own measures but is failing to perform well in relation to its competitors, management needs to be aware of this and take action to recover the situation.

Without competitor information B5 Cars may find that they are out of line with the rest of the industry. They may find that their competitors are offering free finance, as an example, whereas B5 Cars are offering cheap finance at 7% APR; their main competitors may offer free finance for the first year after purchase. This information is invaluable to B5 Cars to ensure that they remain competitive.

Customer information - B5 could lose the sources of information relating to customers. This loss would have a damaging impact on the firm; any organisation needs to know about its market, both existing and potential, to survive and grow. Even if an organisation currently enjoys a strong position in its sector of the market it would be shortsighted to assume that this situation would remain without consideration of the ever-changing market. Predicting market behaviour is challenging enough with access to wide-ranging information from external sources; without these tools the task becomes virtually impossible.

Suppliers - information regarding current suppliers and potential suppliers would be lost. This might result in B5 Cars not making the right decisions or putting in place contingency plans should there be a change in supplier status. It could result in components becoming more expensive to obtain, which would be reflected in the price of cars or a decrease in their profit margin.

Trade/industry - there are many sources of information on specific industries, in this case the motor vehicle industry, which will be lost. Trade Associations established for manufacturers in a particular industry can provide useful information and comparisons about all manufacturers within an industry. The industry provides information with regard to legislation on safety standards and new technology, which could be used to speed up processes or automate production. B5 Cars would not necessarily have the most up-to-date car plants if it loses information from its industry.

The effect on the company's information system

An EIS needs to have access to information, which is up-to-date and relevant for managers to manage the organisation. The loss of access as described above will, in a very short time, produce the effect that the information available via the EIS is inadequate for effective decision-making. The decisions taken will be short-term and reactive.

The system will cease to function as an EIS but will become a transaction processing system, providing a control mechanism. The kind of information the system will produce will be at an operational level (how many labour hours was taken to produce a particular car; how many hours of overtime etc.) rather than providing information to support management decisions. Given the expense of initially setting up an EIS, to use it purely as a transaction processing system would not payback the capital costs of development.

The system would become a closed loop system, working on its own feedback without taking into account any external factors.

The effect on the company's products

Without access to external information, B5 Cars will be unaware of technological innovations; as a result their products will lag behind the rest of the industry and their own innovations may not take full advantage of new technological breakthroughs. There is the danger of 'reinventing the wheel', which will leave them behind in terms of technological advances and incur unnecessary research and development costs.

There is also a chance that products might not meet new government safety standards and might need to be re-worked or even recalled to incorporate new safety features.

External market information would assist B5 Cars to identify trends in the motor industry, from which they could attempt to create marketing opportunities. Without this information marketing opportunities will be forgone.

The lack of market information will mean that the organisation cannot accurately position their products in terms of pricing which in turn will affect their profitability. With accurate market information a producer is in a better position to optimise profits by pricing their product at a price low enough to sell, but high enough to ensure maximum profits.

The Board's decision appears to be misguided which, in the longer-term, may affect the organisation's profitability and future market share.

Answer 2

E-mail

Tutorial note:	
Required	- This question combines two areas of the syllabus – channels of communication and e-mail technology.
	The question is in two parts; in answering the first part you must discuss the impact on work practices of communication by e-mail.
	The second part requires a discussion of the situations where e-mail would NOT be an appropriate communication medium.
Not required	- The communication process using e-mail technology.

Examination tip - Remember the examiner requires a discussion on the impact on work practices.

(a)   Communication by e-mail impacts on work practices in a number of ways. It affects the speed of communication, it adds to the choice of media to use when sending messages or conducting meetings and it accommodates teleworking to suit different lifestyles. There are also negative aspects to the communication channel. It encourages 'chatting' and other non-essential communications and some people use a type of shorthand, which does not seem very business-like.

The speed of communication with e-mail is one of the major impacts on work practices. There is an almost instant delivery of messages, documents, reports or letters. The technology allows the same message to be sent simultaneously to a group of people, such as a committee, and there are no significant time delays, whereby one person receives the information before another. This particular feature reduces ambiguities and helps facilitate co-ordination.

Because people receive their messages as they are sitting at their computers working, there is also a tendency for them to reply more quickly than they would to a circulated hard copy. This means that delays in waiting for information can be reduced or eliminated and time can be spent doing more productive work. Unfortunately, when people send messages that require a response, there is an expectation that it will be instantaneous. When there is a delay it generally creates a certain amount of impatience and frustration.

Another impact of e-mail on work practices is that it increases the choice of communication channel. Many tasks can be completed more quickly and effectively than would have previously been the case without e-mail facilities. It has advantages over traditional forms of communication. Documents no longer need to be despatched by courier. It is more economical than sending letters because it costs less to send an e-mail than the cost of a postage stamp, especially when fast delivery is required. It can be more secure than sending a letter or memo because access can be denied by the use of passwords. Electronic delivery and read receipts can be requested, and a record can be kept of messages, which gives it an advantage over telephone calls.

Because e-mail allows information to be disseminated more readily via circulation lists, bulletin boards and discussion databases, the need for meetings is greatly reduced. Up to quite recently companies had regular committee-type meetings just to distribute information. These types of meetings can be very costly and do not always achieve what is required. The use of e-mail can be a far more efficient and reliable way of keeping everyone informed. There are still some types of meetings where it is not possible for them to be replaced by e-mail, but the arrangements for them eg, the distribution of agenda, can all be distributed more efficiently with e-mail.

Examination tip - *Remember that the downside can also impact on the work practices.*

The downside to all this is that it has obvious implications for employment and the requisite skills of the work force. There can be a tendency for employees to become attached to their computer screens and avoid social contact.

The Internet, with its e-mail facilities, is a part of many people's lifestyle and is no longer considered a form of communication for business only. It has enabled teleworking, with many more people working away from the office environment, changing the entire focus of work. The virtual organisation allows individuals to work on a project or task and communicate with other members of the team, using e-mail, as though they were sharing an office. It no longer matters where people are located or what time suits them to be working. The Internet allows e-mail messages to be sent anywhere in the world at any time of the day or night for the cost of a telephone call. The message is sent to a mailbox and this can be accessed when the recipient logs on to their computer.

There are bound to be some disadvantages associated with communication by e-mail. Because it is very easy to use there may be several messages going backwards and forwards between individuals in a short space of time. This can impact on work practices where people are tempted to use their e-mail facility as a chat line for social as well as work purposes. They can also waste time by distributing items that are not related to work, such as screen savers and games.

Another disadvantage is that messages sent via e-mail tend to be much more informal than traditional hard copy letters and can also be more informal than a telephone call. They are inclined to be very short, without any frills such as salutations. Certain groups have developed a type of language that is only used in e-mail communications. This language uses keyboard characters to denote certain words or phrases. Unfortunately, this trend will have an impact on the language used at work. Employers have been complaining for a long time that school leavers have poor literacy skills and cannot write a business letter. With fewer reasons to practise these skills because of new technologies, formal letter writing will become redundant.

(b)   Like all forms of communication, e-mail has its place and is very useful and efficient. However, there are a number of occasions where it would not be an appropriate form of communication. They include interviews and meetings of a personal or confidential nature, group discussions and training sessions.

E-mail messages are inappropriate for interviews of a personal or confidential nature. One-to-one interviews for a job or an appraisal could not be conducted without the parties to the interview being together. Part of the interview technique is to see how people react to different types of questioning and this could not be handled by e-mail. Disciplinary and grievance interviews are similar but raise sensitive issues, which do not lend themselves to being reduced to short e-mail messages. Some messages are so sensitive that even face-to-face communication is difficult.

Although there are ways of making messages secure and delivering them to the right person, there can be security problems associated with sending messages over a computer network. Within an organisation, messages can be delivered to the wrong person via the internal e-mail system because they have a similar name to the intended recipient. Messages sent via the Internet may pass through several servers en route to their destination and at any of these servers the messages could be read, intercepted or copied.

For planning, agreeing strategies or negotiating, e-mail would be inappropriate. Discussion groups, conferences, meetings and training sessions are all occasions when e-mail would not be a suitable method of communication. It would only take ten people in a discussion group, using e-mail to send items to each other to be discussed, for the messages to become very confused. People participating in the discussion could soon lose track of how it is progressing. Because there is a mixture of oral and visual communication involved in some conferences and training sessions, they are unsuitable for e-mail. It is very difficult to show the subtleties of body language other than at face-to-face meetings.

Answer 3

Monitored Websites

Tutorial note:	
Required	- This question focuses on the role of the management accountant in determining the use and value of information, rather than the actual preparation of information.
	Part (a) requires an explanation of whether the information obtained from the monitored websites is accurate.
	Part (b) asks how the costs and benefits of one particular information source could be determined.
Not required	- Typical cost/benefit analysis techniques.

(a)   There are a number of ways that the analysts at LMC plc could check the accuracy of the information obtained from the monitored websites. They could:

♦   Compare the information from each of the websites and if the majority of the websites are all giving the same information then it is likely that this might be correct. They could therefore discount any information from those websites that are in the extreme in relation to all other websites.

♦   Identify the websites that have proved to be accurate in the past based upon different categories of information supplied. This would enable them to identify those websites that have previously provided accurate information on certain areas and from that they could build up a reference guide for the most accurate websites for specific types of information.

♦   Compare the information received to other sources of information such as the Financial Times, Reuters or Bloombergs. They could also check with government-owned websites. Depending on what type of information is being provided they can check with an independent source.

♦   Check the information with the originating source. They might have to pay for this information or it might take longer to check because of the volume of different sources for the origination of the data. However, they might use sampling techniques to determine which original sources to check with.

(b)   Website monitoring can be an expensive operation. It is not clear whether LMC are using web-agents to monitor the websites or whether this is being done by the analysts which would be very time-consuming.

In order to determine the costs and benefits of website monitoring, it would first have to be determined the cost of alternative methods of obtaining the information. This might involve identifying the costs of reviewing and upgrading the current EIS system and whether the same quality and variety of information could be obtained through the EIS.

In addition, it would be necessary to identify the benefits of obtaining the information. The scenario states that the directors are always interested in the actions of competitors, but if no use is made of the information provided and it is purely monitoring competitor information then the cost of doing this would not be recouped by any benefits.

Some costs are fairly easy to calculate such as the costs of communication, analyst salaries, equipment etc, however, it is always difficult to assess the costs of not having the information because even if the competitor websites are just being monitored without any action being taken this does not mean that action might not be taken on some information in the future.

Evaluating the benefits of the information provided would also be fairly difficult, but generally there would need to be a comparison of the number of clients purchasing information prior to the monitoring and the number purchasing after the monitoring had been introduced.

It could also be evaluated in relation to the profitability of LMC prior to the introduction of monitoring and after the introduction of monitoring. If LMC is spending more money in monitoring websites than it is recouping in additional fees then it would appear that the benefits are not outweighing the costs. However, there are so many other factors which could be affecting 'profitability' which are not relevant to the website monitoring that care would need to be taken in analysing and interpreting the results.

It could be that the website monitoring is the most cost effective way to obtain the information they require, but by carrying out a comparison to assess the accuracy of the information from over 100 different websites they might be able to reduce the number of websites being monitored by eliminating those that have been proved to have supplied inaccurate information in the past.

This could then reduce the costs of the website monitoring whilst still obtaining the same quality of information.

Answer 4

Information Centre

Tutorial note:	
Required	- This question examines how valuable an information centre can be to an organisation, especially when the centre is seen to be a source of expenditure only.
	In part (a) you must be able to justify the existence of the information centre from non-financial benefits.
	In part (b) you are asked to show how a network can assist the information centre in its provision of support to computer users.
Not required	- A justification on financial grounds in part (a).

Examination tip - Marks will be awarded for a memo format. Do not give them away by ignoring this requirement.

(a)   **Memorandum**

To: The Board of JH plc

From: Chartered Management Accountant

Date: 20th February 200X

Future of the Information Centre

The Information Centre (IC) currently consists of 20 staff and has an annual operating budget of £4 million. Its purpose is to support the company in achieving the corporate mission, and set out below are the main justifications for the continuance of the Information Centre on non-financial grounds.

IT systems and standards

JH plc has a high investment in modern IT systems and they are perceived as being the cornerstone to our success in meeting the requirements of our clients. In order to support such a level of investment, an IC becomes essential not only for dealing with Help Desk queries and error reports, but also for ensuring that the correct equipment and software are used and that the maximum efficient usage is obtained from the investment.

It is extremely important that corporate standards are maintained, eg, for file naming and data field definitions. This not only facilitates the sharing of information, but also ensures the forward compatibility of future systems and applications. The IC is a fundamental instrument in ensuring that standards are being used to the best advantage.

Freight business

With up to 2,000 corporate clients, and as a result of the inevitable large range of different products being delivered to many different locations, the propensity for error is extremely high. The reliability and efficiency of JH plc is exclusively the result of earlier investment decisions in IT. It just would not be possible to support such complex operations without the necessary systems. Indeed, our clients now expect this level of service from us. The IC can support systems to ensure they continue to operate effectively and can offer fault correction and fixes in the case of system failure.

Staff considerations

As JH plc has exploited technology to further the company mission, the staff have been supportive. They have adapted readily to IT systems because the IC has been there to 'hold their hands' when needed, to encourage them to develop applications to the fullest extent and to get them out of trouble when systems have not performed as expected.

The staff rely on this assurance and therefore feel confident about using existing systems and readily adapt to new ones because of the IC support. The IC keeps a log of problems and also records suggestions. Without the IC, staff would not have quick and easy access to such information and, as a result, systems will suffer.

Profitability

In order to be the most profitable freight forwarder, JH plc needs sustainable competitive advantage.

We have established a lead with our IT investment strategy because the IC has been closely associated with business objectives. Corporate and individual system requirements have been developed and maintained to high standards. As the IC is staffed by professionals, they are able to translate business requirements into appropriate solutions.

It may be possible to improve short-term profitability by closing the IC and saving £4 million. This, however, puts at risk the considerable investment made in IT systems and will undermine long-term profitability. The inefficient use of technology and the inability to exploit new technology will impact market share and damage our existing competitive advantage. It is, therefore, recommended that, subject to any improvements that can be achieved by analysing external benchmarking criteria, the IC continues.

Signed:

Chartered Management Accountant

(b)   The information centre can use the network in many different ways to provide an enhanced service to the staff of JH plc.

Networks allow bulletins and other messages to be broadcast quickly to everyone on the network. Tips and helpful guides can be sent from the IC staff if there is a particular aspect of a system that staff need assistance with. This can be extended to provide the bulk of training requirements for a system eg, via Computer Based Training (CBT) packages.

The network facilitates e-mail, which is a particularly useful form of communication. Sometimes it is better to see instructions on how to operate a system written down, and so if there is a particular problem, the IC staff can analyse it remotely and send a message explaining the problem, how it is fixed and what needs to be done in future.

With the linking up to external networks such as the Internet, it is important that the integrity of JH plc's network is maintained both from a security and anti-virus point of view. The IC staff can help in educating other staff, and can carry out test checks using appropriate network control software to ensure that all JH plc's systems are protected.

In the case of error reports, it is possible for control of a terminal or workstation to be switched to someone in the IC, so that remote diagnostic tests can be carried out. In many instances, staff may not be sure what an error message means, or may simply not have had sufficient training on a system. Errors can, therefore, be reported which, prior to the network, would have required a visit from the IC staff. This could be costly and time-consuming and the network could, therefore, facilitate remote diagnostic checks.

Answer 5

Information Characteristics

Tutorial note:	
Required	- Management information systems and expert systems can be complementary rather than substitute for each other.
	In part (a) you are required to explain the differences in the information being provided by each system.
	Part (b) – describe the conditions that must exist for an ES to be considered.
	In part (c) you are to outline three advantages of using Expert systems.
Not required	- More than three conditions in part (b).
	Speed and accuracy as advantages in part (c).

(a)   In terms of accuracy of information, the MIS should be accurate and give a true reflection of the medical history of a particular patient. It is the basic record-keeping system for the hospital's patients. It holds the records for each patient including details of past illnesses and symptoms, and has the ability to produce reports either on statistical or individual basis. The hospital uses the MIS to automate the record keeping and, instead of writing out patients' notes to be kept in a paper-based file, this information is input to the computer system to create an electronic file.

The expert system is unlikely to be as accurate or precise as the MIS. It does not have records and data but comprises a knowledge base and an inference engine, which is a rule set from which the likelihood of illnesses can be inferred. It is used to provide several diagnoses with a range of probabilities and precision can only be increased by entering more symptoms or details about the patient or the illness.

The MIS must be complete and up-to-date. The system depends on inputs made to it following a patient's visit to hospital. The doctor may input information during the consultation with the patient and any medication prescribed would be recorded.

The ES depends on being updated to reflect the latest research findings or expert opinion. There is a very good chance of it being incomplete and out of date and not representing a complete body of knowledge. Also, if the knowledge base was created by the hospital, ie the software framework purchased and the information (knowledge) input locally, then there is no guarantee that all the necessary information will be present.

The MIS produces information quickly with typical response times of a few seconds. Most MIS are record-based within a hierarchical or relational database, both types being able to display records quickly at the touch of a button.

In comparison, the ES is very slow because it may need to consider many different combinations of symptoms, rules and information before it can perform a diagnosis. If the patient is showing unusual symptoms, the ES may take a lot longer relatively (ie minutes rather than seconds) before it can respond, particularly. This obviously depends on the sophistication of the inference engine and the speed and capacity of the processors used.

MIS data is only reliable if it has been input correctly. Even if the information is incomplete, the doctor can see from the screen where the gaps are and, with the patient's help, it should be possible to obtain a good indication of their history. The MIS can therefore offer a degree of assurance that there is control over matching the patient to the information.

In the case of the ES the information should never be considered 100% reliable because the doctor or consultant will not know if all the relevant information has been input. For example, some completely different illnesses are identified by similar symptoms. It is very difficult to diagnose appendicitis because the symptoms are similar to stomach problems, constipation problems and pregnancy problems. When the ES creates its diagnostic inference, it will only pick up the information present and could therefore present a faulty diagnosis.

(b) Three of the conditions that should be present if a particular domain of knowledge warrants the building of an expert system are:

Examination tip - Only three conditions are required.

(i) The expertise of the expert system is rare and in demand. This is often obvious when the expert is always too busy answering the questions of others to do his or her own job properly. In many situations the ES is used by people who are experts in an associated field but sometimes need to augment their knowledge with specialised information. For example, doctors who are GPs may need to find out if a particular combination of drugs may react together to give bad side effects, or they may need to find out information about a rare speciality. Lawyers or accountants may need to consult about a complex and/or specialised category of law.

(ii) The problem must be one that is worth solving and it must cost less to develop the system than the cost of non-experts making the wrong decision. Examples include situations where decisions are taken by non-experts, as in some credit rating decisions or when the cost of making a bad decision is so horrendous that the right decision is vital. This often occurs in legal situations.

(iii) The expert is capable of explaining how decisions are made in all situations, and the decisions that are reached are consistent. If the expert might reach different conclusions given the same data, or the decision is taken on 'feel', then an expert system is not appropriate. It should be noted that some experts may find it difficult to explain how a decision has been made because their experience enables them to reach a conclusion automatically. Although the decision may be instant, it is the result of a series of logical thoughts and therefore is suitable for an expert system.

(c) Three advantages of using expert systems:

Examination tip - Only three advantages of using expert systems are required.

(i) Expert systems can be useful training aids in two ways. Firstly, where the trainee makes decisions based on the output from an ES, the manager can be confident that the right decision is reached despite the trainee's inexperience. Secondly, prior training with an expert system may enable a person starting a job to be immediately useful.

(ii)   Experts are able to work where their expertise is of more value because they are released from the mundane task of answering routine questions.

(iii)   The process of building an expert system can provide significant advantages in understanding the problems to be solved. By going through the disciplines that are vital in building a knowledge base, the expert is often able to understand their own decision making better, and sometimes to eradicate bad habits that may have crept into their work.

Answer 6

Management Information

Tutorial note:	
Required	- The Company in this question has correctly set up a management information system. The problem is that the information provided might not be appropriate for the managers that are supposed to be using it.
	Part (a) requires a critique of the current information provision and also to show how it can be improved.
	In part (b) you are asked to explain the information that a management information system cannot provide.
Not required	- The information that a management information system **can** provide.

(a)   (i)   The directors need information that helps them to control the business. This type of strategic information normally has the following characteristics:

   ♦   it contains probabilistic information;
   ♦   it is highly summarised;
   ♦   it is not as accurate as operational information;
   ♦   it is often used to make poorly structured decisions;
   ♦   it is forward looking rather than historical information;
   ♦   non-routine reports will often be required.

The information obtained from the present MIS does not seem suitable for the strategic decisions that the Board of RG Ltd need to take. In particular, the technology involved in glues and solvents is very specialised and new chemical formulae could make old processes out of date very quickly. This is therefore an aspect that the MIS should take into account. The weaknesses in the information currently being provided to the directors include the following:

Examination tip - You must address the problems outlined in the scenario.

Summary business plan - this is forward looking and does give some direction, although two years would be an absolute minimum for most strategic planning. Unfortunately, the plan has been prepared by an inexperienced person who seems to have ignored the information content of past production data. This means that assumptions about growth rates and trends may not be readily apparent and so this plan does not facilitate the required support for strategic decision-making.

Because historical data is not shown on the report, it will be difficult for the directors to assess the assumptions lying behind the report. This is very important when dealing with future estimates where judgement will play a large part and will be especially important here where the author of the report is inexperienced.

Stock balances - this report is much too detailed for the directors and should be presented in a much more summarised form. As it stands, the report would be of use to people much further down the hierarchy in the firm who are making day-to-day operational decisions.

Changes in demand - this may be too detailed, but the directors may well want to have access to this information on demand. Five years is probably going back too far as there will have been many market changes over that time and early trends may no longer be relevant. The report seems to be poorly presented being purely numerical and not allowing the directors to compare different sections.

(ii) The information could be improved as follows:

Examination tip - *The question asked for particular reference to other outputs.*

In addition to the existing reports the following could be useful in strategic planning:

♦ Summary accounting information - although this is historical, future projections may depend on an analysis of past trends.

♦ Sales analyses by product, customer, customer type, geographical area and sales person. Sales value, volume and gross profit percentages should be shown.

♦ A financial model that allows the directors to see the effects of different inputs and assumptions - what if or sensitivity analysis.

The existing reports could be improved as follows:

Summary business plan - this needs to look further ahead and include historical information, projections and assumptions on which the projections are based. It should show income and expenditure on likely new product lines; contain market and competitor information - in particular, competitor analysis and other market dynamics.

Stock balances - should be much more summarised with only important variances or significant balances reported eg, large value stock holding that would require the directors' attention. They should also be arranged in ways, which are of importance to the management of the business.

Summary of changes - information about all sections should be available on the same screen to allow comparisons to be made. The reason behind the changes to the numbers are required to support this report. In particular, any patterns associated with industry statistics, market growth and the changes in market share should be reported - perhaps with the use of text and graphs as well as numerical summaries. This would help the directors to identify important trends and significant events. It might be possible to omit data from over three years ago.

The MIS needs to blend the summaries from RG Ltd's operational systems with externally generated information in order to produce strategically useful information for the directors to use.

Examination tip - *Remember that you are writing about information that any MIS at RG Ltd is unlikely to be able to provide.*

(b) The MIS will predominantly use data that is generated internally by the organisation, though some external data, such as market growth and size can be entered. New products, new applications of existing products and the identification of new markets are all difficult to predict, particularly when there is only historical information on existing product lines to work with. The MIS system will be particularly poor at dealing with the following:

♦ SWOT analysis;

♦ assessing customer satisfaction;

♦ PEST analysis - the effects of political, economic and social changes and predicting technological advances;

♦ making use of information about competitors.

An MIS may be able to provide some information in these areas, but strategic information by its very nature tends to be unpredictable, informal and unstructured and therefore unsuitable for inclusion within an MIS. Strategic information needs to be able to include information on new products, information about new technology and new markets etc. For example, the directors of RG Ltd need information that is specific to the glue and solvents industry such as market measures, industry benchmarks and competitor measures of performance. In addition, government policy towards environmental and ecological matters and the consumer movement in general need to be taken into account particularly if any of RG Ltd's processes result in potential pollution.

As an example of the limitations of the MIS, consider the strategic decision about whether to expand abroad. It may be possible to look up some elementary data on a public database, but it is unlikely that such information will be incorporated into a formal MIS. Most of the work done on this decision will be once off, *ad hoc* calculations. They may be performed on a spreadsheet, but they will be outside the routine reporting systems.

Answer 7

Meetings

Tutorial note:	
Required	- This question looks at the human problems in using e-mail by considering the situation in an organisation before and after e-mail has been implemented. Your answer should investigate the problems that the senior employees have with e-mail and how they might want to revert to the older system.

E-mail is a form of written communication and has many of the advantages and disadvantages of conventional writing. There are, of course some additional characteristics of e-mail, which arise because of the technology used. The problems and benefits of using e-mail are as follows:

Examination tip - From your own experiences, you should be able to show that you can appreciate the human advantages and problems of implementing the system.

Benefits of using e-mail

Information and instructions can be distributed very widely and very quickly within the organisation; distribution could also be cheaper. The speed of communication will be very useful in YK plc where the market is volatile and decisions are required on a daily basis. The latest strategic market information can be made instantly available to all those affected.

With e-mail, many users will prepare and type their own messages. This can be faster than the more conventional method of asking for a message to be typed-up, proofing it and checking corrections.

Written information, if well worded, should be less ambiguous that spoken communication. Even when one wants spoken information to be uniformly supplied to each recipient, spoken communication will contain different words, different emphasis and nuances for each user to whom it is delivered. Some users will completely misunderstand what has been said; some will deny what has been said. E-mail will allow uniform messages to be sent to many recipients.

Written messages can contain a high content of technical content information as the messages can be filed then referred to later. It would be inappropriate to supply this information in any other form as recipients could simply not understand and remember it as it is delivered. They need to be able to look back and study the information.

Written information is more formal. For example, if some company rules change about expense allowances this should be communicated formally using a written memo; it would probably be inappropriate to communicate this informally.

The distribution of messages in an e-mail system can be made very reliable. Once e-mail addresses and circulation lists have been properly set up, messages are unlikely to go astray. Frequently Directors are engaged on other activities and may not always be available on the telephone. Therefore e-mail enables messages to be delivered to them with a certainty that they will receive the message. Message senders can check to see if recipients have yet accessed each message. Recipients cannot later claim that they omitted to do something because they did not receive the instruction.

Messages can be left for recipients even if they are not present. Using data communication equipment such as modems, messages can be sent, retrieved and read from remote locations. Employees can therefore be kept completely up-to-date no matter where they are.

Once an e-mail system has been set-up, users can use it to download information from databases and bulletin boards. It is not confined to using information which has been actively sent. The wide availability of information for retrieval can increase the quality of decisions that are made.

Problems that may arise

Information overload. Because it is easy to create messages and easy to then distribute them widely, people will. It would not be unusual for the Directors at YK plc to return to the office after a few days away and be faced with scores of messages. Many of these will be relatively trivial, but all have to be retrieved and read to ensure that important information is not overlooked. Time then needs to be spent sorting through the individual e-mail messages and prioritising the actions. The consequence is that Directors may become 'tied' to their terminal for extended periods, which can impact on other areas of the business operations. It is preferable if messages can be flagged to give an indication of their importance and urgency.

If there are many items to deal with, a strategic communication could be skimmed over without being fully digested, making it possible to miss important messages. Many users will opt to print out the messages they have received. There can be so many messages that, rather than heading towards a paperless office, consumption of paper actually increases.

Senior managers may spend too long composing and typing their own messages when it might be more efficient for them to delegate this.

Written information lacks important qualities that can only be enjoyed with face-to-face contact. This problem is explained more fully below.

The popularity of face-to-face meetings

Face-to-face meetings are an inescapable part of business life. People will travel (expensively) around the world so that they can hold a meeting and messages appear to be an inadequate substitute for meetings. Face-to-face meetings have the following benefits:

Examination tip - *The question specifically asks you to include an explanation of why the Directors of YK plc are returning to face-to-face meetings on an informal basis*

♦ They are interactive. Participants can respond instantly to information: agreeing with it, questioning it, asking for clarification.

♦ Many participants can participate at the same time, sharing ideas and all gaining mutual understanding. There are enormous benefits in trying out ideas on other people who might immediately see objections or who might immediately be approving.

♦ In meetings, communication is not limited to merely the words spoken. Tone of voice and body language can also convey important information and lead to increased understanding. In some cases, the only effective way for the directors to deal with a matter will be by talking to the individuals concerned.

♦ As no formal record need be kept, participants will often feel more able to let their true views be known and will be more willing to make radical suggestions. People will be less willing to make radical suggestions if these have to be written down and can then be available for public ridicule. Each of the Directors at YK plc manages their own factory and the information exchange between them is seen to be crucial. It is important to be able to be informal ie, off the record and e-mail would inhibit this type of frankness. Also, Directors may not wish to commit sensitive issues to writing.

- ◆ Personal relationships are important in business and other organisations. These can grow best when people meet each other; they can also grow when people speak to each other on the phone; they will rarely grow as a result of electronic messages.

- ◆ People like meetings - provided these do not become too time-consuming and frequent. They fulfil important social needs at work and few of us would enjoy work if we had no opportunity for face-to-face meetings with our colleagues.

Although e-mail has many advantages, it is inconceivable that it will mean that face-to-face meetings become a thing of the past. YK plc will need to reach some compromise involving using e-mail as its core communication vehicle together with some of the face-to-face meetings - though not on such a regular basis.

Answer 8

Incorrect Information

Tutorial note:	
Required	- Provision of high quality information can be hindered by a large number of factors. In part (a), you are required to explain some of those factors, whilst concentrating on the information itself and not on the systems providing the information.
	Part (b) expects you to show an understanding of information centres by explaining what problems the centre can solve.
Not required	- Discussion of various information sources.

(a)   Why information could be incorrect

There are many ways that the information provided by the computer systems could be incorrect. The lack of communication between the sites is the main problem but other problems include the incompatibility, the standards adopted, and the capacity and capability of the system components.

Examination tip - *Make reference in your answer to the problems in JS plc's computer systems and the information being provided by the systems.*

Over a period, the system has been implemented in a piecemeal fashion, without any serious thought for the future consequences. Each department within each site has developed its own independent computer-based transaction processing and management information systems that cannot communicate with each other.

This *lack of communication* can cause errors from the following:

- ◆ *Processing* - It would be unlikely for all the departments to run their batch processing at the same time and use the same data for updating, so the management information system will not be comparing like with like.

- ◆ *Data input* - there are problems if data is input more than once. Information from one system will need to be re-keyed into another, which will inevitably lead to higher levels of input errors. The alternative to re-keying is saving the files to a disk and sending them to other departments or sites by post. Obviously, there is going to be a time delay because of this, so that some files may be up-to-date in one department but not in another. The stock control system may show items taken out of stock, but the information may not have been input into the production department's system.

The incompatibility of the hardware and software can also cause errors eg:

- ◆ *Matching input to output* - from the description, it seems that there is no compatibility between the hardware and the operating systems, and the systems have undergone substantial amendment. This incompatibility probably results in the output from one application not matching the input to another. Files would have a different structure and may not be compatible with all the hardware. It may not be possible to read disks from one system into another. Extra software would have to be written to enable switching between 16 and 32 bit environments.

♦ *Duplicating data* - when different systems are updated with similar data, there are often errors arising because of delays. For example, there could be three systems involved in gathering the data for the payment of wages. The wages department may rely on data from their own database on the employee, data from the sales department about the number of hours worked in the period and data from the accounts department on the amount of commission due on the sales receipts. Any changes to this data eg, increase in commission percentage, paid overtime worked, or increase in salary could easily cause problems to the system.

Duplication of data could show sections, such as sales, production and stock control, having different information about the same thing, and they could all be basing their decisions on this information. The stock issues may show different amounts from stock usage in production or from the sales figures. Because it is not possible to take information directly from one system to another, the management at JS plc will never be certain which information is correct.

♦ *Backing up* - because there is no centralisation, the backing up and storage of files is probably duplicated and non-standardised. This means that the data is not as reliable as it could be.

The lack of *standards* can cause problems with:

♦ *Validation and file handling* - because of the lack of corporate standards and compatibility, variable degrees of validation and file handling would have been applied to developments, leading to some systems being more accurate than others. The operation of the system may be at fault. It may not actually process the data in the way that it was originally specified, or it may process it at the wrong speed. This could result in data and files either not being updated or incorrectly processed, which will lead to inaccurate information.

♦ *Flexibility of staff* - where different systems and procedures are used over departments and sites, any movement of staff between these locations could cause errors while new systems are being learned. Training staff is more difficult over a wide range of hardware and software.

♦ *Interface with suppliers and customers* - the lack of compatibility leads to inconsistencies with the supplier interface. Having no standard interface makes customer queries about their orders/payments/terms of trade very inefficient.

♦ *Testing software upgrades* - where procedures differ between sites and software is upgraded at different times, standard testing is twice as difficult. If there is one department responsible for testing, the likelihood is that only half as much testing will be done in each site.

The *capacity and capability* of the system components can cause errors when:

♦ *Databases are overloaded* - inaccuracies can occur when there are too many fields in a database because it can take a long time to sort. This could encourage staff to delay altering the database until there are sufficient entries or deletions to warrant an update. When all systems are working excessively it may cause database overflows and disk crashes. This can have the effect of corrupting data and subsequent information generated from the system may not therefore be accurate.

♦ *Spare capacity* - during any on-line transaction processing, if the system runs out of memory it can suspend its automatic backup and saving procedures. This can cause a loss of data and problems with making space on the disks to complete the processing.

The Management Information System (MIS) within each department should contain reasonable accurate information in respect of its own function - subject to the inherent weaknesses discussed above - but these systems may be based on false assumptions and incorrect inputs in respect of other departments.

There is also the problem that the information presented to management, from different departments and different sites, will not look the same. Output from the various systems will have a different format or layout. This will make it difficult for management to analyse and assimilate the information. For example, the work in progress reports from production may not be synchronised with either the stock reports or the sales orders. The decision-making support will therefore be faulty in several different aspects and the MIS could present a totally misleading picture.

(b) An information centre (IC) would be expected to provide help and assistance to people who use computers and to each department in respect of system developments. It may also arrange training for users and other staff in order to maximise system development performance and obtain the most value from the systems. It responds to the organisation's need to control technology by:

♦ *Establishing hardware and software standards* - the IC is involved with both the forward planning and development of systems and acquisition of equipment. It can offer help and assistance to ensure that all components, hardware and software products, are compatible within all departments and sites. By becoming a central point for the release of updated software it would help to ensure that information of the same type and the same version of software was being used throughout the organisation. It can also help with capacity planning to ensure that systems do not have to operate excessively. Sizing exercises and the development of proper 'housekeeping' routines can help ensure that all systems operate at optimum performance.

♦ *Approving a range of suppliers of hardware* - companies need to be able to rely on their hardware suppliers to provide guarantees and maintenance contracts for their systems.

♦ *Establishing data, software, testing and documentation standards* - enforcement of company data standards, including field, file and program naming, is essential if information flows are to be improved. Industry acceptable standards can be published and monitored by the IC so that all departments at all sites can ensure developments conform and thereby enable information to be shared across the different departments and sites. JS plc will want to combine the information from the systems in different departments and sites into one corporate database, supported by a single network. This will facilitate data warehousing and is a pre-requisite of obtaining useful and accurate information via a company-wide MIS.

♦ *Enforcing security procedures* eg, backup, problem solving and virus-checking - if a department has a problem the IC may be able to help as it normally keeps error logs and also usually has lists of fixes.

Answer 9

Information as a Valuable Commodity

Tutorial note:	
Required	- This question covers the economics of information and requires you to determine how information is priced and then to explain these factors in the context of the Internet.

(a) *Pricing factors*

The following factors must be taken into account by PC Inc when pricing its information services:

Market factors - the price of anything can only be sustained if someone is prepared to pay it. The generally accepted range of prices within the market is therefore one of the major factors in determining price. The price that can be charged for information will depend to some extent on the nature of the information market. If there are a large number of providers offering similar services it is likely that prices will be low. As there are now a number of Internet service providers, PC Inc will need to take account of their prices and the level of differentiation that it will need to use.

Differentiation - if PC Inc can offer added value by the provision of different or unique services or information, a premium can be charged.

Perceived value - It will only be possible to charge for the information services if customers perceive that the information has value to them. This issue is covered in detail in part (b) but, for example, it is unlikely that PC would be able to charge for access to its website pages containing company data that is in the public domain. It is, however, likely that a charge could be made for research findings.

Cost of provision - although not truly a price determinant, as customers are indifferent to the cost of the service to PC, this is a constraint due to PC's need to make a profit. PC must calculate the true cost of providing the information (including an apportionment of fixed costs and overheads) in order to ensure an acceptable margin is earned. PC Inc is actually providing three things and the cost of each of these can be dependent on different things:

♦ Information within its own website - PC Inc's own web pages will have to be developed using a programming language such as Java. Once the pages have been created, they will have to be maintained. The cost of this depends to a great deal on the functionality ie, if the specialist information can be manipulated or if there is any interactive use of the web pages, then this will make it more expensive to create and maintain. Consequently, the price would need to reflect this.

♦ An e-mail service - the e-mail facility gives rise to capacity considerations. Sufficient processing power (via a dedicated mail server) together with adequate storage for each individual customer mailbox is necessary. Pricing of this aspect would depend on the numbers of mail users. Because most of the costs involved are equipment costs eg, servers and firewalls, the more users the service gets, the cheaper the price that can be quoted.

♦ Internet access to other websites - is the most competitive area and the cost that PC Inc would primarily incur would again be the server and the firewall. The Internet service cost is basically in respect of the communications software and is usually a fairly basic charge.

Nature of costs - the costs have both fixed and variable (time-related) elements. PC Inc would need to distinguish between capital costs and the ongoing revenue costs to support the applications. Ongoing costs are largely dependent on current volumes whereas capital costs are 'stepped' in nature and so periods of over and under capacity may be experienced. There are also the costs of obtaining the information itself that is to be input to the pages on the website.

Most Internet service providers tend to structure their prices as flat-rate subscription charges (usually payable on a monthly basis) together with a usage charge depending on the amount of time on line. This type of charging structure tends to be adopted because of the nature of the costs incurred.

Switching costs - if PC Inc can enforce switching costs, for example a requirement to purchase other software, they could enforce higher prices.

Payment and terms - another consideration that would affect the price charged is how customers intend to pay. If direct debit is used, administrative costs can be kept down and so this can be reflected in the price. Other discounts could also be applied in the case of corporate users who may be able to acquire quantity discounts.

Examination tip - *You will have paid for information at some stage in your studies, probably in the form of textbooks or other study material. Use your own experience to help answer the question from the point of view of the information provided by PC Inc. This answer needs to distinguish between the two different types of service in order to gain the marks.*

(b)   *Factors giving information its value*

The value of information depends on its utility and this may be in respect of time and/or place. Information is now considered to be a valuable commodity and, as such, can be traded in a similar way to any other commodity. The factors that make information valuable are:

Scarcity - if any of the information provided is unavailable elsewhere this will increase its value. This would probably be the case for research findings.

Added value to customers - if possession of the information adds value to the businesses or lives of the customers the price will rise. This could include new developments based on PC's research or faster communication using e-mail services.

Speed of access. Even if the same information is available from other sources, the nature of PC Inc's service may result in a significant time saving for the customer. A saving in time means a saving in cost, which can be reflected in the price.

Quality of information - information of a specialised nature may now be further developed and therefore be more comprehensive, ie use of pictures, text and graphics combined. It could therefore offer better quality for a variety of purposes. This places a value on it that it did not previously possess as it is more suitable for further uses.

Specialist information - if the subject matter is very specialised then the supply of that information is restricted, particularly if a great deal of effort was required to get it to the standard for consumption. Information such as this is usually restricted and subject to subscription; it will conform to supply and demand principles whereby as the price rises more specialist information becomes available.

Location of the information - information possesses value when it can be accessed when and where required. If people do not have to go out for it they may be willing to pay for the convenience of receiving it at home or in the workplace, thus saving delivery costs or the time spent to locate and collect information. This is particularly important for some members of the community and also helps to support people who now work from home.

Relative price - information may have been charged for at a nominal price. If it can be obtained to the same standard, but at a lower price, then people will pay. For example, restricted pages of newspapers are available on the Internet at a price lower than the cost of the complete newspaper. This may suit people who want only summarised information and are prepared to pay relatively trifling amounts, but on a regular daily basis.

Ease of use - if the information is indexed and easy to retrieve, it has more utility, so a premium can be charged as this obviously saves time in searching for the information required. Efficient filing and retrieval can save considerable time and Internet 'browsers' can be used to speedily locate the information needed.

Answer 10

Information Quality

There are several reasons why the information provided to operational decision-makers may not be of good quality. The major problem is that because everything changes over time it is physically impossible to predict future events with any accuracy and so there will always be uncertainty and risk.

Different levels of management take different types of decisions and often require different types of information. Good information is useful to the recipient, it can be relied upon and it helps in the decision-making process. This can be illustrated by the fact that good information provided to operational decision-makers at one level can be poor information at another.

Basically, information for control purposes must be:

(i)   the right information in terms of it being complete, relevant, understandable, accurate and significant;

(ii)   at the right time;

(iii)   delivered to the right person via the appropriate channel;

(iv)   for the right cost.

A holiday company is used to illustrate the points made. Decision-makers in this type of organisation need to manage the types of holiday sold to customers and decisions are very dependent upon such things as areas of the world that are safe, economic conditions, trends, consumer lifestyles and weather forecasts, which are not always that dependable.

Complete - many operational decision-makers do not know what information they need until they need it and the appropriate level of completeness varies enormously, according to the type of decision. A major obstacle in information system design is building in enough flexibility for managers to obtain and manipulate information in a variety of ways. For example, the recent problems with foot and mouth in the UK stock affected holidays taken at home and also the number of visitors to the UK from the USA. Even with complete information about certain holidays, it may not be of good quality to the operational decision-maker if there is a sudden change in tastes. In recent years, many people have abandoned the traditional package holiday in favour of tailor made tours.

Relevant - information must be relevant to the problem under consideration. You often find that reports and financial analyses can sometimes confuse the reader by presenting a mixture of relevant and irrelevant information, or information with unnecessary detail. The information provided to decision-makers should concentrate on the essentials and ignore trivia. Too much information can blind the user to the truly important matters. Management accountants must be careful to present the costs and revenues that are relevant to a particular decision or course of action. For example, apportioning administration costs between different types of holiday is irrelevant when seeking to assign responsibility for the control of those costs to a particular operational decision-maker.

Understandable - information provided to operational decision-makers that is easy to understand is more likely to produce action. Material that is presented in a way that assumes knowledge and abilities that the recipient could not be expected to have is not useful. It should be tailored to the needs and level of understanding of the recipient. The degree of detail required by the credit controller to monitor the level of debt is different from the level of detail required by the chief executive. Because lack of clarity is one of the causes of a breakdown in communication, it is important to choose the most appropriate presentation medium or channel of communication. Modern computer packages contain tables, graphics and charts, all of which can assist in speeding up and improving the understanding process.

Accurate - information should be sufficiently accurate for its intended purpose and the operational decision-maker should be able to rely on the information. However, there is often some trade-off in terms of cost and it is possible to supply information in a much more accurate form than is required. The main question is whether increased accuracy will improve the quality of the user's decision making. Inaccurate information is of little use for strategic, tactical or operational purposes. However, the degree of accuracy or precision of information will vary. The managing director may be concerned with the reporting of profit to the nearest thousand pounds, whereas the sales ledger supervisor will be concerned with a high degree of precision regarding the balancing of the control account.

Information may not always be accurate for various reasons. Most operational decision-makers have deadlines to meet, and actual results may not be available on time and therefore estimated results may have to be used. With a holiday company there will be airline seats and hotel rooms that have to be filled to achieve a breakeven level before deciding whether to reduce prices or cancel the trip, estimates of sales may have to be used when actual figures are not available. The comparison between actual and estimated sales can be made when late bookings have been accounted for. Delays and inaccuracies result in misleading figures and inappropriate decisions.

Significant - part of the art of keeping information simple and understandable is to highlight the significant factors, screening out any facts that are not important enough to affect the operational decision-maker. Information has no value if the user already knows it. The information providers should be capable of highlighting the unusual so that appropriate action can be taken by the recipient. For example, when reporting sales of Caribbean cruises, it is often useful to operate a system of exception reporting. The information that two groups did not receive embarkation details is of more importance than the fact that 150 have been given them without any problem.

Timely - the value of good information declines with the length of time that the user has to wait for it. Occasionally this means a compromise in terms of completeness, as outlined earlier, where the information is not available until after a decision is made, and will be useful for comparisons and longer-term control. Generally, information that is out of date is a waste of time, effort and money. It can only be of use if it is received in time to influence the operational decision-maker. Operational decision-makers in departments dealing with scheduled flights need to know the prices that competitors are charging, especially those selling from 'bucket shops' and over the Internet. Not having the required information available at the right time can lead to embarrassment and lost sales.

Communicated - information must be communicated to the person taking action. Within any organisation, decision-makers have the authority to do certain tasks, and they must be given the information they need to do them. Sales managers, responsible for achieving a certain level of sales within their area, are generally given a target for the year. As the year progresses, they might try to keep the sales buoyant, but unless they know their current total sales to date, they will find it difficult to judge whether they are keeping within target or not.

Cost - the cost of obtaining the information should not be more than its value to the organisation. It is possible to obtain very comprehensive and detailed information. However, this may be very expensive particularly if sophisticated information systems need to be developed to collect and process data. Many firms have to rely on estimates and forecasts because it just would not be economic to improve the accuracy of their information.

Conclusion - for information to have value, it must lead to a decision to take action that results in reducing costs, eliminating losses, increasing sales, prevention of fraud or providing management with information about the consequences of alternative courses of action. The information provided for operational decision-makers helps to make the control of operations and the decision making process that much more accurate. Any improvements to the quality of information can ensure that a better than average success rate is achieved.

Answer 11

IS/IT Strategy

Tutorial note:	
Required	- This question follows a 'define and apply' approach, combining book learning of the theory with the application of it to a practical situation.
Not required	- Explanation of the differences between IS and IT.

The case for developing a strategy for information systems and information technology

Computers have come to dominate the world of business over the past forty years but not more so than in the last decade when the introduction of the microcomputer led to most businesses having access to information technology. However there has been a growing recognition that organisations must plan their adoption of IT carefully and fit it to their business needs. IT can bring competitive advantage to an organisation if the development of their information systems corresponds with their information requirements and business strategy. A company strategy is a statement of their long-term objectives for the business and the way they will be achieved. Planning a strategy is not done overnight and must be done cautiously. Companies need a strategy where decisions have a major impact on the long-term future of the organisation.

Examination tip - Relate your answer to the situation at KLP plc as the examiner has requested.

A company such as KLP plc will benefit from having an information systems strategy (IS) and an information technology strategy (IT) for a number of reasons. First KLP plc have been developing information systems for a number of years and are continually investing large amounts of money in IT. Some people within the organisation may argue that the money has not always been spent wisely. The company need to focus on how much money they will spend on IS and IT in the future and how well the funds are spent.

There is a growing trend towards end-user computing within the company and a growing number of staff are wanting access to computers for CAD (computer-aided design), business modelling using spreadsheets etc. There have even been discussions about CIM (computer integrated manufacturing). All of this costs money, and in the case of CIM, millions of pounds may be spent.

Even with the introduction of the new technology the business may not feel the benefit until the users have been trained on the various systems.

Information systems and information technology have become critical to the operation of the business in KLP plc. The Sales Department could not function without the on-line order processing system. On the factory floor the information system is crucial to their current operations. The company relies heavily on its telecommunications links with suppliers and customers.

The company need IS and IT to give them a strategic advantage over rivals in the market. IT can be used within KLP plc to improve productivity and the quality of services offered. For example moving to JIT (Just-in-time) or CIM the company can couple various sub-systems within the organisation to cut down on stock holdings and increase productivity.

Management and organisational structures can be changed by moving to electronic mail, teleconferencing or even telecommuting. IT can be used to access previously inaccessible markets abroad.

IT can completely revolutionise business practices and whole industries eg banking with their ATMs (automated teller machines) and electronic funds transfer; retail businesses with their POS (point of sales systems) and bar-coding. IT can be both the cause of major changes in doing business and a response to them.

IT now affects every aspect of business life in large organisations and will continue to do so well into the 21st century. Everyone in business will have access to IT and use IT in their working life. IT is no longer a centralised resource.

Well-designed information systems can now provide high quality management information. This will lead to decision support and executive information of the highest level.

IT and IS involves many different stakeholders within an organisation such as KLP plc and external to the company. People who would be interested in the IS and IT of KLP plc might be:

- Other businesses;
- IT manufacturers;
- Consumers;
- Employees and internal users - how IT affects working practices.

Any strategic plans involving IS/IT must consider technical issues. Compatibility of future systems with those already present is a major issue.

Finally the success of any implementation of IS or IT can be influenced by the management. It is essential that they are educated in IS and IT in order that they can make the right decisions in relation to design and development of the business systems.

IS and IT is such a large aspect of business at KLP plc that it requires proper planning and management. IS and IT issues cannot be tackled simply and all implications need to be thought out in advance. Hence there is a need for an IS/IT strategy.

Answer 12

IT Strategy

Tutorial note:	
Required	- You need to explain why an organisation needs an IT strategy and provide examples.
Not required	- More than five reasons.

A strategy is a course of action to achieve a specific objective. The recognition of information as a valuable commodity has led to the implementation of IT strategies within organisations. The five main reasons why it is essential for an organisation to have strategic planning are as follows:

Examination tip - Only five reasons were requested

(i)   for the alignment of IT resources with corporate objectives;

(ii)   as a strategic weapon for the definition of a framework for IT in terms of overall direction, whether to gain a competitive advantage or to create a barrier to new entrants into the market;

(iii)   for the allocation of resources, rate of implementation and level of financial investment (identifying major investment decisions and the information enabling them to be made);

(iv)   developing standards by the creation of the right infrastructure for making decisions on individual projects in terms of organisational priorities and technical compatibility;

(v)   developing the 'knowledge base' by training.

Corporate objectives

The IT strategy will identify the key business areas that can benefit from an investment in information technology. It will further outline the type of investment that the organisation will make, and how the strategically important units will effectively use the technology. An IT strategy allows organisations to make processes more efficient and to employ techniques such as Business Process Re-engineering (BPR) to supplement the strategy.

Examination tip - You will not get the full marks unless you give some examples – the examples must be well-known examples to gain the marks.

IT investment is important for the future well being of the organisation. The travel industry is typical of a lot of industries where IT is seen as an essential element of the business. The successful take over of some travel agents was helped by the organisations having similar IT strategies and systems. This can work the opposite way. It would be very difficult for car manufacturers to merge and benefit from the synergy if their design systems were completely different, yet both up to date technologies. One of the systems would have to be abandoned, along with all the parts specifications, ordering systems, working practices and staff skills.

Strategic weapon

Information technology can be used as a strategic weapon in a number of ways.

♦   It is a potential supplier of competitive advantage to an organisation. For travel agents, choosing and reserving a holiday can be done in much less time and more conveniently when the agent is on-line to the suppliers. IT can also be used in the development of new business. For example, supermarkets can sell the analysis of their sales to market research companies so that trends in product purchasing can be identified.

♦   Information technology and systems can be used as a strategic weapon to improve productivity and performance. Computer aided design (CAD) in car manufacture is an example of this.

♦ Information systems can be used to change the management and organisational structure of the organisation to achieve competitive advantage. Computers with modems enable people to work from home, reducing the cost of travel and office space. Teleconferencing and video conferencing can increase the productivity of managers by reducing the necessity for travel to meetings.

Level of financial investment

Because IT can be very expensive and mistakes or omissions can be extremely costly, the IT strategy helps to plan and control the expenditure. Where IT is used in a collaborative venture, it can change the basis of competition by setting up new communication networks and forming alliances with complementary organisations to share information. Unless the investment is co-ordinated and controlled, the organisation could lose its future business. For example, when Thomson Holidays introduced their on-line reservation system into travel agents' offices, they changed the basis of competition. The new system allowed customers to ask about holiday availability and special deals and book a holiday in one visit to the travel agent. For those travel agents without the necessary investment in technology, the opportunity to benefit from this move was lost.

Developing standards

The IT strategy will give the technology some direction. This will help to develop standards by the creation of the right infrastructure for making decisions on individual projects in terms of organisational priorities and technical compatibility. A strategy enforces standards for current systems and also ensures that future changes are compatible with the existing IT infrastructure. Most organisations rely on information technology and, where there is constant and sometimes rapid change, having an IT strategy helps to ensure that all the relevant aspects work together.

Within the travel industry there are systems such as SABRE where, in order to benefit from its facilities, the travel agent's system needs to be compatible. SABRE is the world's most comprehensive computer reservations system. It offers access to the flight schedules of most airlines, and booking opportunities for airlines, hotels and car rentals.

However, planning the technological direction does not always mean that the organisation gets it right. In the early 1980's two separate types of videocassette recorder were competing for control in the market (Beta and VHS). Although the Beta gave better picture quality, it was easier to find the VHS versions of films in video rental stores, and it became the standard. The less popular Beta was driven out of the market.

Development by training

Part of the IT strategy will look at the implications for the existing workforce. It will identify the requisite skills and identify training needs. This helps ensure that there are no major disruptions in introducing the new system.

When an appropriate strategy is in place and standards are enforced, training becomes a natural follow on. Staff get used to the systems in place and find upgrades easy to learn. For example, in a travel agency, the staff are used to working with menu led screens offering choices of destinations, departure points and hotel arrangements. Any new system introduced would not adopt a different search mode but might offer more choices eg, price ranges. This would be easy to learn as it only adds to the existing system. The same situation applies in many offices where employees are already familiar with a Windows operating system. Subsequent new systems using Windows can be introduced that much more quickly.

Answer 13

Information Systems

<table>
<tr><td colspan="3">Tutorial note:</td></tr>
<tr>
<td>Required</td>
<td>-</td>
<td>This question investigates whether an organisation's information system is really supporting the objectives of the company or providing managers with the information they need.</td>
</tr>
<tr>
<td></td>
<td></td>
<td>Porter's theory of business has been included in the question, although it should be noted that the question requirement is not on the theory.</td>
</tr>
<tr>
<td></td>
<td></td>
<td>For part (a) you are required to explain what inputs are needed for the IS to support inbound logistics, marketing, sales and technology development.</td>
</tr>
<tr>
<td></td>
<td></td>
<td>Part (b) requires an explanation of the outputs from the IS.</td>
</tr>
<tr>
<td>Not required</td>
<td>-</td>
<td>Porter's general model.</td>
</tr>
</table>

(a)   The board of SFA is making a decision on whether to implement a Management Information System (MIS) for all staff to use. Because an information system can support a variety of functions in respect of the monitoring and control of the organisation, the managers are hoping it would help in both primary and support activities.

The MIS should provide an integrated approach to information systems requirements by taking output from the main transaction processing systems of the functions and summarising it into further information for control and decision making purposes. The Board of SFA is particularly interested in inbound logistics, marketing and sales, and technology development. Each of these aspects is considered as follows:

Inbound logistics - the main responsibility of inbound logistics is that the right materials are available, at the right price and at the right time. The purchasing department at SFA needs the support of an information system to help it to get the best price for raw materials. Some production is already carried out using Computer Assisted Design and Manufacture (CAD/CAM) and the company could use output from the CAD/CAM via the MIS to provide valuable forward planning information. As well as monitoring waste or excessive re-work, this information could cover quality aspects and link up with stock control.

The information from the MIS will help the purchasing department to plan and meet future requirements and enable savings to be achieved in respect of supplies. Forward planning will allow negotiations with suppliers to take place in plenty of time, so that SFA obtain the best prices. Information on the quality of stock can provide invaluable information for buyers when dealing with suppliers. The link with stock control will allow SFA to use Just In Time (JIT) methods of purchase, which will help to achieve quality and cost savings.

Marketing and sales - the MIS can provide information on customers and the sales force and ensure that this primary activity is managed efficiently. It could help solve the problems associated with the company's spare capacity. The links with the CAD/CAM system will show the production in progress enabling the sales team to give potential customers information about the garments in production. Similarly, the stocks of finished garments will link with the Outbound Logistics side of the system, showing stock availability, lead time and orders outstanding. This information will help to ensure a better service to customers. The MIS can also be used to forecast demand, so that the marketing and sales staff can see the future pattern and plan accordingly.

Technology development - Because the use of CAD/CAM has been fairly under-utilised over the past two years, the company could use a management information system to look at ways of improving its use. SFA can benefit considerably by using CAD/CAM as it not only speeds up the concept to production development, but also provides for better quality garments.

The MIS can achieve the control and monitoring of CAD/CAM, so that most of the production is managed this way. This will also help customer satisfaction. The system could also be designed to integrate with marketing forecasts and the assessment of the requirements of the large retail shops. The company could use this preliminary information to form the basic information for the CAD database, allowing them to design prototypes and produce samples. This would support the sales function and reduce the lead-time from order to delivery.

The system can monitor the information from inbound logistics, marketing and sales and provide control information about the time from order to manufacture and through to delivery of the various garments. It will be particularly important to project demand levels for the ever-changing fashions and, at the same time, ensure that materials are available to enable production to go ahead. It could also be used to calculate the marginal cost of any spare capacity, which would give the company more information on which to base their future planning decisions.

(b) The outputs from the information systems include those from the CAD/CAM system, the accounting system and the management information system.

The outputs from the CAD/CAM systems are the various performance measures that show how the systems are being used. These outputs are required to show how the design, development and production activities assist the organisation in achieving its objectives. They are used for drawing up any plans for future development.

As well as all of the normal output expected from the accounting system, there would be information on marginal costs. This will provide the basis for negotiation with the large retail shops for special deals, and perhaps own label production runs, to help the marketing and sales staff maximise capacity utilisation and enter into agreement with customers on ways to use the spare capacity.

Outputs from the MIS should provide control reports that show which suppliers and buyers are performing well. It can also outline the 'star' buyer, who is ordering his or her goods at the right price, right quality and right time. When the MIS is linked to input costs via the accounting and procurement systems it improves the information available. The output from the MIS can then indicate the type of corrective action required in certain situations, which can be acted upon quickly, and used to determine the overall value of the activity.

Because the MIS uses information from many sources, SFA can respond quickly to circumstances. The sales requirements can be converted to design and production, and stock control and subsequent monitoring can be maintained more easily.

Answer 14

Website Information

Tutorial note:	
Required	- This question is directed at the advantages of an interactive information presentation medium like the Internet over a more passive paper-based catalogue.
	Part (a) asks for a comparison of these two information provision systems.
	Part (b) examines in more detail how information on an Internet site can assist users in a specific situation.
Not required	- Examples of and comparisons with other similar websites.

(a) There are advantages and disadvantages for SK Products Ltd to weigh up before they decide to provide their information on the Web rather than in a paper-based catalogue. The main advantages of a website over a paper-based catalogue include:

♦ Lower cost - it would cost less because there would be no expense incurred on printing, postage and stationery. SK Products Ltd has a range of over 100,000 items and many customers. They would find that creating and maintaining a website, instead of supplying all of their customers with a catalogue that covers the full range every four months, makes economic sense.

♦ User-friendly - a website can have more impact and be more dynamic than a paper-based catalogue. The designers can use text, pictures, graphs, cartoons, diagrams and moving images as well as sound to advertise the various products. This would be particularly suitable for the complicated electrical assemblies, where added value can be achieved by showing how they work. For example, schematic diagrams can illustrate their place within the final assembly. It gives the company additional ways of attracting customers, by providing further information or installation instructions on receipt of an e-mail address from an enquirer or potential customer.

♦ Ease of update - changes to product lines, prices and visual displays can be made quickly using either the Java code or the HTML, depending on which one was used to create the site. Because a minor change, such as the substitution of images for text, can have a dramatic effect, the ability to alter the site daily (if needs be) without too much trouble can be a real bonus.

♦ Worldwide availability and awareness - this means that the website can potentially reach an audience of millions of people and increase the awareness of both the company and its products. Prompts for e-mail addresses can be included in the site, so that SK Products Ltd can build up an electronic mailing list. This will enable them to send out mail shots of special offers and other marketing material. As well as their own advertising and customer information, the site could offer free software downloads such as screensavers that contain an advertising message. This could generate a lot of interest and make it a much more dynamic site to visit.

The main disadvantages include:

♦ *Set up costs of the site* - creating a multi-media site that is dynamic and interesting needs some careful preparation and planning. This can take up a lot of time if done properly. It may also involve some extra security requirements that include additional equipment and software. Unfortunately, there is a popular misconception that once a site has been created then that is the end of the involvement. In fact, it is more likely just the beginning of the process, particularly with e-business becoming a reality for many organisations.

♦ *Maintenance and development costs* - information that is out-of-date on a website is tantamount to telling the whole world that the organisation is slacking. It is symptomatic of inefficient management, and ultimately will do more harm than being without a website altogether. Maintaining the site can be a chore unless it is documented properly, and supported by appropriate resources. The company should be following a planned upgrade path. However, additional facilities are costly and, where development plans are unclear, it can lead to projects becoming more expensive than they should be. Websites are becoming standard features for many organisations and it is no longer sufficient to have a static site to attract visitors. The expectations of an increasing number of Internet users mean that new sites have to be better than before. This creates a strain on the resources a firm is likely to use to support the site.

(b)   The type of information that SK Products Ltd can provide on its website to help customers install and use its products include: installation instructions; specification details; alternative uses for equipment; and performance and service details.

Because of the type of products sold by SK Products Ltd, installation instructions on the website will be very useful for customers. If electrical engineers need help with installation of one of the company's products, they can use their portable computers to log on or download the instructions to use 'on the job'. This can reduce training requirements, especially where the instructions are provided in words and pictures with on-line help facilities. Customers without specialist knowledge can benefit from having on-line help facilities to use when installing complicated equipment.

The website can provide information on specification details, tolerances, industry and legal standards. Where engineers know that there is a source of comprehensive information that is easily accessed, it saves them from having to use books and/or catalogues. This type of information could possibly attract a subscription premium because of the potential savings.

SK Products Ltd could develop and illustrate additional uses for some of their products. They could also give the customer an opportunity to share any useful or quirky ideas for product development eg, paper shredder used to make packing material or record deck used as a potter's wheel. By showing the various uses of products under safe conditions on the Web, potential customers can see the applications and decide if they are appropriate. This can generate many ideas for product development.

SK Products Ltd can publish information about product sizes, distribution quantities, colours, delivery, suitable applications, stockholding and ordering details on their website. Established and potential customers can browse through the pages and find out everything that they need to know about the 100,000+ items in the product range. The company can also show estimates of life spans of products and performance statistics, so customers can calculate expected replacement periods. This type of information is important when it is not easy to replace components because of where they are installed.

Answer 15

Internet Opportunities

There are many ways in which a business can use the Internet to increase turnover:

Examination tip - There are possibly more examples given below than would be expected under examination conditions.

(i)   To advertise the organisation and raise awareness among non-customers and potential customers. This treats the Internet like a sophisticated business directory, and would allow user browsing for information about cleaning services to read about us. It enables organisations to put their telephone and address details on a website.

(ii)   To deliver information to customers and potential customers by means of e-mailed direct marketing. This uses the Internet as a carrier for electronic mail-shots as an alternative to conventional mail. The organisation could easily invite browsers interested in receiving information to leave their e-mail address on the website.

(iii)   To advertise products or services and provide detailed information relating to them. This uses the Internet as an electronic on-line catalogue. They could put details of the range of cleaning services they provide, and possibly references from satisfied customers. It might even be possible to include some sort of order form for standard services and a request form for them to contact potential customers with specific needs.

(iv)   To facilitate the ordering and selling of products. This uses the Internet as an alternative to a human sales force dealing with customers by telephone or face-to-face, and requires a transaction to be made using electronic data interchange (EDI). Although it is unlikely that our customers would be willing to pay in advance on the Web, they may already be able to use EDI for ordering and billing. This would allow a better service to be offered that incurs lower costs for the customer than those of our competitors.

(v)   Feedback can be received from clients, which will help the organisation to tailor their services to meet customer expectations.

(vi)   Including hypertext links to other organisations could be a source of revenue for the cleaning company. Their website could provide advertising space for other organisations eg, estate agents - people have their houses cleaned after the removals are completed.

(vii)   Information about competing or similar organisations can be obtained from their websites.

(viii)   A web address can give the impression of an up-to-date, technically advanced business.

Answer 16

EPOS and Database Systems

Tutorial note:	
Required	- This question is relevant to several areas in the syllabus.
	The question asks you for a little more than EPOS as such, looking at the strategic reasons for the introduction of the system as well as the operational factors.
	The answer must be in a report format that could be used at the Board meeting.
Not required	- Lengthy discussion of EPOS.

REPORT

To: Managing Director

From: Management Accountant

Date: 28th February 200X

Subject: EPOS and Database systems

Terms of reference

This report summarises the benefits of the proposed Electronic Point of Sale (EPOS) system from the strategic and operational viewpoints.

Strategic benefits

The main strategic benefits of the proposal are as follows:

♦ The proposal gives us competitive advantage, as our rivals are at least 14 months behind us in terms of their EPOS developments. This situation must be exploited, and HS must secure the maximum benefit in terms of increased customer numbers and sales. There is a risk that rivals may be able to implement systems with better features than ours, simply by being later adopters of the technology. We should include an upgrade path in our contracts with suppliers.

♦ The proposal is congruent with our objective of offering the best computerised sales service to customers. Customers should find significant benefits, including shorter queues and better stock availability.

♦ The system will allow us to have access to better information relating to the performance of our business compared with that of our rivals. This will assist with strategic decision-making and allow us to identify further opportunities for competitive advantage.

♦ The EPOS system should significantly improve the profitability of the business, as it will allow us to optimise the use of floor space. This is a key issue, and we will be able to carry lower stock quantities of a greater number of product lines. We should also be able to increase our sales per customer as a result of the wider range on display.

♦ The reduction in overall stock levels should generate a significant one-off cash inflow. This can be used to partly fund the IT investment necessary to introduce EPOS.

♦ The investment of over £50 million is at the customer-facing edge of operations. As we build further applications they will continue to enhance customer service and will be in keeping with the image customers associate with our company.

♦ Although very difficult to measure, we may be able to create a 'high tech image'. This can appeal to customers, as mentioned above, and we have already successfully used computerisation in stock and ordering systems. We may, therefore, be able to gain a reputation for being innovative and at the 'leading edge' of technology and, as such, could gain important psychological advantages over competitors and be treated more favourably by suppliers, particularly when it comes to the further development of their systems.

Operational benefits

♦ The biggest operational benefit is the potential savings in stock levels. Both perishable and tinned goods stock levels are high and the proposed system will reduce these and give us consequential stockholding cost savings. As EPOS results in automatic re-ordering, stock levels can be managed much more effectively. This can be further enhanced by using Electronic Data Interchange (EDI) facilities and Just In Time (JIT) practices, so that stock levels are minimised.

♦ The reduction in stock levels will result in a reduction in waste, particularly of perishable goods. Our general stock management will also improve, as we will be able to identify goods that are approaching their 'sell-by' dates and clear them by discounting.

♦ We can analyse individual products by attributes such as size and colour so that sales can be maximised. This can also be used for store layout purposes, so the most attractive and effective layout can be created by using information in the database. Also, complementary products can be grouped together to bring about additional sales.

♦ The improved management information available from the databases will allow us to exert better control over every aspect of our business. Cash management will improve due to automated reconciliation of sales, as will the utilisation of staff at the checkouts due to improved forecasting of activity levels.

♦ There is the possibility of staff savings within the stores due to improvements in overall efficiency and the elimination of warehouse space. Also it may be possible to reduce the number of staff on counter positions if the system significantly speeds up customer throughput and improves cashiering activities. If this is felt to be undesirable, staff can be retrained for customer support roles, encouraging purchase of high margin products.

Conclusion

There are significant benefits to the introduction of EPOS, and it is likely that the payback period will be short.

Recommendation

EPOS should be implemented.

Answer 17

Strategic Planning

Tutorial note:	
Required	- In part (a) you should indicate the relationship between IS/IT and strategic planning.
	In part (b) do not simply list the IT frameworks that you know. They need to be relevant to the question. The question requires you to look at the existing activities and the future activities of Funtours when examining the role of IS.
Not required	- Supporting diagrams for the frameworks in part (b).

(a)   Strategic planning takes place at the highest level within the organisation.

A strategic plan, based on the mission statement of the organisation, will set out the aims and objectives of the organisation. Once these corporate aims and objectives have been defined then a plan can be made of the way in which they are to be achieved (a strategic plan). This prioritises the aims and objectives and sets them within a timescale - the corporate strategy.

In order to develop departmental strategies, the corporate strategy must be studied. Obviously, any specific, departmental or divisional strategies must run alongside the overall corporate strategy. The same holds true when developing an information technology strategy ie, the corporate strategy must be consulted.

Information is an important resource in an organisation; it can be sold, exchanged, bought and stolen. Information can be described as the 'life-blood' of an organisation - without it, the organisation would cease to exist. Therefore, such an important resource must be properly catered for - Information Systems (IS) and Information Technology (IT) provide the wherewithal to do this.

IS refers to the systems which manipulate, process, collect, capture and disperse information. IT refers to the actual equipment (hardware) upon which the systems run. It is, therefore, essential that these two elements are considered and planned together.

Computers have previously been used and regarded as task processors. Repetitive and mundane tasks have been computerised and word-processors have speeded up the administrative processes. However, with the advancements made in technology, the use of wide area networks and electronic data interchange (EDI), it has now been recognised that IT can provide a competitive edge. Organisations are no longer leaving their IS/IT purchasing to chance, which had previously been the case and resulted in a variety of incompatible computers being introduced into various departments. The recognition of information as a valuable commodity has led to the implementation of IS/IT strategies within organisations.

(b)   The role of information systems

Information technology can be of strategic importance to an organisation because of its:

♦   costs;
♦   criticality to organisational success;
♦   use as a strategic weapon;
♦   macro-economic role in reshaping entire industries;
♦   effect on management levels;
♦   stakeholder involvement;
♦   technical impact;
♦   revolutionary effect on information use within the organisation.

This more than anything else is a justification for examining Funtours' use of IT from a strategic point of view.

Examination tip - *Do not simply list the IT frameworks that you know. They need to be relevant to the question.*

In many organisations, the use of IT has changed over time and with the increasing technical sophistication and cheapness of IT. Applying Nolan's stage hypothesis would indicate that Funtours is past the initiation and contagion stages, and is in the control stage, with IT being controlled from head office and the subject of established budgetary and procurement procedures. Its origins are suggested by the fact that it is the finance director's responsibility, rather than that of a steering committee.

Sam's awareness of the potential strategic importance of IT, however, and the future developments outlined indicate that Funtours is moving, or needs to move, to the integration or data administration stage, where IT is seen to be integral to business issues, and is seen as a resource. However, this does not indicate how important IT should be. Two useful models can suggest IT's existing and future strategic roles.

IT's existing role can be mapped on McFarlan's grid, which relates the strategic impact of existing systems and the strategic impact of future systems.

(i)   Up until now, IT has had a support role in that it dealt with basic accounting and invoice processing, although IT has become very important in processing bookings.

(ii)   The new business opportunity suggests that IT will be even more important, in that it will move centre stage to the effective and basic provision of the firm's business. It will not simply process transactions previously agreed, but will be a vital link in servicing customers, and will be essential if Funtours is to provide bespoke holidays successfully: IT is more than administration, but at the heart of the service.

We must identify Funtours' product - in fact Funtours is providing a service, in which information is a crucial component. Funtours needs up to date accurate information about flight details, prices and availability, hotels to stay, exchange rates. The information embedded in the total service is not as high as that in a newspaper say, but it is higher than, say, in cement. A lot of the service Funtours will provide consists of information enabling the customer to make informed choices.

As far as Funtours' value chain is concerned, how it provides the service is intimately connected with the information it actually gives. It cannot offer information if this is not entered to the system and processed in some way for it to be available for use. The information content of the value chain is also high.

This indicates that Funtours' use of IT for the new strategy is of strategic importance.

Answer 18

JD plc

The main benefit of the IT backup and disaster plan at JD plc is the procedures in place regarding the security of data, particularly in respect of backing up data on a daily basis to an off-site location and to Head Office. Stock balances are updated in real-time, and this means that any customer queries on stock levels will be accurate and goods can be provided in the knowledge that the balances indicated on the computer systems do agree with the actual stock balances.

Other benefits include the virus checking of external inputs and the uninterruptable power supplies (UPS) at branches.

Unfortunately, these measures, while acceptable in themselves, do not go far enough in respect of the organisation as a whole. The weaknesses are discussed below.

Data backup - there are delays between recording the transaction data and its backup - the procedure is to store it in RAM before copying hourly to hard disc and then to transfer it to the communications mainframe. Although the UPS would protect the system in the event of power loss, failure other than a power loss could result in the data stored in memory being lost. The reason for storing transaction data in RAM is not clear. It would be just as easy to store this data on a hard disc drive as transactions take place.

Regarding the daily backups taken from both mainframes at each store, it would appear to be a backup of two sets of data which could lead to inconsistencies should these sets not be identical due to local problems involving the copying of the data from the transaction mainframe to the communications mainframe.

The first annual service of the communication mainframe at one store is likely to be a risk. A switch-off time of 3.40 pm for this computer seems an odd time. When this happens, data stored in the transaction mainframe, which has been labelled incorrectly when they were installed and will be mistaken for the communication mainframe, will not be backed up, as this is done hourly. Because this time of day, (3.40 pm) could be a busy one for the company, the store could be in a position of not being able to trade. Sales would be lost and consequently profits reduced.

Virus checking - this is done only at the stores. Internet accesses and e-mails that originate from outside the company are checked for viruses and this will give some protection. However, some viruses could enter the systems in the store if staff were to use unauthorised software of their own, or if in some way internal e-mails became corrupted. Even where rigorous virus checking does take place, the data is vulnerable from new viruses that are not detected by all virus checkers. The scenario does not mention virus protection at Head Office so it may be possible for viruses to enter JD plc as a result of any external communications Head Office may have, other than with stores.

Alleviation of weaknesses

There should be separate but compatible security systems and disaster plans for both individual stores and head office, and within each store for each computer system. These aspects need to be addressed.

At the Head Office virus checking should cover all internal communications. This could be done quite easily by installing virus-checking software in all the computers used by staff. The UPS appears to be satisfactory at individual stores and although it is not deemed necessary at head office, the facility should be provided as an added precaution. Backup systems should be improved; to maintain the communication systems, dual processors could be installed to handle transactions, one system mirroring the other.

At individual stores virus checks are needed for data entering the system from customers - if orders can be placed this way, and staff use of private software. Most companies introduce controls to ensure that unauthorised use of the system by staff does not take place. Appropriate measures could be included in their terms of employment.

In terms of the data backup, each system should have separate backup facilities. The company should introduce effective controls to distinguish between the two computers; there is no excuse for physically mistaking the computers - it is an example of negligence.

For the future, a more appropriate time should be chosen for the annual services, preferably at a time when the store is not trading, and done on a rota basis throughout the stores.

From a strategic point of view, the management at JD plc should undertake disaster planning (*or* business continuity planning) so that in the event of any mishap, however caused, it will be able to operate as normally as possible This can be done on-site, or through a remote hot or cold site. The use of secure transmission lines would be beneficial in this case.

Answer 19

SKO plc

(a)   The proposal to store information at a central location should be critically evaluated as any other business decision ie, based on whether the benefits outweighed the costs in a cost/benefit analysis. However, other factors would also need to be addressed:

(i)   Information requirements

It is assumed that information analyses (sales, stocks, profitability of product lines etc) are currently conducted locally on each shop's local system. In the event of a central location for information, these information analyses could continue to be available locally.

(ii)   Information comparisons

It is anticipated that SKO plc will want to conduct performance comparisons of each shop in terms of sales, profits, stocks, cash flows etc. This would be available from the central data storage facility and such information could help staff at head office to monitor trends and effect control. The central data storage facility could also be used as a medium for publishing performance league tables, and for establishing stock availability throughout the country - allowing more efficient distribution of stock.

(iii) **Transfer of documents**

Once documents, in both paper and electronic form, are being transferred from one location to another, there are immediate control implications. For example, controls to ensure that documents are received from each shop would need to be implemented. When establishing a central data storage facility the risk of loss, damage or corruption, and delay in transfer must be taken into account.

(iv) **Information storage and retrieval**

The efficiencies gained by storing information at one central location may justify the consideration of methods of information storage and retrieval, which may not have been feasible at individual locations eg, document image processing, microfilming etc.

(v) **Security**

With a central service, security is usually far higher. The central data storage facility will be managed by professional staff. They will be disciplined in the implementation of document storage operations, embracing access security and contingency plans in the event of problems arising.

(vi) **Further considerations**

Prior to a decision being made, further information would be required. For cost benefit analysis, the size and layout of the proposed facility would need to be calculated; other costs would need to be ascertained or estimated such as those relating to secure document transportation and general operating expenses.

(vii) **Conclusion**

Considering the above factors and assuming a positive financial appraisal, with the information requirements - both locally and centrally - being met, then the proposal to store information in a central location should not present a problem.

(b) As the terms of the Data Protection Act 1998 cover data about individuals and not corporate bodies, SKO plc may not need to take any action.

(i) Corporate entities - information on other corporate entities is outside the scope of the Act as it does not fall within the definition of personal data, and under these circumstances there would be no requirement to register under the terms of the Act. However, if data is stored about individuals who belong to those organisations, then there may be a requirement to register.

(ii) Summaries of information - sales by region and estimated market share of each shop do not fall within the scope of the Act. Personal data held for the purposes of keeping the accounts of the data user eg, a record of sales, are exempt from the Act unless the data is used for the purposes of marketing. However, if the sales or market share figures were derived from records of named individuals, then there may be a case to register the use of the personal data by SKO plc (the data user), identifying the type of data subjects ie, the individuals who are the subject of personal data.

Answer 20

JHD Inc

(a) **Alternative policies of charging the costs of the IT Department**

As the information system supports a wide variety of functions in the organisation, and information systems incur significant capital and revenue costs eg, staff, third party suppliers and equipment, it is not surprising that JHD Inc should seek to develop costing systems so that user departments pay for their usage of the IT resource. Accurate and appropriate measurements of cost are important because, if the information is wrong, or it uses inappropriate measures, then decisions about IT investments will be faulty.

These costs can be treated in several ways. They can be treated as part of company overheads, they can be charged out at cost or they can be charged at market rates, generating a profit (or loss) for the IT department.

As part of company overhead - IT is treated as a general administrative expense and is not allocated to user departments. There is no chargeout system and user departments do not have to pay for IT services out of their budgets. One of the advantages is that it is simple and cheap to administer and it avoids potential disputes concerning recharged costs. However, there are a number of disadvantages:

Because managers may be able to obtain the facilities, equipment and services required and at no cost to their departments it does not encourage responsible use of the IT resource.

The IT department management is not given the right cost information to choose between competing projects.

Because there is no rationing mechanism at work, demand can outstrip supply, and funds can be used very quickly with user departments not receiving the service they want.

The IT department has little day-to-day incentive to control costs or use available resources efficiently. IT is a significant expense within JHD Inc and budgetary constraints may be applied. This could mean insufficient support for some departments, and they will have to adopt a 'first come, first served' approach. As the budget is spent, there may be insufficient funds for later in the year.

In the long run, inappropriate measures might be implemented to control user department costs. The departments that are inefficient in their use of IT will have no incentive to improve.

There is no control of IT costs other than the budget and relating the budget to activities can be difficult. Therefore, costs may escalate and poor value for money may be the result. User department managers may perceive this as inefficiencies on the part of IT management.

Individual departmental usage - when IT is charged out on a cost basis it is felt that pricing computer services will achieve two results. Firstly, it will allocate scarce resources according to economic efficiency and secondly, it will regulate demand for computer services within the organisation. This type of chargeout means that users are charged a proportion of the costs of the IT department according to some measure.

Individual departmental managers will want to ensure that their departments are getting value for money. The difficulty here is similar to other aspects of inter-company transfer pricing - the cost components to include and the charge-out mechanism. There are some guidelines to follow:

(i) Chargeout rates should be based on a tangible service that the user can relate to. Examples include cost per transaction processed, cost per page and cost per hour of programmer's time.

(ii) Standard costing systems should be used so that user departments are not penalised for inefficiencies in the IT department and the IT department is not penalised with variances caused by user departments' increased usage.

One of the advantages of basing the costs on individual department usage is that it is conceptually simple. Another is that it motivates user departments to consider the cost of their usage of IT services. It also ties in with costing systems that use responsibility accounting as a means of controlling costs.

One of the disadvantages is that departments would need to be invoiced for the costs of the IT department that they have incurred. This can lead to disputes between users and the IT department that can become very heated, particularly if the users do not perceive the charging mechanism as being fair, realistic or representative of their use of facilities.

As the level of support from the IT department is extensively integrated, it is unlikely that users will be able to choose between the in-house IT department and an external supplier of IT facilities. Because charging may be based on an arbitrary activity it can lead to misleading figures. User perceptions can be distorted as comparisons show that they are not receiving value for money and they may stop the development of new systems if they perceive that they are financially penalised when new developments are implemented. This can lead to further resentment and frustration by user departments.

When contrasting the two techniques, the conclusions drawn will depend on the objectives. If they are to control IT department costs, then treating the IT costs as overhead can provide better control. However, if the objectives are to encourage efficiencies by users in the use of IT facilities and to reduce excessive demands, then charging on the basis of individual department usage would be better.

(b)   Charging on the basis of network traffic

The problems with the proposal to charge the IT department's cost on the basis of network traffic are that they do not reflect the different services offered by the IT department or the services used by the different departments. The IT department is responsible for all IT systems, implementation, servicing of equipment and central file maintenance.

The difficulty will be explaining how the costs are measured. Users will be naturally suspicious of costs that impact on their budgets and any system that cannot be explained simply will not find favour. The relationship of costs to networks is inherently complicated.

Because different departments will be doing different types of work and will have different systems, it is difficult to apportion costs based on network traffic. For example, there is virtually no relationship between some systems development costs, mainly analysts' costs, and network traffic. Some departments may have a very heavy development workload and others may only have mature systems and it is fundamentally wrong to treat these departments in the same way.

An alternative approach would be to base the costs on a tangible service to which the user department can relate. This would have to be done by covering the time spent on the networks and servers, the PCs and peripherals, the central processors and systems development and implementation. These four aspects need to be charged in quite specific ways to each department.

The costs of the networks and servers can be charged to departments on the basis of network traffic. Costing should be based on the volumes of such traffic and the timing of transmissions that affect costs. As networks have to be sized for peak volumes, those applications which cause the peaks should be recharged at a premium rate over and above the standard network transmission rate.

Local equipment such as PCs and peripherals should be charged on the basis of the numbers of units used. This may be a standard cost per unit or actual cost of maintenance and repair charged via the IT department to the local department.

Operating system statistics can be used to determine departmental usage of the central processor. Central file maintenance will consist of both on-line files and those subject to batch update. The costs associated with each type of file processing can be charged on that basis.

Costs associated with systems development and implementation are mainly due to the time spent by programmers and analysts. These costs can be charged on the basis of the number of days spent on each department's system or time spent on development work.

User departments should not be charged with the long term fixed costs of the IT department itself eg, its buildings, over which they have no control. Also, those costs which are actually incurred by the IT department for housekeeping purposes should remain within the IT department cost centre and controlled in that way, rather than passing on the costs to the other departments.

Answer 21

KN Company

(a)   Individual departments compared with centralised database

The KN Company has developed via a pathway described by Nolan, going through the initiation, contagion and control stages. The company now appears to be on the way towards integration, administration and strategic development.

Until the integration step is reached, each department will tend to have developed its own applications; data will not be shared between departments to any extent and the separate systems in each department may not even be capable of communicating with each other.

Integration implies that the separate systems will link together with data being shared. Administration implies that the database stage has been reached with the data being administered and guarded carefully because it is very important to the organisation.

On another level the planned changes can be looked on as a change from a decentralised to a centralised system and there are well known characteristics of each of these types of IT organisation.

Advantages of individual IT systems

Individual IT systems imply a decentralised data processing environment and this is likely to have the following advantages.

(i)   When each of KN's departments was first computerised, the systems developed would have been for specific, very often functional requirements eg, customer service history for the sales departments or stock control for the manufacturing department. Many advantages would initially accrue by virtue of the benefits associated with automating clerical activities.

(ii)   IT development is likely to match exactly each department's specific requirements. The IT applications will be tailor-made for each processing application and are likely to have evolved into efficient systems.

(iii)   The major advantage of specific departmental systems is in respect of data volumes and the degree of control over the information required. Where there is a large transaction-processing load, then the only really efficient way of processing the data and providing the information requirements of the firm is by specific application. Very often this may be a basic application of the firm eg, if KN has a large number of customers that it regularly produces invoices for, then the operation of an individual system is extremely important.

(iv)   Each department has its own IT personnel who are dedicated to serving just that department. Therefore, any problems or system changes required are likely to be dealt with promptly by staff who understand the department's processing needs well. Systems development appears to be responsive to user needs.

(v)   Processing power (hardware capabilities) will have evolved with the departments and their software. As processing is carried on locally, each department can decide on its own processing priorities. Response times are likely to be acceptable to users.

(vi)   Ownership of the data, for example what data is held and under what circumstances it can be changed, will be well understood and its design will reflect each department's requirements.

(vii)   Because data is held and processed locally, there is likely to be local pride in its accuracy and integrity. Users feel responsible for their data and this will tend to increase its accuracy. Separate systems will be resilient to processing failure. Hardware breakdowns, software errors, computer viruses and unauthorised access will normally be confined within each department. Data held in other departments will be unaffected.

Disadvantages of individual IT systems

(i)   There is likely to be a wide variety of processing and security standards; some departments will have high standards, others low. As the importance of IT grows it will be important to ensure that standards are maintained at a high level. If processing is centralised into a database system, it will be easier to impose uniform standards. There is a chance that, because there are many separate IT departments each with its team of experts, the average level of skill will be lower than if IT is centralised. Then, the company may be able to enjoy economies of scale, which will allow fewer but more highly skilled staff to be employed. For example, organisations that have a large database system are likely to employ a database administrator to monitor the access to and development of the database.

(ii)   Security of processing and data can be more difficult in individual or distributed systems. Many people have access to the data, programs and hardware. For example, backups of data should be taken regularly. However, it may be difficult to ensure that all departments are diligent in this; centralising the data and most of the processing in one place under the control of dedicated experts will make it easier to ensure that regular backups are taken.

(iii)   The big disadvantage of individual systems is that they can be too rigid and, as a result, unresponsive to changes. Many systems are designed for a particular purpose and, as further needs develop, they cannot always be enhanced to take account of future requirements. This becomes a problem when access to data and information within a system is required for a subsequent use. Even within a relational database system, data may not always be available particularly if it has not been captured in the first place.

(iv)   There may be duplication of data in some cases and insufficient information, at the corporate level, in other cases. The same data could be stored several times with all the attendant data capture, maintenance and storage costs. In overall terms, there may be gaps in the total information requirements of the firm with each department having just enough data to satisfy its needs, but at the corporate level a shortfall existing.

(v)   Information will be difficult to share between departments. It might be held in different formats on incompatible systems. It is almost certain that different departments will need to be able to access and use data held in other departments. For example, if the company wants to run a large marketing campaign it will need to access all customer records. If it wants to raise and post invoices it will have to have access to the sales ledger, nominal ledger and stock files.

(vi)   Processing will be restricted and limited simply because of the technical difficulties of using data drawn from different systems. Processing should be driven by business needs not inhibited by system constraints.

(b)   The following problems are likely to be encountered when the company attempts to amalgamate the company's data into one central database:

(i)   *Standards* - there will be a problem of amalgamating data that has been developed at different times and under different methodologies. This problem is obvious where the data is very different (for example, debtors ledger and stock ledger) but will also be a problem where the data appears to be the same. Field sizes and content all create standardisation problems when previously separate databases are combined. Files holding names and addresses could have different formats and spaces designated for each field. Duplication of data could arise. For example, two departments could hold information about the same customer but this might not be identified and the customer could appear twice in the final database.

(ii)   *Volumes of data* - centralising all of KN's data into one central computer (such as a network file server), and distributing it to departments when they need it, can create storage and processing problems due to the large amounts of data that will need to be handled and transmitted. This can cause database overflow problems, particularly in respect of data storage. It is essential that users perceive no degradation in the speed of responses.

(iii)   *Control and custody of data* - staff in user departments may be feeling a lack of control and degradation of IT service because providing access for all KN departments will create design problems. The database needs to be structured in such a way that both existing and future applications can access it quickly and efficiently. If people in the user departments have been satisfied with their individual arrangements they may resent control and custody of the data being removed to a central department. A big problem is the migration of the existing data to the new database. As different standards exist at the moment, there could be difficulties in translating existing data into a new format. The design of the database must therefore be carried out very thoroughly. Ideally, no department should find that a facility that it had found useful becomes unavailable when the central database is established.

(iv) *Security* - all the company's data will be held in one place so it is vital that the company designs and enforces stringent security measures to protect the important resource, which will have increasing strategic importance. Loss or corruption of the data would be disastrous. At a departmental level, an individual application disaster can possibly be managed even if there were inadequate back-up facilities. With a central database, back-up contingency arrangements assume much greater importance as KN could not recover from a major disaster without such arrangements. The security measures should include physical access controls, user access controls (for example passwords), back-up procedures, disaster action plans and anti-virus software.

Answer 22

Technological Infrastructure

> *Tutorial note:*
>
> **Required**   - In part (a) remember that quality is more important than quantity. A ten-mark allocation means that the examiner is looking for around four solid points. The answer in part (b) is required in the form of briefing notes.

(a)   To ensure that IT is used effectively within an organisation implementation must start from a strategic level. Once it is part of the overall strategic plan, the IT will be perceived as adding value to the company rather than creating a cost. This is a complete change from the traditional way of thinking, and is said to be 'proactive' rather than 'reactive'.

The marketing manager is correct in believing that IT should be part of the overall strategic plan, as it will only be then that the full competitive potential of IT can be exploited throughout the whole of the company, and the full organisation-wide impact of any strategic initiatives can be assessed. This will allow for the correct level of IT resource commitment to be made by the Board.

By implementing IT at this level, the whole process can be assessed properly right from the end-user, who will be able to feed essential first-hand information on the needs of IT, through the managers who can support this need and assist them, right up to the Board.

Without this overall commitment from the strategic level of the company to the end-user, G&J will continue to fail in satisfying their customers' needs, and also continue to lose its competitive advantage to companies who have seen the potential of IT in its value chain. G&J's competitors have been successful in implementing IT in their order cycle and reducing their costs in increasing productivity, therefore adding value rather than creating costs. G&J must implement the full strength of a new IT infrastructure in order to regain its competitive advantage once again.

(b)   *Briefing paper*

A briefing paper on the benefits to G&J from the integration of IT into the strategic planning process.

          Prepared for: Marketing Director

          Prepared by: Strategic/IT co-ordinator

          Date: February 26th 200X

          1   Introduction

          1.1   This briefing paper has been requested by the marketing director to stress the importance of incorporating IT into the strategic level of the company. G&J have watched the company lose its competitive edge by failing to match their competitors' exploitation of new information technologies.

1.2   It is important for G&J to identify its critical success factors and then appraise to what extent each factor is constrained by information deficiencies. Once identified the costs and technical feasibilities of overcoming these deficiencies can be evaluated.

2   Benefits of IT to the business

2.1   The creation of a technological infrastructure that complements the strategic objectives of G&J could bring immediate benefit to the company. This could be, for example, an on-line sales order entry system, which allows rapid ordering and faster delivery of the products to the customer.

2.2   This new system could be linked to other business objectives of the firm. For example there may be a marketing objective to guarantee delivery within five days. This will depend on systems that can cost-effectively cope with such a demand.

2.3   The systems can be used to rank and select projects and new products for the company. By assessing the customers' wants and needs it will allow a more accurate and cost-effective portfolio of development to be chosen. New opportunities can be implemented more quickly, which would therefore enable G&J to achieve a quicker return.

2.4   As the technology is integrated into the company, other mutual benefits could arise. This could enable closer cooperation between the departments, as information is shared and used. This in turn could bring about an increase in turnover, for example by faster collection of order data, therefore giving improved information capability to the marketing department, who can identify future customer needs.

2.5   There could also be a minimum of data duplication, which could improve the overall efficiency and quality of the service.

2.6   Future opportunities, otherwise unavailable to the company, could now arise owing to the strong link between the end-user and the Board. Information between the parties should be passed on much more quickly and therefore be acted upon more rapidly, producing a more competitive edge.

3   Conclusions

3.1   Overall it can be seen that the benefits of closer links between strategic planning and any new technological infrastructure have to be better than just relying on computer specialists.

3.2   Competitive advantage has to be recovered, and it would seem that closer links between these two areas is the way forward. Being responsive to the customer's needs by introducing IT into the strategic planning of G&J seems to be the missing link between the value chain and the use of technology to achieve their overall aim.

Strategic/IT co-ordinator

Answer 23

Facilities Management

Tutorial note:	
Required	- This question uses as a scenario the situation common to many organisations where the IT function has effectively been outsourced. In this situation, the outsourcing has not gone to plan and you are asked to evaluate the situation and suggest alternatives for the future.
	Use the contract to structure your answer.

(a)   It is not clear from the scenario whether GDC Ltd inherited a system that was already running or whether they were involved in any of the system design and development. Although everyone agrees that the contract between the two parties is legally precise, unfortunately no detailed service level agreement was drawn up. This would have covered the various performance standards that the facilities management company contract would cover.

From the point of view of DS, there are many reasons why it may have received poor service, even though the terms of the contract have been fulfilled. The terms are as follows:

Purchase of all hardware and software

GDC may have a preference for hardware and software that they are familiar with and this may not be a suitable fit to the existing system. Unfortunately, hardware and software become obsolete very quickly and GDC Ltd may not have been replacing it fast enough to keep up with the demands of the company. It could be that they have bought software to upgrade the system eg, moved from Windows 95 to Windows 2000, and they have no staff trained sufficiently to maintain it. A similar situation could have occurred with networking and routing equipment. Problems can occur that are very difficult to sort out without available expertise.

Repair and maintenance of all IT equipment

This is a tall order for any company. When the equipment was purchased, DS should have arranged maintenance service through the manufacturers themselves. There could easily be a misunderstanding over the type of repair and maintenance required from GDC Ltd, for instance whether they are they supposed to fix faults when they occur or perform regular maintenance checks to ensure the smooth running of the equipment. Depending on the terms of the purchasing contract, the decision to repair or replace would be taken by GDC and so it is possible that DS may have received poor service in this respect. Equipment replacement periods should have been agreed under the service level agreement, as well as response times, average downtimes and the Mean Time Between Failures (MTBF).

Help desk and other support services for users

Users often have an inadequate understanding of existing systems and develop unrealistic expectations. This means that they may generate unreasonable and unmanageable volumes of requests for change. If DS relies on a continuous online service, then the service level agreement should reflect this and stress that no downtime is tolerable and hot start standby backup needs to be provided. GDC Ltd might suffer from high programmer turnover rates. Their employees may not have the necessary skills or motivation. Many programmers prefer development work to maintenance work and may be reluctant to get involved in help desk support.

Writing and maintaining software

This could be the area for the most misunderstanding, disruption and cost escalation. There are two main areas of software maintenance:

(i)   Changes to the specification, requiring the software to be changed; and

(ii)   Bug fixes or rectifying deficiencies so that the system performs as originally specified.

Software that is specifically developed encounters many problems and is plagued by time and cost overruns. DS has lost control of this essential element of its business activity by outsourcing. When changes are requested, GDC can charge a premium.

There are three types of maintenance activity:

(i)   Corrective, where behaviour or performance fails to be as specified due to faulty implementation;

(ii)   Adaptive, where a change in the environment has not been anticipated, and causes a departure from the specification. Adaptive changes may arise from changes in the law, alterations in taxation regulations, changes forced by technical advances by competitors and/or the evolution of new standards and procedures.

(iii)   Perfective, where some feature is enhanced though it was within the tolerances of the specification, eg, the program may be made more user-friendly, or the processing speed may be increased.

Because the contract is vague and the scope so large, there are bound to be areas of poor service from GDC Ltd.

Provision of management information

Unless the type, content and timing of the management report required is specified, then there is ample scope for poor service. A new person at GDC Ltd may be responsible for producing the reports and he or she may not know the full routine. The report may have been left in the wrong place, or delivered to the wrong person first. However, the problem may not be due to a fault at GDC Ltd. To obtain essential management reports, the information must be kept up to date by the staff at DS. If the employee responsible for maintaining the database is sick or the files containing the data get damaged or corrupted, then the production of reports is likely to be delayed.

Pricing

The terms outlined - inflation, plus 10% - are very high. Such pricing should relate to unit costs eg, network traffic volumes and assuming a normal rise in activity DS will be paying excessive amounts.

(b)   There are several options available to DS.

The first is to continue with the contract as it stands. This would not be a good idea because the recent exchange of correspondence with GDC Ltd has failed to resolve the problems of complaints and late management reports. Even the staff at GDC Ltd recognise that there has been a fall in the standards of service. Continuing with the same contract means that costs will escalate and the general service will decline, especially for software developments.

The second is to re-write the contract with the help of GDC Ltd so that there is some flexibility but no vague areas and each party knows what is expected from them. Price increases should be limited to industry specific inflation plus a yearly price increase of inflation less two to three per cent for productivity and learning curve gains. This could be done through negotiation while the existing contract is still running. The problem with this course of action is that DS are locked into the current arrangement and GDC Ltd will be aware of the problems it could cause by giving three months notice and leaving DS. They would be in a very strong position to increase the price substantially or restrict their commitment to DS in any negotiations that might take place.

The third option would be to obtain help in re-writing the contract and, when satisfied, give GDC Ltd three months notice and ask them, and other facilities management companies, to tender for the new contract. This may achieve cost reduction but can be very disruptive, particularly if GDC are not co-operative. Another of the problems with this course of action is that DS might just be trading in one company that is giving poor service for another that they do not know. There is no guarantee that service standards will always be as expected.

The last option would be to revert to an in-house IT development and support department solution (a green field approach). This would require a lot of effort and expense and, if new staff have to be recruited, there will be a long period before they could understand the system and be in a position to do what GDC Ltd are already doing.

As a minimum the software development could be in house because it is too important to outsource. This would enable DS to maintain a responsive stance to respond to market conditions, achieving competitive advantage if correctly managed. The main problem with this strategy is that, following outsourcing, the employees with the right skills will probably no longer exist within the organisation.

Because of specialist economies of scale, the repairs and maintenance and help desk and other support services for users are probably better and cheaper if outsourced.

Answer 24

Overcoming Barriers

Tutorial note:	
Required	- Part (a) of this question allows you to show your knowledge of the reasons for the importance of an IT strategy for any company.
	Part (b) deals with identifying and overcoming barriers for three diverse individuals in producing an IT strategy document for the company.
Not required	- List of the advantages of having an IT strategy.

(a)   A strategy can be thought of as a long-term plan. A corporate strategy will set out how management plans the organisation to develop over the next five or so years so that the organisation's objectives can be met. Strategies will have resource implications - capital, management, marketing, human resources and IT. The resources have to be planned and acquired if the overall strategy is to be achieved. If suitable resources cannot be acquired the strategy may have to be changed.

Increasingly, it is important for organisations to have an adequate IT strategy. Profitability, competitive strength and customer service all depend more and more on good information technology. IT no longer merely plays a support role in many organisations; it is a source of competitive advantage. If such organisations neglect the long-term development of IT, it is likely that their long-term survival will be at risk.

Examination tip - The examiner is only looking for the disadvantages of not having an overall IT strategy in place.

The particular disadvantages that can occur without a strategy are:

(i)   Unnecessary costs will be incurred because equipment and software may be purchased which are inappropriate to the long-term direction of the company. The software and hardware might then have to be scrapped early or additional expenditure might be required to carry out upgrades or to make the systems compatible.

(ii)   The organisation's activities may not be properly supported by the IT system, leading to lower staff morale, higher staff turnover and low motivation.

(iii)   Poor IT may drive production costs to become higher than the competition's.

(iv)   Customer service might become worse than that of the competition who can offer immediate real-time customer advice, and competitive advantage could be lost.

(b)   *Examination tip - The question has already outlined the structure of the answer required.*

The senior manager - has little experience of IT. He is fearful of IT because it threatens to expose his weak knowledge and he may feel that he will lose face. He may also worry that, if he cannot cope with IT, further promotion and even his job may be at risk. If the manager is relatively near retirement age he may see IT as an unwelcome extra burden in his last working years.

The manager is also very task orientated. He likes activities, which have to be done now, and which have immediate verifiable results. Formulating strategy is quite a different skill and it requires long-term vision about the future. Results will be slow to appear, may be difficult to evaluate and the strategy may have to be revised frequently as events develop. This is likely to make the manager feel uncomfortable about any strategic planning exercise. He will feel even worse about strategic planning for IT in which he sees no value at all.

To attempt to overcome these problems, the manager must gain an understanding of how IT will be able to help the organisation. Perhaps the best way to do this would be to show the manager how other successful firms make use of IT and how they feel that an IT strategy is vital to success. To develop a more strategic outlook, the manager will need to understand how technology is being used in his industry. Seminars run by the industry trade association might help.

The IT professional - has good technical knowledge of mainframe computers, but little of end-user computing. She is likely to promote something that she is most familiar with, rather than a solution that may be best for the organisation. Her technical knowledge may intimidate other members of the working group who may feel unable to challenge the expert's assertions.

Her attitude that users should accept the information that they have been given is very old fashioned. In terms of Nolan's model of systems evolution in organisations, she is probably not much further on than the control stage. The organisation may need to move much more towards the maturity stage in which IT is seen as a strategic resource and users have a close involvement in its design.

The IT expert may experience some difficulties in changing her attitude. Greater user involvement may imply that the power of the expert declines and she may fear a loss of status and importance. However, this should not really be so; users know the information they want and may be able to handle computer packages, but the more technical aspects of network installation and database administration will stay with an expert. The expert faces her greatest challenge in realising that she may no longer be a technical expert in the new types of system, but she will still have valuable expertise in managing the IT department. It has probably been some time anyway since she was closely involved with the technical side of her department.

Development courses in new systems run by the computer industry and visiting other organisations may help to overcome some of the expert's resistance.

The IT user - is well read in IT matters and will have already gained considerable practical experience within the accounts department as well as good theoretical knowledge. However, the user has spent time only in the accounts department and there is a danger that he will underestimate the information needs in other business areas. He will find costs relatively easy to estimate, but may find it difficult to deal with the benefits arising from IT, many of which will be difficult to quantify.

He is likely to be rather task-orientated and may not have had the opportunity to develop a longer-term strategic outlook. He is obviously very keen and knowledgeable on IT however his experience is purely in accounts and this might cause bias. He will need to gain experience of other areas of work before he can act as a champion of change.

However, with some care on his part, his knowledge, ambition and wish to champion IT should be a great asset to the steering group. Being relatively junior in the organisation he will have no vested interests in adopting any particular system and should be relatively unbiased.

Answer 25

JBCC

(a)   The term 'decision support system' or 'DSS' can be interpreted in a number of ways. Often it is used to indicate a system that helps management make relatively unstructured decisions. An example of this use would be setting price levels and budgets where there are no correct definitive answers but the user can be aided in reaching a good answer. However, the term can also be used more generally to simply imply a system, which helps management make decisions whether structured or non-structured.

The decision-making in JBCC's welfare department will usually be structured because a series of questions will inevitably lead to a conclusion about benefit entitlement. However, the number of rules and the frequency with which they change mean that staff need assistance from a decision support system to apply the rules properly and to keep them up to date.

Hardware - individual laptops

Because staff are often away from the office for long periods it will be essential for them to have mobile computing power with remote access to their head office computer. Each staff member should have a laptop with sufficient power and hard disk storage to deal with the rules and decision-making processes that have to be undertaken.

It is recommended that these machines will need at least a Pentium-standard microchip computer, which has a clock speed of about 700 MHz and a minimum of 64 Mb of RAM together with a hard disk capacity of 20 Gb. The portables would need to be at the lower end of the range in terms of their performance characteristics. Money could be saved by opting for cheaper dual scan screens on the computers instead of TFT screens. Recharger units driven from car cigarette lighters would give staff almost unlimited laptop time.

Each computer should have a modem (either internal or external) so that data and e-mails can be sent and received. A small portable printer would allow staff to print out information for their welfare clients, for example the make-up of payments approved, or a record of information supplied to the welfare officer.

It is likely that officers already have mobile phones. As these are gradually upgraded, it would be worth evaluating the cost of obtaining handsets that allow data to be transmitted and received.

As staff call into the office, it should be possible to plug the laptop into the network so that information can be exchanged easily with the main network computers.

Head office computers

A network system should be set up within the head office to download the latest rules and information and to upload completed claim forms. This will consist of a file server, print server and the required number of terminals. This network would typically work over the telephone lines with dialling-in facilities to obtain a computer link to the central computer system. Some of the terminals can be docking stations for the laptop computers. A docking station allows a laptop to be plugged in and become a fully functioning normal member of the network. The file server and print facilities should meet the needs of the network users.

The file server should be kept in a secure area with restricted access. Backup facilities and emergency uninterruptible power supplies should be used at head office to protect against data loss.

Software

Windows 98 or Windows Millennium front-end is a prerequisite for the system to be easy to use and have the necessary communications software. An integrated package incorporating word processor, database, personal information manager (electronic diary) and spreadsheet facilities would be of general use to staff members. These packages are often 'bundled' with the hardware. Standard applications could be set up at head office to ensure that all users operate the same systems. For example, a database of welfare clients could be set up at head office from which data could be downloaded onto the laptops. Examples of such integrated packages include Microsoft Office and Lotus SmartSuite.

Groupware such as Lotus Notes could be used, allowing many users to share data and ensuring that all officers are using up-to-date data. When the laptops are brought back to head office, Lotus Notes will handle the synchronisation of data and will also record who entered the data. For example, if a staff member were on holiday and another staff member saw a benefit claimant, the decisions made and actions taken by the stand-in would be traceable. When the staff member on holiday returns, his or her laptop would be updated automatically.

The decision support system (DSS) application is likely to be developed from a knowledge-based or expert system whereby the rules, policies and associations of information are all built into the DSS package. This type of application consists of a knowledge base (which contains the rules), an inference engine (which applies the rules) and a user interface (which provides a user friendly front end to the system). The ease of use of such a system, together with the level of expertise that can be achieved, will be particularly useful for JBCC's staff so that they will not need to keep learning new rules.

(b)   Staff retention

The staff retention rate is low due to poor morale. There may be several reasons for this, but probably the two main ones would be the isolation that staff feel when they visit individual clients and the frustration at trying to find the latest relevant information to assist them.

A DSS can eliminate a lot of the frustration by providing accurate and consistent advice, making it much easier for staff members to apply up-to-date rules. The DSS is a rule-based system and will, therefore, be able to replicate the best clerical decisions. Staff motivation should improve because they are able to provide a good service using the latest equipment.

Having up-to-date consistent information available about each claimant will also allow staff members to give more time to addressing the needs of claimants other than just financial needs. The decisions about financial matters will have been substantially automated, allowing more time to 'get to know' the claimants.

The new system will automate the chore of updating rules, reducing the incidence of errors. It will also help to increase productivity by increasing the number of welfare clients dealt with each day satisfactorily.

Having access to the network will lower the feeling of isolation that is currently felt when staff members are away from the office for several days at a time. The new system can make staff feel part of the team and, by providing a facility to log onto JBCC's network, they can be advised of all the latest news not only in respect of the DSS, but also in respect of other aspects of JBCC. This will give staff a greater sense of belonging.

Finally, there will be less stress for staff, as they do not have to rely on their memory for details, or for locating documents or remembering which of the 170 forms to use. All the information they need will be 'on the system' in one form or another and this will help when they are dealing with claimants.

Answer 26

WRF Inc

REPORT

To: The Board of WRF Inc

From: Chartered management accountant

Date:

Subject: Systems development life cycle approach to providing a successful systems changeover

Introduction

The Systems Development Life Cycle (SDLC) is a disciplined approach to developing information systems. It is a model that is based upon a phased approach. There are many versions of the SDLC, and although different terminology may be used the basic intent is similar. It covers the following stages:

(i)   requirements and specification
(ii)   design
(iii)   implementation
(iv)   review and maintenance

The current situation

The systems analyst has prepared the initial proposal, which appears to have been done without following any formal methodology. He or she is on a fixed-term contract, which is due to terminate when the system installation is complete. These two factors represent a risk to the successful system changeover. The solution provided may be satisfactory, but is unlikely to be optimal, especially if the systems analyst's contract terminates at a critical stage of the development.

Before embarking on the phases of the SDLC, it is worth considering that prior to a new system being designed and built, the existing system needs to be fully understood; therefore, it is important that a study of the current system is undertaken.

SDLC is the preferred option for the following reasons:

(i)   Requirements and specification

Initially it is important to ascertain the purpose of the new system, what the new system is required to do, and what level of performance is expected etc.

At this definition stage, the business requirements are clearly defined ie, the inputs, files, processing and outputs of the new system. Resulting from this initial analysis, performance criteria can be set and solutions developed, resulting in appropriate specifications. The specification of a Pentium III processor running at 800 MHz and 128 megabytes of RAM running Windows 2000 was arrived at because the systems analyst 'thinks the users will require' this.

(ii)   Design

This stage considers both computerised and manual procedures, and how the information flows are used. Computer outputs are normally designed first; inputs, program design, file design, database design, and security are also areas to be addressed.

It will also be necessary to consider operability at this stage ie, who should have access to do what to which data?

At this stage a detailed specification of the new system is produced. A Pentium III processor running at 800 MHz may well be considered to be too slow: a Pentium 4 processor running at, say, 1.8 GHz may be necessary to produce the required results.

(iii)   Implementation

This stage may include the building of prototypes and the finalisation of specification requirements eg, 128 megabytes of RAM could be considered insufficient; 256 Mb may be deemed to be more appropriate.

The implementation stage takes the development through from design to operation. This involves acquiring or writing software, program testing, file conversion, acquiring and installation of hardware and training.

When following a formal methodology, implementation and all it embraces should be considered from the initial analysis stage so the likelihood of problems should be substantially diminished.

(iv)   Review and maintenance

This final stage ensures that the project meets with the objectives set, that it is accepted by users, that its performance is satisfactory, and allows for future enhancements and development.

Recommendation

It is recommended that the Board of WRF Inc approve the utilisation of SDLC for the systems changeover.

Not only does this approach encourage discipline during the development process, communication between the developers and the users, and recognition of the importance of analysis and design, but it also ensures that business needs are met and provides a useful basis for future development.

Answer 27

Library Direct Services

This project will require careful management and LDS should appoint a project manager - preferably from their own organisation - to control the chosen supplier.

Six questions that LDS can use to help evaluate potential suppliers for the contract are as follows:

1   Do you have experience in this type of system?

It is essential to find a supplier with experience of producing solutions using complex database management systems and relational databases, as the response time of 30 minutes is a critical success factor for LDS and the system must be capable of delivering this level of performance. It is unlikely that any supplier has experience of legal database design on such a scale, but it might be possible to find a supplier with a history of developing library systems.

2   Will your system be flexible?

Although the new system may well take advantage of modern developments in the human-computer interface such as graphical user interfaces (GUI), there might be demand from the administrators for an option to use command line input as in the present system. This type of issue will reduce user acceptance problems.

3   Will you provide training?

This will also help to manage the problems of user acceptance mentioned above. The supplier might also be willing to allow administrators to participate in the design and development of the new system.

4   Will you write a bespoke solution or tailor an off-the-shelf package?

While a totally bespoke solution will allow a perfect solution to be created, it will lead to increased costs and will require far greater testing and documentation. This may lead to a higher risk of failure than with a less perfect tailored solution.

5   What controls will you impose to ensure continuity of service?

Due to previous problems experienced, LDS will need re-assurance that good controls over system documentation will be in place. They will also seek agreement to a maintenance, upgrade and modification pathway that does not depend on the supplier retaining key individuals.

6   What is the financial position of your company?

LDS will require confidence that the supplier is unlikely to go out of business during or after the development of the system. As this system is a key strategic tool for LDS they would also require a covenant to guarantee a service level in case of a future take-over of the supplier.

Answer 28

Homeworking

Tutorial note:	
Required	- Homeworking has been quite topical in recent years, with many companies experimenting with the idea.
	Part (a) of the question focuses on the effects of society and not on the infrastructure itself. It allows you to explain what benefits and problems homeworking can bring whilst at the same time noting that information technology is not always a solution to all these problems.
	Part (b) requires an explanation of what can be done to encourage staff to accept change. In this situation it means getting staff to participate in the change in some way.

(a)   **REPORT**

To: Managing Director

From: Management Accountant

Date: 22 Feb 200X

Subject: Homeworking

Introduction

The Board of CP Ltd has discussed the possibility of telephone sales staff working from home. This report details the staff benefits and concerns of such a proposal:

Benefits of homeworking for staff

All the data that staff need to perform their job is available on the computer system and staff can therefore spend more time accessing the system. There are fewer interruptions and no disruptions resulting from travelling to work.

The staff can enjoy peace and quiet and freedom from some of the stresses that accompany travelling to the office each day. Also, more flexible work patterns can be achieved which is a significant benefit to those staff members with families.

It has also been shown that absenteeism is less when staff work at home and they can generally enjoy a better quality of life. This also leads to less stress and results in a more focused work effort.

Concerns of staff

The human problems associated with change are very evident. Staff are anxious about future employment prospects, they fear that they will become isolated, and uncertainty about the future is causing stress to build up.

Employees enjoy working in the office environment and the social aspects of coffee and lunch breaks will be missed. Also, there is the support of colleagues in respect of difficult queries and staff are concerned that this will be lost.

In addition, there will inevitably be concerns regarding siting of equipment in the homes of staff and insurance of the equipment and any possible repercussions for their own household insurance etc.

IT infrastructure

CP Ltd's IT infrastructure includes the computer system, access to a VAN, word processing and other systems for producing letters and quotes to customers. This will also support e-mail facilities, which will help staff communications, albeit as a limited form of social interaction. The infrastructure is very modern and sophisticated and meets CP Ltd's business needs. However, this cannot really help alleviate the concerns of staff as many of the issues are of a social nature and it is the human aspects of change that need to be considered separately from the provision of IT support.

Conclusion

The proposal for home working is a very attractive business case, but is dependent upon the concerns of staff being addressed in a satisfactory manner.

(b)   Encouraging staff to accept the proposed change

The following can be done to encourage staff to accept the proposed change

- ◆ Involve them completely from the beginning, so that all the issues can be addressed. Point out the benefits of less time spent travelling with a consequent reduction to stress, the peace and quiet of a home-based environment and generally a better quality of life.

- ◆ Ask them for suggestions on the best way of implementing this change. It may be that a gradual changeover will be better so that the more reluctant amongst them will have more time to get used to the idea. An initial trial and/or a trial period could be agreed, so that staff get the chance of a review being carried out to clear up any aspects that have not worked out.

- ◆ The staff need to be convinced that there will still be social aspects to their work. They will still use the telephone to talk to customers and they will be able to talk to other staff members and therefore continue to support each other. As supervision is remote, some support to deal with difficult matters will be necessary. This can be reinforced if CP Ltd has e-mail facilities within its computer system. Staff should not therefore feel too isolated. Social aspects that will still be needed can be met by having regular meetings at perhaps a centrally located hotel. Regular monthly meetings could fulfil both the staff social requirements and the reinforcement of company directives.

- ◆ Most firms have out-of-hours social activities, such as sporting events or social evenings, and this is another area than can be reinforced so that staff will be able to continue to meet each other. Finally, in view of the savings to be made, it may be possible to offer some financial inducement to staff.

In practice, a combination of these actions could be taken to ensure a successful transition.

Signed

Management Accountant

Answer 29

Intranet

Tutorial note:	
Required	- Part (a) of the question provides an introduction that allows you to demonstrate your knowledge of Intranets.
	The more detailed part (b) looks at the more important area of the effect of placing an Intranet into an organisation and the effect on information usage that this system should provide.
Not required	- Comparison with Internet or hardware requirements.

(a)   A development, which parallels the Internet, is the company-wide 'Intranet', in which departments and individuals set up user-friendly computer sites to provide information and services to anyone on the net. The main objective of an Intranet is to make information flow more freely. This means making it more widely available to those who need to have the rights to it, and less widely available to those who do not. As part of an overall communications strategy, an Intranet offers tremendous potential and a strategy for growth. With control of content, real improvements can be made to the quality and availability of corporate data. Similarly, it is far easier to monitor and manage sensitive data in a secure way. Wider access to more electronic server-held information means the elimination of unnecessary paperwork and more opportunities to improve direct, effective interaction between people who really should know about each other.

At CC the information to meet client requirements is held within each office of the company and there are 20 offices. A lot of the information used is duplicated and could be server-held centrally with everyone having access to it. This would reduce the need to maintain it at each office and any changes or updating of the information need only be done once. There is also less risk of it being out of date or wrong if all the employees are using the same information.

There are occasions when e-mail can lead to better provision of information. For example, when an individual employee is privy to information that could benefit the whole company, communicating this information to everyone concerned could lead to cost savings within the company. Answers to questions and solutions to problems can be found quicker if an e-mail can go to over 2,000 people. Shared information on appointments diaries can lead to co-operation if an employee is unexpectedly away from the office or delayed with a client.

(b)   The hardware in the company is quite old and only just meets the minimum specification for the provision of an Intranet, Internet access and e-mail. Consequently, the Intranet will run very slowly and employees will be discouraged from using it. The best way for CC plc would be to get the supporting technology right first - a slow Intranet is worse than no Intranet at all - and to choose it with rapid growth in mind.

There are often problems and lack of trust because no one knows who is controlling the information. The management of CC plc need to establish standards straight away and decide what software is going to be used, who is in charge, who owns the Web servers, who runs and manages them and, above all, who decides on content. If the site content is not up to date or relevant to those people who need to access it, then they will dismiss it as useless and revert to their previous system. The solution to this problem is obvious - the site needs to be interesting, relevant and the information must be correct. Someone from the management team must keep on telling everyone what is happening, advertise new intranet sites and new applications and encourage new grass roots applications. A custom website could be used for this.

Any new communication system is going to worry some employees and make them unsure about their position if they relinquish their cache of information. CC plc need to get everyone in the company to buy into the process and need to make sure that everyone knows the benefits, how the technology works and what is in it for them. They need to set goals and deadlines, tell everyone involved what those are, and tell them when they have been met or missed, and why.

There may be a reluctance to share information because of reduced job security, a fear of broadcasting sensitive information and losing customers or the feeling of 'I have had to work hard for this, why should I give it away?' To counter the fears of job security, CC plc need to stress that people who can be seen as a source of valuable information will be highly regarded. Also, more data will be available in return than will be given. Knowing what is there and where to get it will be the skill of the future, rather than having the knowledge itself.

To answer the fears of broadcasting sensitive information, the management must make sure that firewalls are placed in the system and that access to the information is restricted to the employees that need to know.   To address the last type of reluctance, employees must be told that the information is not being given away, it is being put where it will have the maximum impact. Only companies that use all of their resources in the most effective way will prosper.

Answer 30

Information Overload

<table>
<tr><td>***Tutorial note:***</td><td></td></tr>
<tr><td>**Required**</td><td>- This question covers the situation of a manager suffering from information overload. In many areas of work, managers find coping with the volume of information difficult, especially where information is being presented in a wide variety of formats.

In part (a) you will need to explain what is meant by 'information overload', both from a theoretical point of view and by applying the concept to the specific situation in the scenario.

Resolving the problems produced by information overload is also an important task and you are required to show how information overload can be managed in part (b).</td></tr>
</table>

(a)   *Information overload*

Examination tip - *For each aspect of information overload that you address, you must remember to explain how it could affect the working efficiency of Mr A.*

In the case of Mr A at the JB Company, information overload can occur where he is in receipt of so much information from a variety of sources (such as e-mail, telephone calls, verbal reports from staff, clients and the company's databases) that he is unable to sort out the information that is relevant and necessary to advise clients correctly. Too much information may result in some of it not being used where it should be, and some irrelevant, detailed information being given prominence in his decision-making processes.

From the information given in the scenario, it would appear that too much of his time is spent gathering information from the various sources. Between 30 and 40 e-mails are received from staff and clients each day, and it can be assumed that many of them will require immediate responses. On the other hand, much of the information received may be 'junk' mail. Widely circulated messages from both within and outside the organisation may be of little interest or value to him. Sifting through all the messages may be very time consuming.

Mr A will also be affected by the telephone calls from information analysts and clients. In many cases, queries will have to be answered at once, and therefore he should be in a position to give quick and accurate replies. He also receives information from Internet sites every hour or so. This again can be time-consuming, especially if he is interrupted by staff seeking face-to-face discussions.

Although there are no details, for example, of the number of people who see him personally, or the number of telephone calls he receives, the mere fact that there are 129 offices worldwide, plus a potentially large number of clients, could result in just too many queries for one person to handle. (His workload needs to be reduced, as discussed in part (b) of this answer.)

The overall effect of Mr A having to cope with information from a variety of sources will be to reduce his effectiveness as a human information processor and this, in turn, will affect the way he does his job.

(b)   *Reducing the information overload*

Given that Mr A is suffering from information overload, then there is a need to tackle the problem from several different points of view, including:

♦   his overall workload in terms of the number of clients he deals with;
♦   the information he needs to deal with them;
♦   the way in which the information is collected and assembled for each client;
♦   the use of IT in helping him to handle the information.

Organisational Procedures

One way of dealing with Mr A's workload would be to review the need for him to deal with so many queries personally. The scenario states that the team of information analysts review and summarises information, which Mr A presumably sends to clients. The need for Mr A to be dealing with clients directly must be questioned - this could be a job for the specialists themselves. Some analysis of his actual job is needed. It could be that what he does is not appropriate for a senior accounts manager. His actual day-to-day workload may be at the wrong level for too many clients. Clarification of details, for example, is effectively being done on a second-hand basis. It may be more suitable for Mr A to concentrate on the need to guide the analysts on the type of information they provide - he would then be fulfilling more of a strategic role as possibly befits his seniority.

Some form of re-organisation of responsibilities and duties may be required. Mr A does seem to be involved in many operational tasks and the company should consider the way in which information is collated before being presented to him. A personal assistant could be appointed to him, who would have the responsibility of handling incoming telephone calls and e-mail. There is a risk here that, unless this assistant is suitably qualified in this respect, there may be times when information required by Mr A does not get through to him.

There also seems to be some duplication of effort, with Mr A reviewing Internet sites every hour or so. This alone could be more than enough work for one person, depending on the number of sites visited. The analysts may already be doing this. Mr A may only need to know what significant changes have taken place in the areas in which he is interested. A considerable amount of time could be wasted here.

Depending also on the number of clients Mr A deals with, it may not be realistic to receive so many telephone calls, requiring him to retain the information mentally, as is also the case where face-to-face discussions are held. It would seem that he simply has too many queries to deal with, hence the need to re-organise his responsibilities, so that he deals only with those decisions that it is necessary for him to make.

IT Procedures

Better and fuller use could possibly be made of IT in helping Mr A. The Intranet could contain all information sent to clients, but it could be organised on a client basis, to make its retrieval more effective. E-mail messages could be prioritised so that Mr A is aware primarily of only the urgent ones. Defining 'urgent', however, could be a problem; if left to the sender, there is the danger that all messages could be classed as urgent, and hence the effectiveness of the system would be compromised.

Clients could also be given access to the Intranet where they could access the information or also be re-directed to other sites containing additional information. There may also be areas where support systems such as Expert Systems (ES) or Executive Information Systems (EIS) may be employed. The latter, in particular, could be designed in such a way that although much detailed information can be built into it, and updated by the specialists, Mr A would have the ability to enter it at a higher, summarised, level but 'drill down' for additional information should he require it.

Answer 31

Implementation Problems

Tutorial note:	
Required	– This question investigates the situation where sales representatives do not want to use an improved system because it adversely affects their power and remuneration.
	In part (a) you will need to relate to why the reps do not want to use the new system and provide specific reasons for this.
	Part (b) asks you to suggest how the situation can be resolved.

(a)   *Reasons why representatives have stopped using the system*

From the information in the scenario, it would seem that Q Ltd had a valid reason for wanting to change the existing procedures of having individual databases. Not only were customers' orders being lost but although not specifically stated, it is quite possible that the systems maintained by the individual representatives were not fully compatible. It is also apparent that the whole project was poorly managed and controlled for a number of reasons, the end result being that the new system was rarely used after six months. These reasons include:

Implementation was hurried, resulting in a lack of proper validation.

Final user acceptance was not achieved. Representatives would be unlikely to use a system that they had not fully agreed to, particularly if they were satisfied with the existing system. The new system should give added value to the users in respect of its usage and the information provided, if they are to accept the system readily and willingly. Any system is primarily designed for users who, after all, are the ones who will make it succeed or fail.

Implementing the system in a hurry meant that user acceptance testing did not take place. This would alienate potential users from the outset.

The fact that the programmers were allowed to make changes shows poor project management and control. It would appear that this was done without consulting the users of the system.

These changes were at the expense of some of the user-friendly interfaces. The Human Computer Interface (HCI) aspects of any system are paramount, no matter how efficient the system is in terms of running speeds (provided that they are acceptable).

The fact that most of the representatives were not trained in the use of the system again shows poor project management, resulting in their reverting to a system with which they were familiar and which also meant that they would be in control of their own sales and hence their own commissions. This, in turn, would mean that information would not be shared, leading to sales being lost to the company as a whole.

The scenario does not state to what extent the salaries of representatives are dependent on the commission they earn from sales. The fact that all the representatives would have access to information on all customers through the Intranet could lead to a situation where an order initially dealt with by one representative could be finalised by another. Arguments could arise as to who should receive the commission. Representatives would tend to protect their own financial interests.

The fact that they were allowed to return to their own systems is also important, and indicative of the failure of the whole project planning process.

The over-riding reasons why the representatives may have stopped using the new system are a lack of proper user involvement at all stages in the design and implementation, together with poor project management.

(b)   *Actions to be taken*

A number of steps need to be taken to try to get the representatives to use the new system:

♦   Consult the representatives to explain the reasons for the new system and to find out their reasons for not using it. Even though they were consulted originally, it would appear that the unauthorised amendments mean that the system no longer meets their requirements. Draw up a revised schedule, with agreed milestones and deliverables, for the introduction of the new system. This may require a 'fresh start', although a significant part of the groundwork will have been done.

♦   Re-define the users' requirements in view of any comments they may have made during the new consultation period. Re-design the system, as far as is needed, to ensure that user requirements are fully met, with appropriate user-friendly interfaces. Users must agree that their requirements are being met.

♦   Establish proper controls to ensure that no unauthorised amendments are made to the system. Ensure user involvement at all stages, including testing and acceptance.

♦   Draw up a special training programme (or series of programmes) for all representatives. The original schedule, coinciding with staff holidays, was obviously not well thought out, and is not an acceptable basis on which to implement a system.

These measures should result in the representatives regarding it as their system, have ownership of it, and using it effectively.

The system whereby sales representatives' salaries may be wholly or partly commission-based may need reviewing, as it tends to make the representatives protective of their own customers. They regard customers as 'their own', rather than the company's, and hence sales are being lost when they are unavailable. A commission-sharing scheme may be investigated, whereby representatives dealing with colleagues' customers receive part of the commission available.

Answer 32

Human Problems

Tutorial note:	
Required	- This question investigates what a typical over-worked management accountant may be facing. You are required to explain what these problems are and find some workable solutions.
	Credit will be given for practical solutions, which take into account the fact that the company will not have infinite resources to provide solutions.

Human problems facing the Management Accountant

It appears that the volume of work the management accountant is dealing with is excessive. His responsibilities cover management and financial accounting, IT, Human Resources (HR) and all of the taxation areas. It would be difficult for anyone to keep on top of such a workload because it is spread over many functional areas. You would not normally expect the personnel aspects of the job to be combined with the maintenance of the transaction processing system. The management accountant may well possess the knowledge required for accounting matters and some of the taxation elements, but he will probably not be trained to cope with the information technology and human resource management roles as well.

M O'B does not delegate enough of the interesting work and his subordinates are demotivated. This could be because he does not trust the junior accountants or that he feels he could do the work faster himself. Whilst under time pressure he is unlikely to be able to take the time to check work done and ultimately he still has to take responsibility for their standard of work.

We are told that M O'B is working long hours and is making mistakes. This could be as a result of stress. It is not possible to sustain such a level of work, to any reasonable standard, over the longer term and he is therefore suffering from fatigue.

Human solutions

Unless other areas of work can be removed from the management accountant's area of responsibility it will be impossible for him to delegate and train his staff effectively. An alternative could be that they 'shadow' him and learn by watching and then by doing. This would then alleviate the need for checking their work and would not put more time pressure and responsibility on the management accountant.

Depending on where the management accountant's skills lay, it might be advisable to relieve him of some of the personnel work and/or the IT work by appointing specialist professionals. Obviously, this would depend on the manpower planning within the company and any budget constraints that may exist.

Whatever reason he has for working excessive overtime, the Board needs to implement procedures that will enforce a separation of some of the management accountant's duties. A reappraisal of the role of the management accountant within the company may be appropriate. The Board also expect rather a lot of reports on many areas within the company. If any of these could be eliminated then the time spent on them can be diverted elsewhere.

IT Solutions

If the system were networked, so that all three accountants accessed the same information, it would ensure that the information was shared as well as improving operational efficiency.

It should be possible to automate many of the processes so that routine monthly reports are generated within the system. This would give the management accountant and his assistants more time for investigation and analysis. If the executive information system (EIS) and the transaction processing systems ie, the support systems were developed, the Board could have direct access to as much information as possible. This would reduce the dependence on the monthly reports and would satisfy most of the ad-hoc enquiries that may arise from the information provided.

Specialist software packages in human resource management and in completing tax returns could also help relieve the management accountant of some of the work.

TEP plc

Answer 33

Sources of Information

Tutorial note:	
Required	- For this question, you are required to provide examples of information, from both internal and external sources, that could be used to support two competing investment decisions. While the scenario will provide an indication of some of these sources, you will have to apply your knowledge of external information in particular to produce relevant examples.
Not required	- Capture of information.

Sources of internal information

The main internal information sources are the employees, the current information systems and the results of market research undertaken recently.

Employees of the theme park - will be a useful source of internal information. Because the employees are in close contact with customers and are able to observe how the park operates, they are in a good position to comment on current operations, as well as make suggestions for future changes. It could be that the employees have preferences about the future plans. There may be a reluctance to operate rides suitable for younger children because they are not exciting enough. Current employees may not like the idea of a complete change in business as far as the hotel is concerned. Very few people enjoy change in their working life and the information that the employees can give will aid management in their decision.

TEP plc's current information system - together with the directors' EIS, can provide internal information on the numbers of customers, the most popular rides and the type of products that sell well. Because the company has information from the previous seven years of operation, they could use it to establish the trends over that period. It may be possible to analyse the effect of the introduction of new rides and give a more precise estimate of the effect of investing in a major new ride each year. Further processing of the existing information system could reveal more information regarding the type of customer paying by cash or credit card eg, whether families are more likely to pay by credit card and younger customers by cash.

Market research - other information exists within the company eg, market research findings and information gathered from its own questionnaires. TEP plc are monitoring the competition because they recognise the distinct advantage gained from providing technologically advanced rides. This type of information is derived from the details of visitors per ride, queue length and average waiting times.

Sources of external information

The external information sources include the customers, demographics and economic information, findings from complementary services, and an analysis of the competition.

Customers - this will be the main source of external information. It is important in competitive markets to understand what the customer wants and from this to try to predict trends. The information gathered would enable the company to put the customer requirements first. Some of this information can be collected from gate receipts eg, type of customers, method of payment etc. Further information can come from carrying out surveys or market research exercises. Questionnaires that are completed by visitors when leaving the park could indicate their activity preferences. Questions could be posed to find out what they enjoyed most about the park at this visit and whether they were planning a trip in the near future, and what they would most like to see or experience. Information on the customer's postcode, mode of travel to the park and proposed length of stay will also be useful.

Demographics and economic information - another source of external information is available from government agencies in respect of demographic and economic information. The demographic information will be particularly useful to determine the number of family units that are close enough and likely to visit the park. The broader economic outlook is most important because all investment decisions are made on the basis of uncertainty and risk and this type of information should be scrutinised before commitments are made for such large sums of money.

Findings from the complementary services industry - information that is gathered from all the services surrounding TEP plc will help in evaluating the investment alternatives. These services include:

♦ trading partners that supply the food, refreshments, gifts and other associated services within the park;

♦ companies that provide security services within the park;

♦ general cleaning and car parking services;

♦ travel agencies and travel companies eg, rail, bus and coach;

♦ local hotels, boarding houses and camping sites.

Competitor analysis - information about other theme parks will enable the various options to be evaluated. The information will include:

♦ prices;
♦ number of visitors;
♦ type of visitor;
♦ popular attractions;
♦ facilities offered;
♦ catchment area (advertisement spread); and
♦ future plans (advertisement claims and company literature meant for investors).

Examination tip - *The question requires that the changes should enable the directors to receive the information needed to evaluate the success of this investment. Make sure that you have explained this.*

TEP plc needs to consider carefully their business aims. The new venture would represent a radical change in the objectives previously set. Before any decision is made, detailed costings will need to be established with potential suppliers of goods and services eg, manufacturers of specialist rides and quantity surveyors etc. This information is useful to build into the decision-making processes together with a comparison of the appropriate cash flow projections, which are important to assess before any major capital expenditure is approved.

The evaluation of the decision will be most dependent upon marketing information, for example, the numbers of customers likely to visit the park because of the rides available as opposed to the numbers of customers who will be attracted more by the hotel, shopping and holiday package services. Marketing assessments for each of these investment alternatives are therefore crucial.

Answer 34

Executive Information System

Tutorial note:	
Required	- In this question you are expected to be able to explain how a well-designed EIS will assist the directors of the company.
	The examiner will expect your answer to focus on the EIS design itself and not just on the information that will be displayed by the system.
Not required	- Explanation of other management information systems.

The current Executive Information System (EIS) is seven years old and can allow the directors to view daily totals from the theme park's information systems. However, the directors hardly ever use the EIS because of its limited functionality. The changes that need to be made include the full provision of facilities that a modern EIS now tends to provide. This would consist of:

♦ easy to use, screen-based systems with mouse, icons and touch-screen facilities, giving easy access to data;

♦ presentational aids, by pictorial or graphical means, so that information can be conveyed without too many trivial choices of scale, colour and layout. The EIS should be able to provide information pictorially, and in an easy-to-use format, so that the directors can overlay the trend information from one variable on top of another to check for correlation etc.

♦ summary level data, captured from the organisation's main systems, which might involve integrating the executive's desktop PC with the organisation's mainframe;

♦ a facility which allows the executive to drill down from higher to lower levels of information;

♦ data manipulation facilities such as comparison with budget or prior year data and external information that can be superimposed onto the organisation's information eg, sales forecasts with information from the Meteorological Office about the weather;

♦ tools for analysis, including ratio analysis, forecasts, what if analysis and trends;

♦ a template system which allows the same type of data eg, sales figures, to be presented in the same format, irrespective of changes in the volume of information required.

The directors need to have information about TEP plc's performance and also details of competitors, particularly comparisons in respect of new rides. In the initial stages of the development, the changes to the EIS should give the directors the following capabilities:

♦ Control information on the investment, because an investment of at least £6m over a relatively short period can cause many problems unless sufficient project management controls are in place.

♦ Control information on costs and progress of the new hotel development.

Once the hotel has been completed the EIS will need to provide details of the effect it has had on results. It will need to provide:

♦ Details of the effect of the new investment, with the results broken down to give information on customers visiting the park and the number and duration of stays at the hotel. The EIS should be able to provide information pictorially, and in an easy - to-use format.

♦ TEP plc's performance results compared with similar details of competitors eg, comparisons of new rides.

When appraising this investment certain assumptions about the numbers of customers who will attend because of the enhanced facilities will be made, together with increases in spending on souvenirs, food and refreshments. The EIS will need to have:

♦ Facilities to monitor the level of operational expenditure. For example the running costs of the hotel will be monitored, especially as it is new, and TEP plc has no previous data on how the pattern of maintenance costs will emerge.

♦ Manipulation facilities to process the data from the components of the feeder systems. The hotel will have its own range of merchandising and the EIS needs to be able to extract and integrate this data in order to provide the full picture.

The EIS can be changed and improved to provide full functionality and provide the data required. The ability to track critical data that has been collected from different systems means that the directors can use the EIS at every stage of this investment.

Answer 35

Communicating via the Internet

Tutorial note:	
Required	- This question is about the use of the Internet to provide services. You are required to consider the effect of this change on employment and society as a whole.

The growth of the Internet over the last few years for every type of application and communication is phenomenal. Most companies in the UK would feel behind in technology if they did not have either an e-mail address and/or a website.

Advertising on the Internet is an extremely powerful marketing tool. It allows full multi-media capability, including sound, colour, graphics and movement. These can all be combined to create maximum impact. High-level languages like Java and HTML are used to create the websites and they can have an assortment of interactive 'buttons' that give you access to further information when clicked on. The displays may be words, pictures, photographs or short video sequences.

TEP plc's site could guide the potential customer through a number of pages containing information on the hotel, the park, the extra amenities and the rides. For the hotel advertisement, as well as the tariff and details of any special deals, there could be a combination of sample menus, photographs of the rooms, leisure facilities and children's play areas. For the park and rides, if the programmer writing the advertisement was very creative, he or she could write screens that took you around the park as though you were in a train.

The booking system could be organised in a number of ways. It could be a series of menus and forms, allowing the customer to check availability and place a provisional booking, which would be confirmed upon receipt of the deposit.

The effect on society - when booking, buying, communicating or browsing over the Internet, there is no social interaction. It is very different from booking by telephone or in person, which usually means talking to other people and exchanging the usual social pleasantries. Booking via the Internet involves filling in a screen-based form with details of the product or service required, together with the appropriate payment details. There are advantages and disadvantages to both methods when it comes to booking a hotel room or a visit to a theme park. The amount of information available when browsing through pages of advertisements on the Internet is far greater than a person would find available from a receptionist in the hotel or sales person at the park. There are no closing times on the Internet and no annoying music on the telephone line because you are held in a queue. The customer should have access to the same information as the staff at the park and, if more information is required, there should be a means to leave a message on the site for someone to contact you.

One of the disadvantages is that some people are reluctant to use their credit cards on the Internet. This is probably because of the fear that security is not what it could be. In reality, most credit card frauds are the result of using the carbon copies of credit card slips, rather than via the Internet.

Employment

The Internet allows people to obtain advertising information, view and purchase products whenever they want. It feeds the current desire for instant gratification and so its use as a booking medium will grow because it gives an instant response. People are no longer limited by the distance from the shops or by the opening times of the different outlets.

There are obvious employment implications for sales staff, both retail and commercial, and for people who work with transportation. Fewer people will be required to answer telephones or attend to enquiries. If potential customers can receive the information they want at home they do not need to use their cars, or public transport to search for the products they want to buy. The overall effect on employment will be that the skill mix within organisations will change. Instead of having socially outgoing, sales-oriented employees, organisations will need to employ the skills of computer programmers to make their websites more sophisticated and web managers to keep the information up to date. This will be the way to increase sales. The employment of staff may therefore depend on their logical skills rather than their people skills.

Answer 36

Information Sources Required

Tutorial note:	
Required	- This scenario is based on the telecommunications industry. It investigates the current industry and how it is expected to develop over the next few years.
	The question asks you to explain appropriate sources of information that can be used to set the price for a future integrated digital service. While the concept of obtaining internal and external information will be familiar, the question is complicated in that the service will be provided in the future. This will limit the information available and encourage you to think more deeply to identify the appropriate information sources.

Information can arise from sources both within and outside the organisation. For example, in making 'selling price decisions', information about production possibilities and costs will arise from within the organisation, whereas information about potential demand for the products will be found by market research, which is an external source. Information concerning competitors' pricing policies and other aspects of 'market intelligence' is also external.

Sources within LT plc include the employees, the current information systems and market research findings.

Employees will be a useful source of internal information, because they are in close contact with customers and in a good position to comment on current operations, as well as make suggestions for future changes.

LT plc's current information system, together with any EIS, can provide internal information. There are usually several information systems collecting internal data. These include formal systems for producing accounts, production statistics, sales analyses and personnel records. In most organisations, the accounting system is one of the most powerful internal information systems because it is the only one that expresses the firm's inputs and outputs in the same unit of measurement. Because the new integrated digital service is currently available for trial runs with the Asymmetric Digital Subscriber Line (ADSL), the basic costs of producing this service are already available. This should provide a basis for a pricing policy.

The sales analyses could provide a lot of information on LT plc's customers. This can range from the numbers and types of customers, the average spend and the type of services that sell well. Because the company has information over many years of operation, they could use it to establish the trends over that period. LT plc must have introduced other services in their recent past eg, Integrated Services Digital Network (ISDN) and call back services and they could use the information about how they set the price at that time. Further processing of the existing information system could reveal how many customers have changed to a competitor, for either their main telephone line, or to add a line for cable television and fax/Internet use. They can also find out from the itemised billing system how much time and money is currently spent on Internet connections.

Customer services within LT plc may have gathered information on customer enquiries about the service. Customers returning to the UK from America or certain European countries may already be aware of ADSL and be expressing an interest in connecting in the near future.

Market research information will exist within the company eg, market research findings and information gathered from its own questionnaires. Information will be available from surveys carried out when the company introduced its ISDN service. These customers will probably be amongst the first to switch to the new service because it is faster, runs on a normal phone line and does not need expensive switching gear from the phone company.

The external information sources include market research, customers, demographic and economic information, external record-based information, environmental scanning services, the industry and an analysis of the competition.

Market research exercises will find out the opinions and buying attitudes of potential customers.

Customers will be the main source of external information. It is important in competitive markets to understand what the customer wants and from this to try to predict trends. The information gathered would enable the company to put the customer requirements first. Some of this information can be collected from the itemised bills eg, type of customer, method of payment etc. Further information can come from carrying out surveys or market research exercises. Questionnaires completed by customers could help identify the target market for the new services and get some idea of the price range that would be acceptable to them. Trial runs of ADSL in certain parts of the country will enable LT plc to test the market for a range of prices to see what the take up rate is. Certain Internet Service Providers (ISPs) will also be test marketing ADSL and their reactions to different pricing structures will be available.

Demographic and economic information is available from government agencies. The demographic information will be particularly useful to determine the number of new business start-ups, the number of people working from home and the number of schools and colleges requiring Internet services. The broader economic outlook is also important because of the investment required to launch a new product or service.

External record-based information provides the type of information from external databases that is used by strategic planning departments, financial planners and other user departments. However, with the increasingly turbulent business environment, LT plc will want to co-ordinate their use of such external services, as well as combine internal and external information to understand the industry trends better. Examples of formal external record-based information include:

♦ Legal and regulatory update information: changes to company law, tax employment law, accounting standards, environmental protection, etc. Any changes that have a cost element are important for LT plc.

♦ Research intelligence: information about technology changes or new discoveries, which may have an impact on the new service.

♦ Other forms of market intelligence: for example the formal collection of feedback forms from customers, sales representatives and others 'in the field', such as maintenance staff.

Environmental scanning services have been available for many years. They browse the Internet, review publications, clip out pertinent articles and create abstracts of articles, then pass them on to their clients. A newer development of this service is the delivery of the information directly to an organisation's computer where managers can interpret it.

The telecommunications industry will have societies established specifically for providing information and comparisons about all the companies in that industry.

Competitor analysis - information about other companies offering similar services will enable LT plc to evaluate various options. The information will include prices, numbers and types of customers, services offered, number of central offices and plans (advertisement claims and company literature meant for investors).

Answer 37

Integrated Service

Tutorial note:
Required - Although this question appears to be speculative in nature, the potential effects on society should not be too difficult to determine.
You will have to apply your knowledge from the effect of similar technological changes like television or the use of home computers.

In the near future, it is expected that telecommunications companies will be able to provide a fully integrated service of traditional telephone, digital cable TV, Internet access and home shopping to most households. The system will enable consumers, in both domestic and overseas markets, to order their shopping, browse the Internet, view films on demand and make telephone calls, possibly with integrated video, from their living room. This will have a profound effect on both employment and society.

It will be particularly significant for businesses in the retailing, media and entertainment fields, speeding the development of electronic home shopping and banking, and the 'interactive' communication between a business and its customers. The Internet and electronic commerce technologies will be used to link an enterprise to its customers and to its other external business partners. Many organisations are setting up websites with product or service details for people to access from anywhere in the world. Within the banking and financial industries, EDI and related applications are revolutionising the entire system of moving funds. Supermarkets will deliver shopping ordered over the Internet, selected from a list of more than 20,000 different items. International e-mail systems will enable businesses to communicate cheaply and efficiently around the world. E-mail also side steps busy facsimile machines and increases the ease of communicating across time zones.

Enterprises will not need to be tied to any particular building or country. People will be able to telecommute because communication between computers will enable people to work from remote sites. By combining many different businesses via communication links, a virtual company could be created. This will encourage the development of staff working from home and offer the benefit of flexibility. The organisation will be able to save money on office space and travelling costs might also be reduced if more business can be done with employees using their own telephone connection linked to a computer. It will make part-timers and freelancers easier to use, as they may be happier to work from home. People can work when they want to, rather than during office hours. There will be no routine manual chores of handling and processing data and information. An integrated digital service will mean that a business's human resources can be used more effectively and efficiently for innovation and planning production, decision-making and the servicing of customers' needs.

Developments in 'video conferencing' via personal computers and the telecommunications' system mean that companies can arrange 'electronic meetings' between executives and business partners in different countries. The growing use of video conferencing will reduce dramatically the amount of time and money spent by business executives travelling between subsidiary plants and offices located in different countries and continents.

Never before have there been so many options in terms of how, where, when or with whom to work, learn, buy and sell. Teleworking, telelearning, teleshopping, telebanking and telemedicine are transcending barriers of organisation, distance and time. Because browsing on the Internet knows no boundaries, it is possible for consumers to buy with confidence after comparing specifications of goods available throughout the world. From the comfort of their living room, people will be able to study, work, organise their finances, do their shopping, browse the holiday destinations and book a holiday, chat on the telephone or send an e-mail and choose from many different channels of television. The Internet has been described as a 'network of networks' resembling a computer network co-operative. With a connection to the web, users have access to a huge, up-to-date library of information, which is on line 24 hours a day normally at the cost of a local telephone call. With video on demand, you can pick different films, documentaries, comedy shows, operas, dramas or whatever without having to juggle videocassettes.

Answer 38

Supporting Strategy

Tutorial note:	
Required	- This question investigates the strategic problems faced by LT plc. You will have to think what the effects of the organisation's policy (ignoring the home market) will be on its overall strategy.
	Although part of the answer will be that the company has some significant failings, you will have to explain these in the context of the organisation and then provide some application of knowledge to show how these failings can be overcome.

LT plc is finding it difficult to obtain information on the home market. The development of its Executive Information Systems (EIS) has followed the strategy of the company, providing summary and detailed information about overseas competitors. This has had the effect of losing focus on the home market. In an attempt to provide more timely decisions and meet the demand for new services, they have set up four autonomous business units within the organisation.

Early indications are that there are common problems facing all units. These are outlined below.

A lack of information on how to set prices for new services

The setting of prices is often a complex process. Businesses frequently reference prices in a number of different ways before deciding on the consumer price. Usually it becomes a compromise between prices generated from product cost data eg, cost plus methods and customary pricing, which is the level expected by customers and determined by the market leaders. LT plc will have internal systems collecting data on production costs and R&D spend. Sales staff or other employees often supply pricing intelligence because they get feedback from customers and information from colleagues. Information available on the Internet about similar systems that are up and working will help decision-makers arrive at a price. Seattle's telephone company run a system and there are systems being test marketed in the UK (Hull) and in France (Paris). Telecomm's Netissimo service costs from as little as £25 per month.

Lack of understanding on how to use the existing IT system to stop the fall in market share

LT plc's market share is being eroded in all areas partly because the company cannot match the offers on price terms and partly because of the time taken to make strategic decisions to offer competing services. There is a bit of foot dragging at the moment because the monopoly on the UK's 'local loop' - the equipment at each end of the piece of copper between the exchange and the customer's telephone - will not end until the summer of 2001. Asymmetric Digital Subscriber Line (ADSL) will run alongside a regular telephone service on the same line (when it is freed from the monopolist). The voice line stays put and the ADSL signal is modulated on top of it at a different frequency. However, when the new service is introduced, it will kill the lucrative ISDN and KiloStream services and this is causing the current dilemma and delay. At the moment, the main threat to new services comes from cable modems, although there is one electronics company (3Com) that makes both cable modems and ADSL equipment.

The management at LT plc need to decide whether they are going to wait until after the monopoly ends and risk losing many more customers to cable companies, or offer a superior solution with ADSL equipment and an ISP at a reasonable price to ward off any competitors.

Lack of available capacity in the existing IT infrastructure (bandwidth) to provide enhanced services to domestic customers

Because LT plc are totally committed to providing the enhanced services, they will find a solution. If the problem is one of capacity, because the ADSL connection is 'continuous on' and no charge per call, then the service will have to be limited to certain areas in the initial stages and gradually extended to cope with the extra traffic. Alternatively, the problem could be the current bandwidth on the existing lines. There does seem to be a way around this, because some companies are offering both a 'continuous on' Internet service and video on demand by squeezing extra bandwidth out of the existing connection. They install an ADSL modem, which reserves a 4KHz channel for your ordinary telephone traffic and divide up the rest of the frequency spectrum into a number of 64Kbs/s channels. These channels are then aggregated. An upstream channel is set aside (128Kb/s running in both directions) to convey commands from your handset and, by interlacing, it is possible to squeeze a 115Kb/s bi-directional pseudo-channel out of it. What you get will be slightly slower than a two channel 128Kb/s ISDN line, but with no call charges, and should supply the bandwidth necessary to deliver an MPEG 2 full-motion video stream.

Lack of critical success factors (CSFs) for each business unit

The first step for each business unit is to set the SBU's goals and objectives. Once the objectives are identified, they can be used to determine which factors are critical (the CSFs) for accomplishing the objective. Then, a small number of prime measures for each factor can be determined. Examples of CSFs might be forecasting of demand variations or supplier performance in terms of quality and lead times. The use of critical success factors can help determine the information requirements of senior management, which in turn assists in identifying the information system required by the company. Unfortunately, without knowing what the objectives of each SBU are, it is difficult to suggest a range of CSFs for LT plc.

Lack of understanding on the social and economic impact of the enhanced services on society.

This type of enhanced service will change society in ways that can only be guessed at now. The identification of major trends can be built into the construction of scenarios as a way of analysing environmental influences. Scenario planning is useful in circumstances where it is important to take a long-term view of strategy and where there are a limited number of key factors influencing the success of that strategy. It is an attempt to construct views of possible future situations. Once these are drawn up, they can be used for sensitivity testing of possible strategies.

Answer 39

Improved Decision-Making

Tutorial note:	
Required	- This is a straightforward question on an EIS. You should be familiar with them and be able to provide a good overview of the type of information that an EIS can produce.
	The question requires you to show how decision-making will be improved by provision of information from the EIS.

An Executive Information System (EIS) is an interactive method of allowing executives and managers to access information for monitoring the operations of the organisation and scanning general business conditions. The type of information that could be provided by an EIS and how it would improve decision-making at LT plc is outlined below.

(i)   *Internal communications such as personal correspondence, reports and meetings* eg, a government report on cables or the minutes of a meeting held where industry representatives discussed future developments in video technology. The Board may use information of this type to set up a committee to look into ethical and moral issues that might arise from providing video on demand.

(ii)   *Company performance data on sales, production, earnings, budgets and forecast* - this type of information can be collected over a period of time and used for comparison with current figures. If 'sales' is chosen from the menu, then the executive will be presented with a primary view of that data eg, sales by region, by distributor or by service. He or she can then drill down and interrogate the system further. If the executive were to choose to examine the budget comparison, he or she may find that there is a variance in the last month that warrants investigation. It would then be possible to return to a previous menu and select analysis by region against budget to establish which region is behind budget. If this proved inconclusive, the executive could examine the results by service or distributor etc, until he/she found the information that allows a decision to be made on the deviation from budget.

(iii)   *Finance reports* - the Board could obtain control information on costs and progress of any new developments or details of the effect of any new investment, with the results broken down to give information on the type of customer buying the new service.

(iv)   *Competitors' results* - by comparing LT plc figures with those from the main competitors, the Board will be able to ascertain whether the company's market share is increasing or decreasing. Changes in market share have to be considered against the change in the market as a whole. The market could be expanding, and a declining market share might not represent a decline in absolute sales volume, but a failure to grab more of the growing market. A further breakdown of the competitors' results could show the sales by employee and the overhead costs. All of this type of information would help in the setting of objectives when the Board is discussing strategic options.

(v)   *Environmental scanning for news on government regulations, competition, financial and economic development and scientific subjects* - LT plc will use this type of information in three specific ways. Firstly, to avoid surprises by anticipating any major changes in their business circumstances. Secondly, to identify threats and opportunities. Companies continually have to make almost daily responses to small changes among their customers, suppliers, workforce and other stakeholders. Those who discern the longer-term patterns in these day-to-day changes can judge more quickly whether they pose a threat or an opportunity and can therefore obtain a head start upon competitors. Thirdly, to improve planning by acting more effectively once threats and opportunities have been identified.

Answer 40

IT Strategy for Large Companies

Tutorial note:	
Required	- This scenario covers the use and implementation of IT strategy within a company.
	Part (a) of the question requires you to explain why an IT strategy is necessary for a company. The question allows you to display your knowledge of strategy whilst at the same time putting it into the context of a specific company.
	Part (b) investigates the problems that a company can face when the IT strategy starts to become more important. Your answer should identify the specific points that are relevant to the IT investment that is taking place, rather than concentrate on the generic advantages and disadvantages of diversification.

(a)   Strategic planning is particularly important in the following circumstances.

♦   There are long timescales - for example in developing new systems.
♦   There is heavy capital expenditure - for example on new equipment.
♦   The success of the organisation is at stake - for example in gaining competitive advantage.

McFarlan's grid can be used to show the strategic impact of IT within an organisation. Under this classification ARG would be shown as a strategic user of IT. Not only is its IT important in the day-to-day administration of the airline (billing, ticketing, bookings) but it will also play an important strategic role in helping the airline to gain competitive advantage. Here are three examples of how ARG could make strategic use of IT.

♦ By monitoring how many bookings are made for a flight, fares could be continually adjusted to maximise revenue. If a flight is well booked early on, few seats need to be released for cheap fares. If a flight has few bookings it would be worth reducing fares to attract marginal revenue.

♦ Code sharing with other airlines can give passengers a better, more comprehensive service.

♦ In the light of bookings, assigning different aircraft to flights to control costs.

IT will be so fundamental to the success of ARG that without a successful IT strategy its success will be at risk.

(b) Many companies have thought that diversification away from their core business looked attractive. In particular, diversification may have offered some reduction in the risk profile of the business, as revenue could be obtained from more than one type of activity. Undoubtedly, some businesses make a success of diversification but success is usually a result of careful planning.

Success in diversification is also more likely if the additional activities are in some way related to the original activities. There is then some chance of economies of scale, and management will have some knowledge of the new businesses. For example, diversification into travel agencies or contract aircraft maintenance would appear to offer better fits to the existing business. If diversification into computer services is pursued, ARG must realise that it will be competing against large special companies that will already possess an enormous expertise and presence in their market.

The decision to diversify into computer services has not arisen as the result of deliberate planning. The company has found itself with surplus computer capacity and has attempted to find a strategy that can produce revenue from the spare capacity. The supply of computer services is unrelated to running an airline, and it is unlikely that the new business will generate any synergies or that existing management will have expertise in that area. On the other hand, it must be said that the diversification is likely to be small in comparison with ARG's main business.

The apparent over-investment in its WAN facilities should be regarded as a sunk cost when deciding whether or not to diversify. The potential advantages and disadvantages are as follows.

Advantages

♦ Additional contribution to the group – additional revenue streams with, perhaps, relatively low marginal costs.

♦ The portfolio effect – for example, when the airline business is in recession, the data transfer business could stay buoyant.

♦ Exposure to competition will help to keep the company in touch with the most up-to-date developments.

♦ Revenue earning will elevate the importance of computer services and may give additional incentive to the business to keep up-to-date.

♦ Charging for services in a competitive market will encourage cost control, as the services will have to be provided at a competitive rate.

Disadvantages

♦ Additional risk arising from a lack of expertise in the commercial provision of computer services – the company will face powerful competition.

♦ Competition for top management time and attention.

♦ Competition for processing resources – data being processed on behalf of customers may begin to take precedence over the airline's own data, and airline operations could be adversely affected.

♦ Competition for financial resources.

♦ ARG appears to have installed a system that is not industry standard – a risk analysis should be performed to assess how robust is the system and to ensure that clients' data could not be put at risk unduly.

As seen above, diversification offers many potential advantages. How serious the disadvantages are depends to a great extent on the scale of the new operations and the relative priorities assigned to those and to the original airline business.

Answer 41

Information Characteristics

Tutorial note:	
Required	- This question is very straightforward. The characteristics of information are easy to list. However, the challenge is to show why those characteristics are important to the company

Like all information, the information provided across the WAN must possess certain characteristics for it to be of value. The most critical characteristics are:

Accuracy

The information provided across the WAN to the ARG offices must be accurate. Each office needs information about flight schedules and destinations for example, and it would be virtually impossible to operate an airline without this information being accurate. The WAN itself should have error correction built in, so that information is not corrupted in any way and to ensure that it arrives intact at the right place and at the right time. Networks generally conform to the OSI 7 layer model, which ensures all aspects of the information being transmitted are safeguarded.

Timeliness

Each office has access to information on aircraft location and servicing history and it is extremely important that such information is available in a timely manner to ensure safe and efficient operation of the airline.

Completeness

Each office provides information on airline services, flight times and destinations and it is important that this information is comprehensive and complete and up-to-date, as well as being transmitted in real time. Without this characteristic, schedules could be severely disrupted, with some flights being over-booked and others having available seats/space.

Integrity

The offices provide access to individuals who wish to make reservations. This access is presumably via the WAN, which could interact with other networks such as the Internet. The critical characteristic here is the integrity of the access. The WAN should allow only authentic transactions. Therefore, each local office will need to carry out some validation checks before allowing the transaction onto the network. This will also help ensure that information placed on the network will be in an understandable format. Many validations consist of computer terminal input forms so that the information relating to the transactions can be clearly understood.

Security

Each office also has access to confidential data, some of which is extremely sensitive such as aircraft service history, personnel and salary information. A critical characteristic for information on the ARG WAN therefore would be appropriate security measures for transmissions. Data encryption should be used to prevent unauthorised 'eavesdropping'. In addition, standard network control protocols should be used to protect the data 'en route' to ensure that it arrives intact and not corrupted. The WAN itself will be accessed by terminals and these terminals may need to conform to 'tempest' specifications. This suppresses electromagnetic radiation impulses from monitors, which could otherwise be received on appropriate equipment by unauthorised third parties.

Terminal access should be restricted to authorised users only with a combination of PINs and passwords and, where appropriate, two-tier transaction authorisation as necessary. These measures will ensure the information is protected not only from loss or corruption, but also from unauthorised disclosure. The type of information on ARG's WAN would make such security measures essential if it is to avoid potential hijacking or terrorist risks.

Answer 42

Internet Access

Tutorial note:	
Required	- Use of the Internet has been increasing over the last few years. Although many companies are still to be connected, there has been concern about the security of the system and the threat of computer viruses being transmitted over it.
	This question asks you to evaluate the potential dangers and benefits, both to ARG and to its potential WAN users, of providing Internet access.

(a)   The main potential dangers are as follows:

Internet access would mean that individuals accessing ARG's network via the Internet could create many problems. These problems can range from inadvertent mistakes to malicious damage or corruption of information and files. For example, in the case where the local office had allowed access to the passenger booking system, there is a risk that individuals might be able to make bookings and/or cancel them at will. This is potentially an extremely dangerous situation and the entire operation of ARG could be put at risk if these accesses are not properly controlled.

The Internet contains material that can be offensive and it can be an offence to be in possession of such material, so if ARG staff download any such files, then this could present problems for ARG. ARG WAN users could access such material by accident or design. Also, business operations could be disrupted, which may result in ARG's staff accessing the Internet via the WAN and wasting time looking at irrelevant information that may be of interest to them personally, but not of much commercial value to the company.

Internet security is not as comprehensive as it could be and it is possible to download virus-contaminated material. The first conviction in the UK, under the Computer Misuse Act, was in respect of an individual who introduced viruses onto the Internet. Hacking generally is a problem, which, as a minimum, results in an unauthorised disclosure, but can also be far worse if data is manipulated leading to all sorts of misleading information.

The cost of using the Internet over prolonged periods of time can be expensive particularly if staff fail to log off for example. So it is important that access to the Internet is controlled and appropriate standards followed.

The benefits of Internet access fall into two main areas:

Marketing

By providing information about ARG via a World Wide Web (WWW) site, 'visitors' to the site can see the range of services offered, the prices, schedules etc. ARG can effectively use the pages contained within the site to market its services by providing additional information to encourage sales. Similarly, third party users of the WAN could also create WWW sites for marketing and information purposes. It is important to keep such information updated however, as the WWW is subject to advertising regulation standards like any other media.

Transactions

In its simplest form, the Internet can be used to exchange e-mail although this can be extended to the electronic exchange of trading information between businesses and individuals. The Internet could be used by travel agents, eg to effect reservations with ARG's offices. Again, the third-party users could also use this facility to handle such things as purchase orders and invoices etc. As the volume of business conducted over the Internet is expected to rise considerably over the next few years (US research indicates $45bn for the year 2000) then there is a real advantage to be gained by having the necessary infrastructure in place to support this activity.

The security aspects of the Internet are continually being improved and many of the dangers should disappear over time. The trading and business aspects of the Internet will become increasingly important to all businesses and ARG would be at the forefront of applying this technology.

(b)   It would be essential that security controls are put into place in order to minimise the risk of virus or hacking.

Passwords

Passwords would be used to verify a user on the system. This would relate both to ARG employees and to its external WAN customers. When anyone logged into the system their user code and password would have to be verified before admission to the system.

Encryption

Because some of the data being transferred by ARG to its other offices is highly confidential and because of the guarantee of security it is offering to its WAN customers, they would probably have to set up encryption facilities. Data would be encrypted before transmission to ensure that if the transmission was intercepted it would be difficult for anyone to read the data.

Firewalls and Gateways

At each gateway into another system firewalls would have to be put into place to stop unauthorised access between systems. ARG employees should not have access through the network to the other WAN customers' systems and vice-versa.

Partitioning controls

If ARG and its WAN customers are going to trade through the Internet then it will be necessary that they partition off their databases. The product, stock or booking systems that would be available for viewing and booking by customers should be completely separate to the management information systems of ARG and its WAN customers. Partitioning controls will need to be put into place to ensure that customers cannot gain access to company management systems.

Answer 43

MQS Ltd

(a)   MQS Ltd production report

A report of this type is necessary under the current system of sharing out responsibilities. Senior managers need information about the progress of projects that they are responsible for. However, in its present form this report has little relevance to the purpose for which it is used. The following are weaknesses identified in the format and transmission of the report:

Completeness

The production report is incomplete because, in addition to the report, senior managers need to collect further information from production managers and technical journals.

The report is also deficient in the amount of information relating to project profitability. It does not make it easy for the recipient to interpret precisely how costs and profits are determined; or what production cost and manufacturing cost means. There is no explanation of how many batches are produced, how production costs and manufacturing costs are related or how profit for the week is derived from the overall sales value and cost figures.

The recipient presumably knows whether different projects use the same materials because there is no overall summary of usage, cost and stocks of each of the different materials.

The report lacks budget figures. There are no standard costs, weights and variances and no comparative information on the previous week's figures. There is no indication of how many weeks the project has taken to date. Comparisons cannot, therefore, be made between actual and planned performance, which is unsatisfactory with regard to both control and decision-making.

Timeliness

The report, relating to the period ending 30 April 2001, is generated on 19 May 2001. This diminishes its value substantially. Any decisions which need to be made relating to the input mix would need to be made quickly, so a report relating to a period 19 days earlier is of little use and may even lead to incorrect decisions.

Presentation

The report lacks consistency and clarity in its presentation.

It is not clear to the recipient whether the units reported are in millions or thousands. Some figures are given 'per batch', others are 'per week' and some are 'to date'.

Some figures appear to be rounded - in the case of sales value, to the nearest £10,000 - while other figures are entered to the nearest penny. Input tonnes and stock appear to be rounded - assuming stock is measured in tonnes - while the cost of materials is given to the nearest penny. Inconsistency with decimal places means that, within individual columns, figures are not aligned.

Despite not containing all the information required by senior managers, in this format the whole report must be a mass of figures over several pages because of the number of projects and their associated materials. The layout means that although project A's financial details can be compared at a glance with input mix data for project A, products use a large number of chemicals and the input mix data for project A is likely to be some way down the page or on a different page, making comparison difficult.

Delivery

Information which managers receive, both from the report and from other sources, is not compatible; in some instances there is duplication, while in other cases there is insufficient information.

The medium of e-mail and on-screen viewing is not appropriate for information of this complexity. Senior managers are irritated, increasing the likelihood of errors, and their time is wasted printing out material that could have been sent to them in hard copy format - especially given its lateness. This situation cannot assist in the decision-making process.

Proposed amendments

To be effective in assisting the senior managers with decision-making, the factors particularly relevant to decision-making need to be clearly identified in the report. If the report is to judge profitability, to assess production and manufacturing cost (including input mix control) and stock control, as well as measure progress of all of the projects, it is probably trying to fulfil too many purposes at once. It might be more useful and effective to produce several shorter reports. Prior to any amendments being made, an analysis of the information uses of the report needs to be carried out.

The most effective media should be employed to present the report, displaying the main elements required for decision-making in graphical, text and numerical format. All the relevant information should be contained in the reports, and variances where corrective action is necessary should be clearly identified.

(b)   Weaknesses in information provision

As well as the problems identified with the production report, there are several others related to the information provision at MQS Ltd.

(i)   MQS Ltd's decision-making structure is inappropriate and suffers from lack of support from its computer system. The order, production and information processes have not been adequately defined and analysed and, as a result, are cumbersome and time-consuming. This does not assist the senior managers to operate effectively and, coupled with the fact that they are not able to make their own decisions, could potentially lead to demotivation. The procedures currently adopted at MQS Ltd appear to have small regard for the requirements of the customer and information relating to profitability is ambiguous.

(ii)   The Chief Accountant authorises most of the decisions in MQS Ltd based on recommendations made by senior managers, who have the time-consuming task of collecting the necessary information for decision-making, which includes:

   ♦   collating and producing weekly management progress reports

   ♦   manually transferring information from the computer system to his/her own summary reports

   ♦   obtaining verbal reports from production managers

   ♦   retrieving information from the weekly production meeting

   ♦   researching details from technical journals

(iii)   Given the variety of sources, and the way in which information is obtained, the whole process is extremely error-prone and must eventually lead to communication problems, particularly because of the extent of reliance on verbally reported information to supplement the written reports.

(iv)   Senior managers have a large number of projects to keep track of over a long time span (up to 4 months). Inevitably, some areas will regularly be overlooked because of the piecemeal nature and slow pace of information provision.

(v)   The computer systems, such as the technical database and the company's email system are not used effectively due to a lack of co-ordination between systems support and operations. The technical database is difficult to access and presents information badly. Inappropriate use of the email system means that it is not used - the telephone, which is far more intrusive, is used instead.

(vi)   The current office layout does not provide an environment conducive to productive and efficient operations. An open-plan office of 50 people, together with their printers, telephones etc. can lead to potential communication problems.

Suggested changes to overcome the problems identified

The following action should be taken:

(i)   Improvements to the production reports and systems such as already suggested should be implemented. This will help to address problems of completeness, clarity, accuracy, and timeliness of information provision, and problems of incompatibility between the formats in which information is provided.

(ii)   The use of email should be encouraged and developed. However, the way in which it is being used needs reviewing. For example, the senior managers' perceived requirement to print out the reports rather than retaining them in electronic form requires investigation.

(iii)   The company's technical database should be modified to improve access and presentation of information. This might include better networking and database software, a more powerful server, a better database structure, training in the use of the database, and regular updating to include information from the latest and best technical journals.

(iv)   The Chief Accountant's role should be reviewed. The authorisation of the Chief Accountant before implementation of recommended actions represents a potential problem. A bottleneck could develop in the system particularly if he/she was not available for a period. Due to the quantity of reports involved, it is unlikely that all of those submitted for approval are effectively reviewed.

(v)   Empowering the senior managers with decision-making could improve the process as would delegating or automating it. Information collecting and collating is essentially a clerical activity that could either be delegated to less senior staff or automated. Senior managers could then concentrate on their management role. Managers should not have to buy their own technical journals: the company's own technical database should be the single source of such information.

(vi)   A re-examination of the human/computer interface is required to produce a fully integrated, automated office. The working environment could be improved by installing printer hoods or buying quieter printers, and by partitioning the office area. Improved layout or relocation of managers closer to the production managers they deal with may reduce the need for constant phone calls, and may provide extra space away from the area of main activity, which could be used for meetings.

(c)   **Assuming that MQS will change its ordering and production process**

(i)   **Critical success factors**

Three critical success factors, which could be used to judge the success of the change of MQS Ltd's ordering and production process, are time taken, product quality and costs. **(Two CSF's only are required)**

Time taken - currently each order takes four months to complete; MQS should examine ways in which this can be reduced. The process is conducted sequentially but there are processes that could be carried out concurrently, and each possible instance of this should be identified. The time taken from initially receiving an order to delivering it to the customer would be the measure used for this critical success factor (CSF). At each of the four stages, performance indicators could also be used and management control information can be provided to ensure these are attained.

Project control techniques, such as Gantt charts, can be used to monitor the progress of each customer's order, in terms of elapsed time.

Product quality - Although production only takes one week, quality control takes three weeks. This points to a major quality problem - probably caused by inadequate systems for ensuring a consistent quality of inputs and for adjusting the input mix as required. Changes could be considered successful if material ordering and production were to 'get it right first time'.

Exception reporting could deal with instances where rectification work is necessary, indicating the cause and the extent that it is due to inaccurate specification of input requirements, poor quality materials or failure to adjust the mix in time. Other measures could be adverse comments from customers and returned products.

Costs - a second area where improvements could be sought is that of the costs associated with the ordering and production process. A standard cost for carrying through a customer's order could be developed and the critical success factor would be the comparison between current costs and the new standard cost. Again, performance indicators could be used at the relevant stages to support the CSF.

Substantial cost savings can be made in the area of material ordering. Currently 10 staff are employed to negotiate 'savings' of £25,000 per year; these savings could be achieved with much lower associated costs by, for example, negotiating a standing order arrangement with the three suppliers and thus making significant savings on staffing costs.

Further cost savings could be made by improving procedures; quality checks, for example, could be carried out during the production process rather than taking place post-production.

(ii) The potential benefits of the change to MQS Ltd as a company, and to the staff employed by MQS Ltd

From the point of view of the company - the principal benefit will be that it can give customers a much faster service, whilst maintaining or even improving the quality of the product. Processes throughout the company will be geared to satisfying the customer rather than to maintaining a cumbersome bureaucracy.

The company's efficiency will increase - it looks as if an order could be fulfilled about four times faster than at present. In theory this ought to mean that the company has the capacity to fulfil four times as many orders. If the demand is there, this should have a positive effect on profitability.

There is some potential for reducing costs - stock levels, for example, could be reduced and rectification costs avoided. Again this will impact upon profitability. It may be possible to drop prices, which will help MQS to compete more effectively in its market.

A reduction in bureaucracy and its associated costs should attract more custom; the company should be easier and cheaper to deal with. Staff appear to be frustrated by the current methods of working and are likely to welcome change and offer more commitment to the company's mission and objectives than they do at the moment. Barriers between different departments (for instance material ordering and production) are liable to be broken down, improving staff communication and understanding of the task of the company as a whole.

Processes are carried out concurrently, paperwork is reduced and staffing costs are reduced. New systems and better recording and storage of information should mean that the company's ability to reach ever better-informed decisions, to measure its performance, and to identify areas for further change will improve. Customer satisfaction is improved as they receive their order more quickly. These improvements pave the way to a more dynamic approach to conducting business.

From the point of view of the staff, the benefits may include the following:

(i)   Changes in the decision making structure eg, empowering the senior managers, will lead to managers taking responsibility for their actions, which should make work more rewarding for senior and production managers. Morale and motivation should also increase with the introduction of improved procedures and empowerment. Staff at all levels should be affected positively by these changes and, committed to the objectives of MQS Ltd, should provide a high standard of service to their customers.

(ii)   New information systems will also help managers to do their work more effectively and spend more time on challenging work. Projects will be completed more quickly because managers do not have to remember and keep track of issues that first arose three or four months ago. However, this benefit may be lost if MQS attempts to take on many more projects.

(iii)   The working environment will be more pleasant and relationships will improve (senior managers are at present 'hostile' to the information provided by production managers).

(iv)   Increased productivity and profitability should mean increased pay for staff. Remuneration can be results-related, and the performance of plant managers could be evaluated based on output variances.

(v)   A change in the culture of an organisation is often associated with business change. Greater trust and responsibility is given to staff, as the organisation becomes more self-regulating with fewer controls. Changes that enhance the success of the business benefit the company, its staff and its customers.

Although the question asks about benefits it ought to be noted that change is never put into effect without some resistance. It seems likely that the company will have to deal with opposition from the Chief Accountant and from the purchasing department, and these staff have the potential to undermine the effectiveness of changes if they cannot be persuaded of the merits of new practices.

The company must maintain good communication with staff, provide training in new ideas and skills, and offer fair deals for those who are no longer needed because the changes are successful.

(iii)   How time could be saved

The information provided on the initial input requirement and pricing tells us that this stage takes two days. No solution is given about improvements to this stage.

When assessing processing requirements, because each order is made to individual customer requirements it is likely that some time needs to be spent working out the implications of tailoring the processing to meet these needs. Three to four days have been allowed for, in the absence of further information. This may be an underestimate, given that the quotation process currently takes about one month.

Some care is needed in drafting the quotation, given that the company may be tendering against competitors. Some liaison between production, purchasing and marketing will be needed to ensure that one department is not making undertakings that other departments cannot meet and that considerations such as the likelihood of repeat orders are taken into account. One day is allowed for this.

The time spent sending the quotation to the customer and waiting to receive confirmation is likely to be very variable, as it depends on the customers' decision-making processes. One day is allowed for the quotation to reach the customer and four for the customer to consider it and reply. However, more time may be needed if the customer is obtaining and comparing several quotations. Fax or email would speed up this process, of course, if this method were acceptable to customers.

Major savings in time can be made in the area of ordering and obtaining materials. The savings achieved by negotiating prices only amount to £25,000: this must be far outweighed by the cost of employing ten staff. The process of obtaining three quotes, looking for discounts and accepting the lowest quote should be dispensed with. The material ordering department should identify reliable suppliers of good quality materials, perhaps negotiating long-term contracts in return for guarantees about quality and delivery quantities and time. Following negotiation, orders for delivery of ex-stock should be placed with suppliers to Just-in-Time delivery within the same week. Having set up arrangements with the suppliers, the requirements for expensive and time-consuming negotiations for each order placed is eliminated.

There is no need for a quote to be authorised for acceptance by the Chief Accountant. Expertise in this activity resides in the purchasing department. Authority limits could perhaps be set at an appropriate level, if controls are felt to be necessary.

Assuming that suppliers are reasonably local and delivery times are fairly short, we can allow three days from placing of the order to receipt of the goods. EDI links with suppliers may reduce this time still further.

Production need not hold up ordering of containers or organising of a courier. Quality control can continue into the following two-week period while awaiting delivery of the container. All of these can be done concurrently over a maximum time span of two weeks - the time it takes for containers to be delivered. We assume that this time cannot be reduced because the containers are 'specialised', but the delivery time should be investigated for potential savings in time.

The time taken to perform quality checks can be reduced by using better quality materials, by using better information systems and devolving authority to allow faster decisions on input mix and by substituting in-process quality controls for post-production ones. The latter may mean that production takes longer than a week, but time will be saved overall because less work will be needed to put things right.

While carriage is being organised with the specialist courier, the goods can be checked into the container. Fourteen days for production, quality control checks, obtaining containers and organising the courier, overlapping with the packaging and shipping arrangements, is assumed to be sufficient.

Currently the time taken to service an order is four months. Following the above process, the new ordering and production process could be reduced to about five weeks. Further time may be saved by investigating procedures further eg, whether spare containers could be kept on site; reducing the delivery time of the container, the time taken to carry out quality control etc. As well as reducing the production time, other savings such as staff costs, have also been made.

The suggested revised timescale for order fulfilment is as follows:

Stage	Work days
Initial input requirement and pricing	2
Assessing processing requirements	3-4
Drafting quotation and internal authorisation	1
Sending quotation to customer and confirming order	5
Ordering and obtaining materials	5
Production/quality control checks/obtaining containers/organising courier	14
Total working days	30-31

Answer 44

SF Group

(a) **Sources of information**

The different sources of information that will be required to monitor the quality of bread are:

The quality control department (QCD) - the stated function of this department is to compare bread samples to standards to give assurances that legal requirements have been met in respect of the allowed additives. The quality control department must have access to the latest regulations governing additives and will perform chemical analyses on the bread to assess additive content. Variance analysis can be used to compare against the quality standards that JTK Ltd uses and if variances are large some batches may have to be withdrawn from sale. The variances will tend to concentrate on output rather than input and reports will therefore be restricted to comments on the look and texture of the product.

However, there are a number of problems with the operation of the QCD including hours of work, number of loaves sampled and the timing of the samples. Production is overnight, ending at 4 am, yet the quality control department operates from 12 noon until 10 pm. Most of the production takes place when no quality control facilities are available and most of the bread will be delivered to shops before the quality control department starts again. Presumably, other quality measures are used as well, such as assessing the bread for look, texture, taste and keeping quality. However, we do not know how these important characteristics are measured. Some, such as taste, are purely qualitative and will need to be assessed by experts; others, such as texture, may be susceptible to more objective measurement.

The production department - the QCD can also monitor production runs ie, the amounts of materials used and overall control of batches of bread baked. This will be more in keeping with ensuring that overall costs of production can be measured, so that profitability as well as quality is maintained. The production department will be able to monitor input and output quantities and to perform classic variance analysis - price, mix, and yield. Some production information specific to bread making eg, cooking times and temperatures, should also be recorded for later analysis.

The ingredients and production details will be key determinants of the quality of the bread and significant departures from standards are likely to lead to quality problems. However, it may take some time for variances to be calculated and reported, and samples should be taken throughout the production run for quality assessment. This is particularly important because there are some old machines that appear to be unreliable when delivering ingredients, especially at the end of production runs. It should also be pointed out that having the information about quality is one thing, but JTK Ltd needs to be able to take corrective action when necessary by varying the input mix but the present production process would tend to indicate that this is not possible because all raw materials are combined in a set formula.

Customers - if quality falls to a very poor level, customers will eventually complain. Before that point is reached, many customers will have switched brands and sales will have been lost. JTK Ltd has had adverse publicity twice within the last 20 years and therefore needs to monitor this aspect continually. Customers tend to have long memories and it can take a great deal of time and effort to rebuild perceptions of a quality image.

However, waiting for customers to complain or detecting a decline in sales is too late and too reactive. Information should be obtained direct from customers by way of questionnaires or surveys on a regular and continuous basis. This will enable the quality satisfaction of customers to be assessed. The company can offer blind tasting of its own bread and that of rivals to help it to identify what customers really want.

Competitors - quality is really one aspect of the information assessed from competitors. If formal benchmarking techniques were in place, then quality would be one of several attributes assessed in comparing JTK Ltd with the rest of the market.

Having 15% of the total bread demand, JTK Ltd should be something of a market leader and so it should be able to exercise some influence regarding standards within the market. It may well be in a position to instigate benchmarking with other firms. The information this would provide would enable an independent comparison to be made about JTK Ltd's quality performance and JTK Ltd would therefore be able to use this information to improve quality.

Suppliers - the final quality of any product is very heavily dependent on the components or raw materials that are used in production. The standards used by JTK Ltd are all based on internal measures and more information is therefore required on the quality of inputs from suppliers. Although there is no evidence of alternative suppliers, the quality and consistency offered by competing suppliers should be monitored and those who are unreliable should be no longer used. Information regarding quality of inputs eg, in respect of the various types of flour, will be essential if quality is to be maintained. No doubt, many of the ingredients used in bread making can be graded as to quality, and quality specifications should be built into supply contracts. Suppliers may also be able to offer suggestions about new ingredients, which come onto the market, and they may even be willing to give advice about how these can be used.

Trade and research organisations - often produce useful data. For example, they may have developed ways in which certain qualities can be assessed or they may have commissioned large market surveys on consumer tastes and trends and what consumers perceive as important in generating quality.

(b)   Limitations of controlling the process as a 'closed loop' system

There are benefits that can be associated with closed systems such as monitoring of inputs and evaluating outputs and this can be important in respect of ensuring legal requirements are met. JTK Ltd's system also provides for the purchasing of raw materials on a regular basis. Therefore, there is an element of control over the production process. Unfortunately, the system acts as a closed loop feedback system and there are inherent weaknesses with such systems, including time delays before corrective action can be taken.

The technical definition of a closed loop system states that its environment has no effect on it. Such systems cannot exist in the long term as they will slowly degenerate and eventually fail. The process of degeneration is known as 'entropy', a scientific term meaning that all systems tend towards greater disorder and chaos. A simple example of this happening in JTK Ltd would be a failure to take into account changes in consumer preferences and in competitors. The control system would continue to operate as it always had, but the whole system would become increasingly irrelevant and useless as a way of ensuring survival of the business.

In addition, the Law of Requisite Variety states that successful systems should have enough flexibility of response to deal with all the events that can happen. The production process itself is inflexible and the ability to control it seems limited as inputs are combined in a set formula and the old machinery makes the quantity of input difficult to manage on a consistent basis.

This system appears to be unable to respond to changes in consumer taste, competitor action and changes in production techniques. It demonstrates a lack of flexibility and the information emanating from it follows the law of praxis rather than responding to dynamic or innovative requirements.

The major weaknesses are:

Lack of flexibility - JTK Ltd is reluctant to change - demonstrated by the fact that the board members wish to continue as they have done for the last 20 years. The overall process seems dated and the flexibility to produce a variety of different types of bread in response to customer demand is missing. The system is certainly not responsive enough for today's economic conditions, which involve greater consumer awareness and discernment. If JTK Ltd cannot satisfy the very demanding requirements of today's consumer (and the current system does not appear able to do this) then their market share will fall and it will lose customers.

Supply management - JTK Ltd's procurement processes appear to be very casual. There is no evidence of competitive tendering and stock levels are rising. The EOQ (economic order quantity) has not been adjusted for 15 years when, almost certainly, production quantities and mixes will have changed. This provides another example of entropy in a closed loop system. The EOQ is normally independent of the reorder level but at JTK Ltd the EOQ appears to have been set as the reorder level. Without control over ordering the consequences of increased stock are increases in wastage and deterioration. Not only can this be expensive, it can have quality implications as the ingredients themselves may deteriorate.

The company should investigate more modern supply systems such as just-in-time systems, with its close co-operation with suppliers so that the right ingredients, of the right quality, are supplied at the right time.

Production process - the main ingredients are transferred to production and then combined in a set formula to produce the bread. It is not clear why the input mix quantities are altered on a monthly basis. The quality of the output will depend critically on the input mix so for consistency of product one would expect the input mix to be constant. As the machinery is old it makes the inputs difficult to manage towards the end of the production run. At the very least, more attention should be given to testing at the end of production runs. The major weakness here is that no advanced production techniques are in place. This will result in variable quality meaning that JTK Ltd will be unable to respond to any changes required. Ideally, errors in production would be prevented from occurring at all, though this may require new, more reliable machinery. The Management Accountant wishes to invest in new systems and equipment to alleviate this weakness.

Internally focused - the production process resembles a closed loop system because it is almost totally internally focused. Organisations cannot operate in isolation of their environment and therefore external information eg, from customers, suppliers and competitors, is essential if meaningful quality control standards are to be applied. In a competitive environment, organisations have to respond to and counter competitor action. If they do not, competitors are likely to win market share.

Quality control - only 10 loaves are taken from the *start* of each production run. This may be inadequate for statistical purposes and taking the entire sample from the start of production is almost certainly unsatisfactory. Samples should be taken throughout production ensuring that each batch is sampled and subject to quality control prior to being placed in finished goods stock.

Following on from acceptable quality control inspection, the batch can be placed in finished goods ready for despatch. This obviously has implications for the quality control department as their hours of work are 12 noon to 10pm. They must work the same hours as production so that quality checks can be carried out and continuous monitoring and feedback can be provided in parallel with the production runs. Quality control should also be extended to include the testing of the quality of supplies, so that supplier quality performance can be monitored.

Feedback

The feedback from the quality control department needs to be compared with JTK Ltd's company standards, but more importantly with external information, particularly customer satisfaction questionnaires. Nowhere does the feedback control system appear to take any account of customers. The overall isolation of the system from external information means that the company can become completely out of step with market requirements. Comparisons should also be made with competitors' products perhaps by an independent panel.

Conclusion

The current system is not suitable for today's needs and will be unable to cope with future demands. Long-term business survival depends on being market-orientated - determining and anticipating consumer demands and preferences. The need to be continually aware of environmental factors and the ability to respond in a dynamic way is of paramount importance to all businesses.

(c)   Future demand

The market survey information concerning future demand for JTK Ltd's bread contains two elements: the probability of a demand change; and the change in the demand. Both of these will be very difficult to estimate with any accuracy because they will depend on many variables including the economy, competitor action, consumer taste, prices and health fads. It would seem that the market survey information is ambitious in attempting to predict probabilities over a three-year time scale. A one-year forecast can be reasonably accurate as it is relatively short-term, although if the product is dependent on certain conditions eg, dieting then this can add a further element of unpredictability.

A particular danger arising from using the quantitative information provided is that it has been stated with such precision that users may believe that it is accurate and reliable. It is unlikely to be so, and must therefore be used carefully. The survey information about the natural bread states that demand will increase with *certainty*. That is a rash statement and, as this bread is likely to have a relatively high price, demand will certainly depend on economic conditions. The lack of quantification about the increase means that it will be more difficult to create a convincing economic argument for investing in production of this bread.

It is also difficult to use the forecast information that is available. The demand profile for cheap bread is inconsistent. There is a 10% chance that demand may actually increase over the period. Although, with a 90% chance of a decrease, it seems more likely that demand will decline, but by how much is almost anybody's guess. The normal way to use such information would be to calculate the expected value of the demand and to make judgements based on that. However, an 'expected value' may be a value that will never actually occur. In addition, the risks - in particular the downside risks - of any decision should be carefully assessed.

Risk is the measure of the degree of uncertainty or the degree of probability of any particular outcome occurring. It is clear that the information provided by the market survey alone is insufficient for the decision now facing JTK Ltd and that, although risk is an inherent part of decision making, it can be reduced by appropriate access to relevant information. This information should include demographics, gross domestic product, socio-economic groupings of consumers etc.

(d)

Critical Success Factors (CSFs) and performance indicators to justify expenditure

Justification of expenditure on new equipment and computer systems would normally be subject to the standard management accounting investment appraisal techniques such as discounted cash flow (DCF), internal rate of return (IRR) and Payback. These techniques depend on a number of CSFs, which are the areas of the business in which an organisation must perform well if it is to succeed. Financial CSFs focus on financial success and typical performance measures include those for return on investment and profitability.

To justify further capital expenditure, the following could be used:

Return on investment - this CSF needs to be controlled in order to ensure wise investment decisions are made. However, there are problems isolating the effects of the investment decision from the return achieved from normal day-to-day operations. Performance indicators that can be used are

(i)   Return on Capital Employed (ROCE) - at the Group level, SF may be able to use ROCE as a performance indicator, although this ratio can also be subject to other factors that go to make up the calculation. The success of JTK Ltd would be measured over the long-term achievement of ROCE, which is dependent on appropriate investments being made at the right time.

This ratio is often used by outside analysts to assess how well management is using the capital at its disposal. Directly after new investment, ROCE can decline as there is suddenly much more capital but it has not had time to produce additional profits. This short-term effect can deter managers from making investments, which would enhance the ROCE in the long-term.

(ii)   Internal Rate of Return (IRR) - at the subsidiary company level, JTK Ltd would be expecting this type of project to pass a hurdle rate of return based on the DCF of the project. The main problem with this performance indicator is in estimating benefits. However, the evaluation gives a good indication of the success of the investment.

(iii)   Net present value (NPV) - this is another discounted cash flow technique. A positive NPV for an investment project means the organisation and its shareholders become richer. To calculate NPVs, the future cash flows have to be estimated together with an appropriate cost of capital to use as a discount rate. As it seems that the company may not have had many large capital projects recently, it is unlikely to have a discount rate readily available.

(iv)   Cash flow - the cash flow generated for both the group and the subsidiary, is another performance indicator for the investment.

Profitability - because the overall objective will be to generate profits from the investment this measure is a CSF that can be used to justify expenditure. The performance indicators include:

(i)   Annual profits - at group level, overall annual profits of JTK Ltd will be the main performance indicator in achieving this CSF; profits growth - often leading to growth in earnings per share, is evidence of success. The performance indicator will highlight whether the business is being run efficiently and whether correct investment decisions are being made. However, the problem here is that retrospectively it can be difficult to analyse which changes in profits can be easily ascribed to a particular investment.

(ii)   Sales volumes and values - are also performance indicators that can be used to support the profitability CSF, although these are dependent on other factors, such as general market conditions, as well as decisions to invest, and so cannot be relied on exclusively. There are underlying assumptions about all investments at the time they are made including the prospective behaviour of customers and competitors.

(e)   Problems with using a notice board to display quality control information

The main problem with notice boards is that staff will only see the information if they make the effort to visit the board and there is no way of determining exactly who has seen a particular notice.

Various messages may be displayed and staff may not take much notice of hand written notes pinned to a board. Quality-related information may become mixed up with other information on the board. As a medium, it is uncertain and inconsistent eg, there might be delays in updating the information: it might not be updated reliably; or old information might not be removed.

A notice board does not convey a professional image and will not, for example, instil the necessary discipline for staff to look at it at the start of each day. The low-tech, possibly unsatisfactory, display of information may reduce the importance with which quality is regarded in the organisation. The nature of the note may be variable as it is difficult to enforce standards ie, some staff may take a great deal of time and show headings for categories of input etc, whereas others may simply write down numbers in what they perceive to be a logical order, but which may not be readily apparent to others.

During the course of a working period, there may be various emergency situations where staff are required to take immediate action and therefore they may not be able to spend time looking for the latest note amongst other material on a notice board. Similarly, they may not have time to produce updates themselves for subsequent QCD staff who will need the information the following day.

The advantages of a computerised bulletin board

With a bulletin board urgent messages can be distributed immediately to everyone concerned. When QCD staff log on to their terminals, the system can send a prompt to remind them to look at the bulletin board for the latest update. The system could actually display this as the first screen following log on.

Information could be generated automatically by the monitoring system or it can be input immediately by processing staff.

A computerised bulletin board can facilitate standardisation with screen-based 'forms' that can be completed easily with information always presented in a straightforward way. As the information is displayed on a terminal, not only will it be legible, but also ergonomically better as it will be presented in a standard way and the whole production situation can be assimilated much more quickly, especially if colour and graphics are used to highlight important information.

The bulletin board system can be linked to any other systems that the QCD staff may need to use so that following input to one system, they are again prompted to go to the bulletin board and update it. Alternatively, the systems can be automatically linked so that the inputs are taken directly into the standard forms within the bulletin board.

Answer 45

SPK plc

(a)   (i)   Characteristics of information

Strategic level of management - this type of information will be used by the senior management team at SPK, including the Chief Executive and main board directors, who are mainly concerned with overall policy and the strategic direction of SPK plc. The characteristics of the strategic information required at this level include the following:

♦   It will be primarily forward-looking, to allow strategic planning decisions to be made. In this type of industry it would be reasonable to plan strategically over a five to ten year period.

♦   It will relate to both internal aspects of the business and the external environment. Internal information relating to, for example, sales and costs will be used in summary at the organisational level with additional analysis required to individual revenue and cost headings. External information such as competitor sales figures or customer satisfaction survey results might be obtained from inside the organisation or from external information providers such as public databases.

♦   It will tend to be unstructured and made available on an *ad hoc* basis by enquiry from an Executive Information System (EIS) terminal using a sophisticated graphical user interface (GUI). Most of the output would be in the form of screen-based graphics or tables of summarised comparative figures.

Tactical level of management - this is the level within the company where middle managers exercise management control of individual projects or departments of SPK. The strategic level plans are translated into departmental budgets and the general characteristics of the information include the following:

♦   The information used for planning over the medium term will be more detailed, and for control purposes. It will be a combination of historic and forecast, probably to the end of the current year or the end of the relevant project.

♦   Most of the information will relate to the activities of SPK and focused towards internal results and performance measures, although some limited external information that is specifically relevant would also be provided. Examples include market shares for the marketing manager and supplier prices for the purchasing manager.

♦   Although the information may contain external benchmarking type information, tactical information relating to departments is typically delivered via Management Information Systems (MIS), which are based on the company's internal support systems. To help project managers in their specialised planning and control activities, a specific decision support system (DSS) might be used.

Operational - at this level the information would be required by first-line junior level managers for day-to-day control of small parts of the organisation such as a work-team or production line. The information might be provided by the organisation's transaction processing systems in the form of a regular weekly or monthly report in hard copy format. Additional information might be available on a real-time basis by enquiry from a PC or terminal. The information characteristics are:

♦ much more detailed and required to address short-term tasks with analysis at the cost and revenue code level

♦ focused on specific, sectional targets where action can be taken to correct variances

♦ related to revenues earned or internal costs incurred during the current or previous period, often compared to the budget for the period.

(ii)   Information provided in the reports

Memo from the Chief Executive

Provided more information is given, the Board have agreed in principle to the concept of the new production line. The CE's report gives a very broad outline of the proposal to build the new production line. Although conciseness is an important quality of information, particularly at the strategic level, this report is far too brief for a project of such size and importance and there is insufficient information to assist the Board. In terms of completeness, the report should give a far greater level of detail.

The specific content of the report is also weak in a number of areas:

♦ The success measures required to control the project are missing from this memo.

♦ There is little external focus in the CE's memo. Apart from more marketing information, external information on suppliers and competitors is also required. For example, what do other motor vehicle manufacturers use and is it proving successful?

♦ In terms of the relevance of the information, the report covers some of the required areas such as costs, technology and market impact, but the understandability is significantly reduced by the lack of logical structure. A series of separate sections would improve the report so, for example, a 'technical' section should contain all aspects of the CAD/CAM system including the showroom interface, with broad estimates of development and implementation costs and timescales.

♦ An assessment of competitor reaction to SPK plc will be needed, once the system starts achieving growth.

♦ There is only one assumption about market growth, with no justification given. It would be better to have a range of scenarios, and to see the effect of different growth rates on the revenue of the project. Although the CE mentions 20% pa growth over a five-year period, no estimated sales values or market segment analysis (particularly how existing sales will be affected) is provided.

♦ The critical success factor mentioned is not relevant to the project being considered. It would be better to use a break-even level of increased contribution as a direct result of the investment.

Memo from Production Manager

At the tactical level the Production Manager is naturally concerned with departmental plans and budgets and the logistics of the new production line. However, the information provided to the CE in this report is also too brief for a project of this magnitude, especially as the Production Manager has had almost one week to produce it. Although additional detail is supplied on disk it is possible that the Chief Executive will be unable to gain access, as the new spreadsheet package may be unavailable outside the production department.

Specific criticisms of the content include the following

♦ Once again there is only one underlying assumption (15,000 units production) with no explanation or justification. A range of scenarios should have been provided eg, optimistic, most likely and pessimistic, with detailed justification and a probability of occurrence for each. The production budgets need to be 'flexed' over a range of different outcomes.

♦ Numbers of this magnitude should be rounded and the whole report could be presented more professionally.

♦ Greater detail should be given of the costs, separating out fixed and variable elements.

- The expenditure details are unclear and, although materials and labour would both tend to be direct costs, they may need further analysis eg, materials split into metals and plastics. Similarly, the figure for automation expenditure may include capital investment items as well as software development and maintenance.

- Comparisons should be given with the present cost structure.

- The sales forecast should form part of the marketing department's report and the production manager's assumption of average selling price could be misleading, especially as SPK plc could probably charge a premium for the level of customer service that the new production facility will be able to offer.

- The manpower requirements and the relationship of the numbers of staff to the level of CAD/CAM investment should all be summarised for the chief executive so that the necessary degree of assurance on the feasibility of the proposal can be established.

Memorandum from Operational Manager's Assistant

Considering that the information may well have been assembled quickly, this report contains a reasonable level of detail, but the format makes it difficult to understand. The decision, in principle, has been made and what is now required are feasibility criteria. The operations department should be looking at how it can meet the demands that will be placed on them if the proposal goes ahead.

Specific criticisms are as follows.

- The use of the term 'best guess' does not inspire confidence. An estimate of probability or use of degrees of confidence would be preferable.

- The section on personnel requirements is difficult to understand and should have been structured better for the reader to assimilate the information more easily. A schedule for the labour price elasticity of supply, along with the probabilities of success would have communicated this information far more effectively.

- Staff turnover rates should be expressed separately, and compared to the current case.

- The information is not focused on the new production line and drifts off into comparing industry sickness rates, which seems irrelevant to this decision.

- The presentation of the materials section leaves a lot to be desired and it is difficult to see how the averages have been arrived at. The cost breakdown supplied is based on a single scenario, and the figures supplied require analysis into further detail and between the classifications of costs. The materials used are not actually mentioned eg, the body will consist of both metal and plastic components, the interior possibly leather, plastic, cloth etc. This information does not assist in the overall process of planning and budgeting for such a new product.

- The estimate of factory costs of '£5 million to £20 million' is similar to the CE estimate for a new factory although it may be the manufacturing costs. It is just not clear - it could be an annual cost, a one off or up front capital cost. The CE would need to query such information to obtain clearer details.

Conclusion

The new production line is off to a bad start as none of the three reports provide the information required to fully consider the proposal at any of the management levels. It is difficult to see how the project can progress based on the information provided.

(b) **Importance of IT to new production system**

The proposal is for an integrated system to take customer requirements and translate them into a finished, bespoke product. The sub-systems are likely to be as follows:

Showroom facilities - the showroom equipment will probably consist of a highly modified client workstation. The hardware will have to be inviting and give the impression that using it will be easy and fun. Because the design is effectively 'on-line' to the factory, it is unlikely that mistakes will be made. What the customer sees on the screen will be what they ultimately get. It may be possible to place the hardware inside a vehicle interior or otherwise disguise the fact that it is a computer - it can be enhanced by a Virtual Reality (VR) interface so customers can truly get the 'feel' of the vehicle they are designing. This is far more effective than using brochures and forms and will be a major factor in the success of this project.

Communication - the showroom equipment will be linked to a central server via a wide area network. The customer is effectively engaging in computer-aided design (CAD) and this facility should be integrated on a real-time basis with the computer-aided manufacturing (CAM) at SPK's new production facility. Electronic communications from the showrooms to the factory are essential so that the CAD/CAM interface can work both effectively and quickly. This will allow rapid response and automated instruction of the manufacturing facility. This could not be achieved without appropriate data communication links.

Expert system shell - the whole system needs to be controlled from the central server by software capable of evaluating the customers' input and recommending or insisting on changes if the design prejudices safety or is impossible to manufacture.

Production planning - motor vehicle manufacture is traditionally based on batch production where a 'production run' of a particular model is made when enough orders have been received. The ability to change specifications during production requires very sophisticated production planning software for scheduling and controlling. Without such systems the risk of a mistake is high, with consequent higher costs of reworking and/or scrap.

Manufacturing facility - the CAM facility will require a series of computer-numerically- controlled (CNC) machines, organised into a series of cells to form a flexible manufacturing system (FMS). This hardware will be capable of self-selecting tools and jigs to allow total flexibility while eliminating the need for human intervention.

Cost considerations - by ensuring continuous production is carried out and by automating as much of the process as possible, costs can be kept to a minimum. This is crucial to the success of this system as there are alternative competitors available who can supply the same service, but who are currently more expensive. Information technology is critical to enable an efficient, cost-effective process to be maintained.

In summary, it is unlikely that any of the elements described could function without the use of Information Technology.

(c) **Data security at the strategic, tactical and operational levels of management**

The term 'data security' generally relates to the effective storage and protection of the data from misuse, abuse and/or corruption. There are responsibilities for data security at all levels within an organisation.

Strategic level - at this level, the Board of SPK plc has a responsibility to ensure that the overall management of information security is carried out in the correct and proper manner throughout the company. Their responsibilities for data security are in two main areas.

(i)   Establishing a code of practice and policies for the security of data throughout the organisation. The British Standard Code of Practice (BS 7799) sets out the obligations of senior management in respect of a security of information policy and the need to define roles and responsibilities of all staff involved. It is important then that the Board takes appropriate action to ensure that policy is disseminated and the organisation of security defined.

(ii)   Ensuring compliance with relevant legislation (eg Data Protection Act 1998) on behalf of the organisation.

The actions that the Board should take include the following

(i)   Ensure that Data Protection registration is completed and continually reviewed to take into account any changes to data items held or data subjects covered. This may be an issue with the proposed new design system for such data items as customer details.

(ii)   Ensure that the organisation has a clear Information Systems strategy that includes reference to security of data.

(iii)   Because those at the strategic level tend to have privileged access rights as well as the ability to connect to external systems, they need to ensure their own personal security disciplines of confidentiality and disclosure are maintained.

The CE and Board are users of information and as such place reliance on how that information has been created, processed and provided to them. The security of an information system should be the responsibility of the owner of that system which in this case may consist of several owners dealing with different sections of the system. The CE and Board will place reliance on the security features that systems owners have had designed into their systems.

Tactical level - at this level management are responsible for the planning and control of individual systems projects. This responsibility covers ensuring that projects support the Information Systems strategy of the organisation, and managing the development of solutions so as to retain or improve overall systems integrity. Managers must decide who can access the systems and establish an appropriate level of protection. This includes sufficient back up and recovery facilities, which should be tested on a regular basis.

The responsibility for designing appropriate validation and correction mechanisms within systems may rest with this level of management. However, like all aspects of systems security, individual responsibility can be delegated to individual user managers or service providers.

The actions that should be considered at the tactical level include the following.

(i)   Create a series of project steering committees to control individual system developments.

(ii)   Contribute to the specification and design of new systems to ensure adequate data security measures are built in.

(iii)   Conduct post-completion and continuing reviews on all systems to ensure data integrity and security are maintained.

(iv)   Registration within the terms of the DPA needs to be undertaken and all staff should be reminded of their obligations under this Act.

Other actions that need to be taken are independent reviews of systems and procedures to ensure that the security of the information systems within the company is maintained to a sufficiently high standard.

Operational level - at this level system users will be responsible for:

(i)   maintenance

(ii)   'housekeeping' routines

(iii)   the verification of data on entry to the system

(iv)   the implementation of data security controls on a day-to-day basis, particularly in the case of personal data relating to staff, customers and possibly suppliers.

The operational levels rely on systems being able to support them in their routine activities and so are dependent upon the strategic direction of overall information security management policy. Equally, they are reliant on the design control features that the managers at the tactical level have insisted upon at the development stage.

Actions will include regular changes to passwords, the backup of software and data, and periodic audit and reconciliation of data sets.

All levels - of employee within the company are responsible for their own actions in terms of maintaining password secrecy and the integrity of the information that they deal with. There is also personal as well as corporate liability in respect of breaches of computer-related legislation such as the DPA and also the Computer Misuse Act 1990, and so it is the duty of all staff to act responsibly.

(d)   Hardware and software elements of the human computer interface (HCI)

Before discussing the hardware and software elements of the HCI it is necessary to determine the level of user skill and the objectives of the users. It is assumed that most users of this type of system are customers who have limited computer literacy. They wish to use the system to design their own car in a totally non-technical sense, while having fun, and with confidence that their design can be translated into reality.

The elements of the HCI include the positioning and user friendliness of the equipment, the interface, user support and technology.

Positioning and user friendliness - the actual positioning of the equipment should be considered first. It must be laid out in an attractive way and look interesting. It must also give the right impression of the cars that SPK plc makes. For example, if safety features are the main criteria then the design facility should be solid and robust and fit with this overall perception of the company.

SPK plc does not want to lose sales because potential customers find the system daunting. It must be extremely easy to use, so a user-friendly front-end to the system with graphical user interface (GUI), a customised terminal, keyboard and mouse with 'point and click' features is essential. This easy-to-use front-end could also have characteristics such as:

(i)   a conventional windows-style interface which allows the customers to select icons and pull down and pop up menu options, help bubbles and icons;

(ii)   CAD-style engineering tools and three-dimensional views of the car during design;

(iii)   touch-screen facilities so that colours, components etc can be selected by touching the appropriate picture on the screen;

(iv)   voice recognition/enhancement to capture information and to describe features;

(v)   access to multimedia such as video to support the design process.

Interface - a sophisticated control system will be required to handle the simple input from the customer and simultaneously translate it into complex engineering solutions for the flexible manufacturing system. The software needs to be presented in a reasonably structured way so the customer is not continuously going backwards and forwards between engine specification, body shapes and interior features. It should also contain design expertise so that minimum safety/performance constraints are not violated.

Screen-based virtual reality packages are commercially available that can place the customer in the driving seat and show such things as the inner workings of the engine compartment. The car can be shown against various backgrounds eg, an estate car could be shown driving on country roads, a compact car parking in the city etc.

User support - context-sensitive help to use the system is essential so that if the customer is having difficulties the system can then put them 'back on the right track'. Because the process may take quite some time, it would be very frustrating to lose a file during the building stage of the design due to the computer terminal being accidentally switched off for example. So it is important that the system is designed to take care of these aspects and developed using robust components from a variety of software packages and applications. In addition to these elements, customers will also require on-line support either through the workstation, by telephone or from a member of the showroom staff.

The technology - will include the equipment to use standard GUI packages with the CAD/CAM system. Also sound, video and virtual reality can all be used via a single terminal to create a full multimedia application.

The system will need to have the intelligence to analyse inputs and evaluate the feasibility of engineering solutions. This will require access to a database of technical design and manufacturing expert knowledge.

The control system will need to access rules relating to the use and application of the knowledge in order to give the customer immediate feedback on their design.

Customers will need confirmation of their design requirements together with a supporting schedule of information and also a series of pictures of their car. This output will require high quality colour printing, probably from a laser printer next to the workstation.

Answer 46

KJ plc

(a)   Alternative systems

A strategy is a general statement of long term objectives and goals and the ways by which these will be achieved ie, the necessary level of operational support. The main objectives of the IT strategy have been to:

(i)   ensure goal congruence between the different sections so that they are all working together to provide good customer service;

(ii)   provide good customer service (from the point of view of the customer);

(iii)   maintain an acceptable Transaction Processing System (TPS).

Both of the alternative systems currently under review will support these strategic objectives and the strengths and weaknesses of each can be considered and compared.

Alternative One

Goal congruence - the system structure and the information to be provided sounds similar to the existing transaction processing system. The main difference is the addition of a strategic planning module. Although its use would be for the MD, there is no reason why other managers could not use the facility in time. The large, centralised computer will provide efficient and economic operation, and the common database will ensure that this system would support goal congruence between the different sections, because everyone would be working from the same information.

To evaluate any system there must be an analysis of both the current and expected future size of KJ plc's business. This analysis must include the number of transactions that the system needs to process. Provided the centralised database is large enough, it could provide a suitably congruent solution and any future organisation changes could be accommodated within such a structure if required. However, organisational changes may detract from the level of congruence that this alternative could support.

One of the disadvantages with this alternative is that it does not enhance the decision-making opportunities of the managers or facilitate change to the management structure, although the MD has recognised that this is an important issue. In the long term, overall goal congruence would be achieved, but the MD would retain control of the decisions regarding the computer system and individual departmental development might be limited. This system offers no impetus to change the management structure and if it is selected other organisational development techniques would need to be employed.

The other disadvantage is that there is no provision to transfer the historical data from the old system to the new system. Employees would have access to it up to six months after the system changeover, but this might cause problems with goal congruence and affect the service offered to customers.

Customer service - this system offers improvement to the two top-ranking factors in the customer survey - speed of delivery and availability of product. The promises on same day delivery in major cities for orders placed before 11am will make a valuable contribution towards customer satisfaction and support the IT strategy based on meeting customer needs. Because the system is fully integrated, stock-outs can be rectified in half the time. As well as ensuring a better service to customers, these new features could also be a source of competitive advantage for KJ plc.

The lack of historical data from the old system might be a disadvantage. Although it would be available for up to six months after the systems changeover, this is insufficient to enable some analyses to be performed effectively eg, full trend analysis and monitoring of sales demand. This could have an effect on future business planning and the further development of the IT strategy, especially if middle managers take a more active role in decision-making in the future.

The maintenance of an acceptable TPS - KJ plc's current supplier would supply this system. We could assume that the supplier knows KJ plc's business and has provided support for the existing TPS over the last five years. The DP department would probably have formed a relationship with the suppliers, and know who to contact when there are problems. This can be an important advantage to the DP department and the other departments in KJ plc because the business knowledge would tend to minimise the disruption caused by undergoing a systems changeover. It would also be a relief to the employees in the DP department as this system needs to be maintained by a specialist department so there would be little disruption to their employment contracts.

Because the suppliers are well established, it means that other organisations with similar TPS to KJ plc may be available in the locality to co-operate in a mutual aid contingency plan to provide hardware backup in a crisis situation.

The downside to the system is that it is not industry-standard. This could cause problems for KJ plc in respect of future upgrade capability. They could find themselves in a similar position as the current one in less than five years. Technology moves on quickly and there is a better chance of upgrades being available for standard hardware and software than bespoke systems. There is also a risk that continued support might not be available from the current supplier.

Alternative Two

Goal congruence - a de-centralised system with no centralised database will not support goal congruence as well as a centralised system. However, it will improve the motivation of the recently appointed middle managers because this type of system will facilitate delegation to departmental managers. It will probably alienate the long-serving managers who are happy with the status quo. Because each department would be responsible for maintaining its own computer systems and making its own decisions on the use of those systems, it is unlikely that department managers would be working together to provide good customer service. The potential for sub-optimisation is high because individual managers would have responsibility to make tactical and operational decisions for their own departments. This would force them to focus on their own goals and objectives rather than the overall strategic corporate objectives.

The current system allows employees in the sales department to take the order details, check the stock in real time to ensure the order can be fulfilled and then to transfer the order to a central warehouse for delivery to the customer. This alternative system would require the information to be transferred and updated without having one comprehensive view; it would break down the processing into separate 'compartments'. Each department would have its own version of the data and there might be delays in updating, accessing and communicating information across departments. Because the speed of delivery of the goods is likely to be adversely affected by this system, the staff are going to blame other departments for causing these delays and it is not going to aid goal congruence. All departments will not be working together to provide good customer service.

Customer service - the extra facilities of e-mail and Internet over fax and telephone give this system a big advantage. Most modern companies use e-mail, and the Internet is becoming more popular as companies use it as a marketing tool. The ability to use a wide variety of communication media, together with the focus on KJ plc's own branded products, would help organisational improvements, which may give KJ plc a competitive advantage over their competitors. However, these extra facilities would not be addressing the customer requirements outlined in the survey. Ease of ordering and brand image are not very highly rated in the list of desirable attributes.

There will be a full range of information (operational through to strategic) provided by this system. The powerful database query tools will allow full trend analyses to be carried out with key historical information being available to the new system if managers can afford to make the transfer from their own budgets. The ability to draw up these reports could improve customer service by producing individual customer demand profiles, which would help in avoiding stock-outs and would minimise manufacturing delivery lead times.

Although this system offers several new facilities, it does little to improve on the current response time when accessing certain databases. Customer service staff would be unable to be very helpful if the system response time was so slow that both staff and customers became frustrated. As this factor is ranked third most important characteristic of the customer survey, it must be taken into consideration.

Acceptable TPS - a de-centralised system is a more modern approach than the existing centralised computer system. The advantages are those associated with client/server developments. The processing is distributed across a network of servers to PC-based desktop clients. To evaluate this system there must be an analysis of the speed of access on the internal Intranet system. Estimates should be made using the current number of transactions and the expected future transactions that the system will encounter. If extremely high volumes were involved, the Intranet may not be able to cope and a large centralised facility might provide better response times. This would have a major impact on the customer service staff and affect the customers.

The supplier for this system will provide industry-standard equipment that is IBM compatible. Because many organisations have IBM systems, future compatibility, maintenance and upgrades are more assured. Even if their supplier goes out of business, KJ plc will have the ability to purchase the equipment, network and database management software from leading companies that specialise in these areas. IBM compatible equipment would also make it easier to find an organisation in the locality to co-operate in a mutual aid contingency plan, providing hardware backup in a crisis. These advantages would make it easier to maintain the strategy of an acceptable TPS.

A disadvantage with this system is that the DP department would have to change. Each department would have the responsibility of maintaining their own system and the managers may not choose to use staff from the existing DP department because they may not be experienced enough in the new system maintenance. This could cause problems during the system changeover and may affect the service given to customers.

Conclusion

Alternative One shows marked improvements over the existing system. There is ample support for goal congruence, and improvements to facilities concerning customer service. However, maintenance of an acceptable TPS may cause problems in the future because of the future upgrade limitations, but the future of the DP department looks assured if this alternative is adopted. This system would achieve the objectives of the IT strategy to provide good customer service, but it would not address the management structure or motivational problems. Enhancing the decision-making opportunities of the elite group of managers would need further organisational development.

Alternative Two addresses the motivational aspects of the majority of the managers and would provide some improvements to customer service, but not in the high priority ranking factors outlined in the customer survey. The benefits of future upgrades and use of modern standardised components are also advantages of this option. This system represents a possible acceptable basis for the customer service and maintenance of the TPS objectives of the IT strategy, but it would not address the goal congruence objectives. It might provide other organisational advantages concerning the morale and motivation of most of the managers, but it would leave the future of the DP department needing further organisation.

There is a difficult choice for KJ plc because both systems would provide an acceptable basis for some of the three key areas of the IT strategy. The company could focus on the internal improvements offered by Alternative Two or could concentrate on providing better customer benefits offered by Alternative One.

Transaction processing systems provide the raw material, which is often used more extensively by management information systems, databases or decision support systems. The TPS might be used to produce management information such as reports on cumulative sales figures to date, total amounts owed to suppliers or owed by debtors, total stock turnover to date and value of current stock in hand. However, the main purpose of the TPS is operational, as an integral part of day-to-day operations.

(b)   KJ plc's current system

The current TPS allows for the continual receiving and rapid processing of data which validates and updates the files with every transaction. There do not seem to be any problems with response times from the system. The reason it is being replaced is because of the increased maintenance and other costs due to the system's age. It provides a vast amount of information, which is used by managers at all levels in the organisation. There are very few complaints concerning the amount or the quality of information that is normally supplied. The MD makes most tactical and strategic decisions and, whilst this suits the long-serving managers, the majority of the managers want to take a more active role in decision-making. As the current system only allows the managers to implement the objectives of the MD, it is difficult to say whether the information available would support them in the traditional decision-making role of middle management. We understand that there is ample information available to them in their role as administrators but they are not using it to exercise any form of control over the business.

The TPS currently supports the three main areas of the IT strategy but the ability to bring about change has been restricted because only the MD authorises changes to the system. The scenario does not mention whether the current system could support enhanced decision-making by middle managers, only that the MD does not know how to implement an acceptable solution.

If Alternative One were adopted, there would be additional benefits to customer service and customer satisfaction would increase. However, unless this brought about more business, it is doubtful whether the information emanating from the system would show this improvement.

All staff would have access to the centralised database. In the future, managers might be given the authority to make more decisions and this type of system would facilitate control. Unfortunately, the current situation would prevail in the short term and the managers would be in no position to influence matters. The management structure would remain unchanged, with the MD retaining control of the major decisions regarding the computer system.

Because historical data would only be available six months after changeover, this could create problems at KJ plc. Full trend analyses would not be possible and managers would find it difficult to produce some reports eg, stock levels in relation to sales and purchases. There could also be lost opportunities in recognising the potential of new products.

The strategic planning module that comes as an extra with this system would allow the MD to use the information from the TPS in a different way. He would be able to consider a number of alternatives and evaluate them under a variety of potential conditions. However, unless he shares this facility with the managers and gives them the opportunity to exercise some control over their departments, they would probably be indifferent to the information provided by the new system.

The information to be provided by Alternative Two includes a full range of strategic to operational information, with database query tools to access as much information as KJ plc want from the TPS. The key historical information would also be available at extra cost. The system offered by Alternative Two will only satisfy low-level customer requirements in the short term, but could bring about a significant change to the marketing and sales procedures with the introduction of e-mail and the Internet facilities. These facilities will make more information about KJ plc and its products available on the Internet for customers and potential customers. They can also be used to obtain environmental information to help in the decision-making process. The internal management processes of the company would be improved with a de-centralised system, and a revised management structure could bring about enormous change.

The facilities offered by this system will affect management style and, because of the nature of the information and how it is disseminated, can provide the necessary catalyst for change. As managers would have the responsibility to make tactical and operational decisions, more information would be required for control purposes. The Intranet can be used for information that ranges from the financial data that management needs, to the scheduling of workgroups within certain departments, down to the latest changes to the staff handbook. The database query tools will enable specific items of information to be obtained from the TPS. This should improve the motivation of managers, because they will be taking more control of their departments and the decision-making process. Managers should also be able to develop the system and produce reports tailored to their departmental needs and information to suit their requirements, provided that the query system uses a structured query language that is fairly simple to master. Motivating the managers and supporting organisational change could bring about significant cultural and attitude improvements, allowing an information infrastructure to be developed. Communications and information flow could be improved and put into practice by a well-motivated workforce. As the control over departmental systems is localised, then potentially each department can maximise the use of its systems to provide the information required by managers.

(c)   Financing methods

KJ plc has a choice between obtaining the new computer equipment either by outright cash purchase or by an operating lease. The strategic and operational advantages of these financing methods for the new computer equipment are outlined below.

Strategic - outright cash purchase

One of the strategic advantages of financing by an outright cash purchase is that the new computer equipment can be purchased in the same way as any other asset. However, the opportunity cost of using the cash for this type of purchase would have to be taken into consideration. The main advantage of purchasing the asset is that ownership would allow the management at KJ plc to make any changes deemed necessary to the equipment over time eg, make upgrade changes when required. They would not have to seek permission as they would from a leasing company, nor have the worry that permission may not be granted by the lessor, because of the requirement to maintain a standardised configuration.

Assuming that finance is available, equipment can be replaced when required, and certainly before it becomes obsolete, without having to wait for an agreement to be completed or pay a penalty for early cancellation. This helps longer-term cash planning and ensures a fit with the strategic direction of the organisation. However, because of the very rapid changes that occur within the computer industry and the risks of accelerated obsolescence, outright purchase may not always enable the company to keep up with the changes required.

Operational - outright cash purchase

For KJ plc, the benefits of buying rather than leasing are that they will have complete control over the systems use and a better choice over the type of hardware and software to use. Operating fixed costs will be lower as its users will own the system. The equipment can be treated in the same way as any other asset. It can be depreciated according to expected life span and the costs, capital allowances and interest payments can all be managed in the usual way, making the procedures easier to deal with at the operational level.

Strategic - operating leases

There are a number of options available to KJ plc to finance the asset over the longer term. A leasing arrangement is mostly undertaken through a finance house for a normal period of between three and five years. The lessee chooses the computer then negotiates as for a direct purchase transaction. The leasing company (lessor) pays the supplier's account on behalf of the lessee after installation, and the lessee then begins payment of leasing charges to the lessor. Leasing contracts normally give the user an opportunity to upgrade the equipment on attractive terms at the end of the contract. Operating leases are really rental arrangements, the main advantage being the flexibility that is offered. Many specialist suppliers have variations on this type of lease eg, exchange hire. With this scheme, the equipment is rented at a set price for a given period. During this period, if the equipment is replaced or upgraded, the exchange hire agreement is used to switch equipment in or out of the overall package. This has the obvious benefit of maintaining the flexibility required for a modern computer installation and keeping an up-to-date configuration at all times. However, it may be a disadvantage to be committed to a long-term agreement from a strategic point of view.

Another form of financing this type of asset is a contract hire purchase agreement. The company might consider this method if the equipment was part of an overall long-term IT strategy requiring considerable and continuous IT investment.

Operational - operating leases

This option is also easy to administer as regular monthly or quarterly payments are made and cash flow can be managed accordingly. Capital otherwise tied up in equipment is now available. Leasing charges do not alter during the primary period and they are often reduced after lease renewal. The biggest operational advantage will be that all the expenditure is treated as revenue and so this option avoids the potential confusion that can arise as to what constitutes maintenance and what should be classified as capital enhancement.

(d)(i)   Motivation of the managers

Alternative Two would help the motivation of most of the managers because of the improvement in planning and decision-making, participation, communication and delegation.

Decision-making and planning - because the system is de-centralised, each department manager will make his or her decisions regarding the use of their computer system. The managers would also be responsible for making the tactical and operational decisions necessary to run their own departments.

The maintenance of the systems will also be the managers' responsibility and the amount of departmental information that they make available, and try to receive, on the internal Intranet is also their responsibility. The quality of the data and the information used in the decision-making process will be dependent upon their involvement with the system and their ability to interrogate the database. This should ensure that the information is available when required and of a suitable standard to base their decisions on.

Because planning is considered one of the main functions of a manager, and the managers at KJ plc have not previously had the opportunity to do it, it will help to motivate them in the initial stages. The ability to use the Internet to gather external environmental information, and the powerful database query tools to analyse old databases, will give them the tools for their own planning. They can produce reports on trends from the information available that will enable them to look to the future and, as they will have the ability to influence outcomes, they can make the most appropriate decisions.

Participation - every employee in an organisation likes to feel that he or she is playing a part in its success. As we have just noted, this system will provide the capability for managers to extract information for planning, control and decision-making purposes. These functions all help to motivate the manager, who feels able to participate in the business. It will also be available for the rest of the staff to carry out their duties well, so that everyone in the organisation can be involved in participating in its success. Participation and teamwork can create an environment that encourages creativity, which can lead to more development opportunities for the organisation. This can further enhance motivation.

Communication - Motivation is improved when people feel that they know what is going on in the workplace. Alternative Two has the most up to date technology for communication. Information is available through the internal network and via e-mail, as well as the traditional methods that were already in existence. The introduction of an Intranet also helps to disseminate some company information throughout the organisation whilst directing other, more personal or specific, information to the correct recipients.

Delegation - delegating the running of individual departments to managers allocates the authority to go with the responsibility they already have and therefore motivation will increase. Instead of just identifying problems, they can actually do something about them. A large part of a manager's job is getting things done through people. This means inducing people to work to the best of their ability and enabling them to achieve some satisfaction from their efforts. The manager can delegate some tasks to his or her team and they can all work towards a common purpose. Lifting the spirits of the team not only motivates the team members, but is a morale booster for the manager as well. This will lead to increasing job satisfaction and the managers will be able to feel that they are making a contribution to the organisation.

(ii)   Actions that can be taken

Middle management consist of two distinct groups - a minority of long serving managers who seem to be generally happy with the MD making most of the strategic and tactical decisions, and a majority who have been recently appointed and would like more responsibility. An unwillingness to accept responsibility by the long serving managers may just be one symptom of a wider problem. There may be fundamental problems that no new system could address. Because they have been doing the same type of work for a long time, and have been protected from risky decision-making and planning by an authoritarian MD, a combination of organisational development, bringing about a cultural change, and a programme of personal development will need to be considered. This will involve training the managers concerned, and this must be co-ordinated within a whole programme of change.

These managers will now require a different set of skills. Specific training courses can help to cope with the new methods of work, such as negotiating for additional information. They will also need help to acquire knowledge about how the information systems can be used to their advantage. This could be arranged using some form of guidance or mentoring.

When the confidence of these managers is raised and they realise that they can make decisions without making too many mistakes, the improved communications and information flow of the new system can help managers accept more responsibility. If they understand the system and can participate by making the tactical and operational decisions necessary to run their own departments and computer systems, they will be exercising their responsibility and authority.

Once the managers understand the new system, they will be able to deal with the maintenance issues and the decisions regarding their own departmental computer system. This will help them to focus on their developmental targets, become involved and take on the responsibility necessary to achieve their objectives.

The extra effort that the managers will be putting into their work will need to be rewarded. KJ plc can introduce an organisation-wide performance appraisal system, using developmental targets and departmental objectives to measure the managers' success or otherwise. Encouragement by reviewing, supporting and counselling the managers can be used as part of the overall process to help them overcome their unwillingness to accept responsibility.

Answer 47

Criminal Justice System

(a)   **Costs and benefits of Alpha and Beta**

Introduction

There seem to be more instances where the costs, rather than the benefits, of information systems can be quantified. For this reason, costs can more readily be split into tangible and intangible ones. Benefits, however, with a few exceptions such as reduced system costs or an improved cash flow situation, tend to be mainly intangible, for example, 'improved decision making, due to a better use of information' or 'greater control over the operational processes' or 'improved customer service'. Following an assessment of both the hardware and software currently in use, and the requirements of the new system, the costs and benefits can be identified as follows.

System Alpha - Tangible Costs

The tangible costs for this system include the following.

(i)   Where manual systems are in place, or where systems are out-of-date or not compatible with the proposed system, suitable hardware will need to be purchased for each Court. Depending on the size of the systems in each Court, this may be based on powerful PCs or mini-computers, with suitable memory, processing speeds, backup and storage facilities, printers and CD ROM drives. Larger computers may be necessary to handle all the Statute and Case law.

(ii)   Designing and implementing new systems to replace the old ones, whether manual or computer-based, along with the cost of transferring existing data from the old systems to the new ones and adding any additional data will incur costs.

(iii)   There will also be the cost of the new Management Information Systems to collate the operational information.

(iv)   The availability and cost of expertise within the Central and Regional Court Systems should also be taken into account. It may be necessary to use contract specialists or bring in consultants to oversee the project.

(v)   Users and the Court Administrators will have to be trained to use the new systems, particularly if they have been used to manual systems in the past.

System Alpha - Intangible Costs

Although there is a courier for urgent information from the Central Court, the distribution of information by CD-ROM may mean that it is out of date by up to one week. Obviously this delay could be greater if there are problems with the distribution through the postal service eg, information may be lost or damaged in transit.

In some cases these costs could become tangible ones eg, where Court procedures are held up and costs are incurred because of this. The lack of correct, up-to-date information may lead to an incorrect decision being reached on a case. In these circumstances the whole trial process may need to be repeated.

System Alpha - Benefits

The operation of the criminal justice system in the country could benefit from this system in the following ways:

(i)   By introducing information on common databases it would mean that each Court was working to the same standards. This could help with the transfer of data throughout the system, particularly with the proposed use of CD ROMs. Common systems would also ensure that the reliability of the information is improved and there is consistency in the decision-making process.

(ii)   System updates are easier with common systems, equipment and procedures. The introduction of standardised working practices would allow staff to be transferred from one Court to another, on either a temporary or permanent basis, to deal with variations in workloads.

With this option, individual Courts would still retain the ability to manage their own local systems relating to schedules, fixed assets and salary information, allowing them to retain some independence in decision-making and making them more likely to accept new systems.

System Beta - Tangible Costs

The tangible costs associated with the Beta system include the following:

(i)   The provision of a new computer configuration, probably a medium to large mainframe, to handle all the information relating to common data on Statute and Case law.

(ii)   Communication links and dial-in facilities to each Regional Court and the costs of operating the file server.

(iii)   Backup facilities.

(iv)   Software to update the regional databases.

(v)   The set up and running costs of a central data processing and distribution department for the Central Court Data Services Department.

(vi)   Management Information Systems to collate operational information (as with the Alpha system).

(vii)   The costs of regional Courts accessing centralised information (this could outweigh the costs of maintaining their own databases locally).

System Beta - Intangible Costs

Disagreements could arise because responsibility for information systems would be split between the Head of Court Data Services and the individual Court administrators over who should do what. It could also lead to goal incongruence because data relating to cases could be held in different places, and may not be up-to-date in each location.

Poor motivation and dissatisfaction of Court Administrators, due to the reduction in their control over the databases, could cause staffing difficulties.

The transfer of data may also cause problems - especially if information went missing when being transferred. The use of dial-in facilities using public telephone lines could lead to security problems. If confidential information were to be obtained by outsiders, then it could lead to cases being dismissed perhaps on technical grounds. However, potentially high costs could still have been incurred at this stage.

System Beta - Benefits

A number of benefits could ensue from the introduction of this system:

(i)   Only one database is needed, making it much easier to update.

(ii)   The cost of maintaining and updating local databases would be reduced, although this must be weighed against the costs of accessing a central database.

(iii)   The cost of upgrading the common database in the future, or maintaining it, would be cheaper.

(iv)   Staffing costs associated with this approach could be reduced.

(v)   The availability of common data could mean that decisions made by courts would be consistent.

(b) (i)   Critical success factors and performance indicators

Critical Success Factors (CSFs) are elements or activities or the key operational goals vital to the success of an organisation. They are used to establish organisational information requirements. Performance Indicators (PIs) are measures of performance that indicate whether the CSFs have been achieved or not. Some measures use factual, objectively verifiable data while others make use of softer concepts such as opinions, perceptions and hunches.

The criminal justice system is a not-for-profit organisation and will not calculate all of the standard financial performance indicators used by profit-making organisations: ROCE, profit levels etc. However, it does have an equivalent of income and expenditure. Income comes from the government and costs include salaries, premises, equipment and other running costs such as electricity and administration. Therefore, there may be a need to justify this expenditure on a political or social basis.

In general, such organisations are more concerned about the level of service they provide than about any accounting surplus that may arise. Of course, this does not mean that they can afford to neglect financial disciplines, only that the focus of such organisations is less directed to the achievement of financial targets than would be normal in a commercial organisation. There is often pressure to ensure that whatever service is provided is done so cost effectively. It is reasonable to assume that 'value for money' and 'quality of service' are required, although value is difficult to determine and could be rather subjective.

Even in a public service organisation, such as the Court system, there needs to be some way of measuring efficiency, if the organisation itself wishes to ensure that it is not wasting the resources allocated to it. Given that this is the case, relevant PIs are needed to assess whether or not the new agreed CSFs ensuring efficiency have been met. These will have to be more than a simple measure of whether the money has been spent so that it relates to the quality of the expenditure ie, whether or not it has been spent efficiently on necessary services. No quality control currently seems to be applied. The percentage of Court utilisation may indicate that courts are being used, but does not say how effectively they are being used. Time may have been spent inefficiently on lengthy minor cases. Trials may also be speeded up, to the detriment of those involved, to ensure throughput and improve utilisation.

(ii)   Performance indicators (PIs) to support the new CSFs

The two new CSFs are:

♦   internally - to ensure efficient allocation and use of the public resources that the government commits to Courts; and

♦   externally - to minimise the time taken for cases to be taken through the Court system.

The PIs that could be used to support the internal CSF are:

♦   the amount of money distributed to each court, relative to the population served;

♦   the number of cases heard;

♦   the number of successful prosecutions;

♦   the amount of money spent by each regional court on the various areas of expenditure, eg maintaining the fixed assets register, salary information, maintenance of the database systems, heating and lighting;

♦   the relative amounts of expenditure on actual court proceedings and administrative overheads;

♦   variations in expenditure, together with the reasons for them.

The performance indicators for the external CSF are:

♦   the average length of each court case;
♦   the time taken for the case to be heard;
♦   the classification of court cases, eg minor or serious offences, and the time taken for each type;
♦   variations in the time taken for similar types of cases, with explanations for the differences.

In each case, comparison could be made between the various Courts and other institutions both at home and abroad.

The PIs are appropriate because the government needs to know where the money is going and what it is being spent on. It needs to know that the money spent is a necessary expense on items that are needed. It may also need to know where necessary expenditure is considered to be under-funded in case efficiency is being compromised.

(c)   The input data

The scenario indicates that with both proposed systems the Court Service Information System (CSIS) will be used for operational information only. With alternative Beta, however, it is also mentioned that responsibility for information systems would be split between the Central Head of Court Data Services and local Court Administrators and it must be made sure that the CSIS could meet this requirement.

The current information systems provide details on:

(i)   Statute and Case law
(ii)   Court organisation schedules
(iii)   Fixed assets register
(iv)   Salary information relating to Court officials

The new Court Service Information System (CSIS) will therefore need to provide similar information.

Court organisation schedules - includes lists of judges, jurors and Court officials who will be present in Court on any given day and details of the cases that will be heard in each Courtroom.

The nature of this information means that it is needed on a daily basis, along with the ability to amend details at short notice. Hence some form of forward planning is needed. Details relating to judges, jurors and Court officials will need to be input. Some of these details that will need to be input, regarding judges and Court officials, may be semi-permanent eg, names, addresses, areas of the law in which they specialise and duties. Juror details may only be relatively fixed with regard to their names and addresses; their availability on a particular day may need to be amended at short notice should they not be available eg, due to illness.

Similarly, although the details of cases to be reviewed may be known in advance, last minute changes may have to be arranged to establish a particular day's schedule. Last minute changes to pleas could affect the whole day's schedule of a particular Court, as would the withdrawal of a case. This is an area where the CSIS needs to be capable of being flexible, holding as much basic daily data as possible, with the flexibility to enter up-to-date amendments at short notice, in order to produce daily schedules.

Longer-term information may also be needed, along with past trends and future predictions, relating to population levels and crime statistics. This would facilitate planning and decision-making on the Court's workload in the future.

Fixed assets register - contains details of the assets under the control and ownership of the Court.

Once these details have been entered, amendments are not likely to occur too frequently so this would be a simpler system to operate. Details required would probably include:

(i)   assets purchased eg, land, building and fixtures and fittings - with the date of acquisition, price, current value and methods of depreciation

(ii)   assets disposed of - with relevant data.

Once again, an analysis of trends in assets would allow expenditure to be budgeted. Monitoring of the expenditure should take place at regular intervals.

Salary information - relating to Court officials

As the Central Court pays the judges, this is likely to be a fairly standard payroll system for Court officials. Because the term 'salary' has been used, we can assume that officials are paid on a normal monthly basis. The CSIS will require data relating to names, addresses, annual salaries, bonuses/overtime if applicable, tax, insurance and whatever other details are needed to replace the systems currently in use. The system will also need to cater for amendments to salaries and grades and the addition of new members of staff or the removal of those who leave.

(d)   Virtual Private Network

Although the Gamma alternative system has been rejected as being too expensive to install, the main benefit of a Virtual Private Network (VPN) is that it is a way of balancing an organisation's need for remote access with a need for tight security. Other advantages are that information relating to common data about Statute and case law could be held and updated more easily and the amount of equipment held locally would be reduced.

We can assume that the major cost that was affecting the decision not to adopt the Gamma system was the installation and use of the dedicated leased lines, although they can be cheaper to operate than normal telephone lines. Even though the VPN would provide a secure way of handling information, this must be weighed against the practical effectiveness of the system. It is not certain that it would meet the needs of local users in the regional courts. In fact it is reasonable to assume that the main workload in providing information lies within the local courts and the central system may not provide sufficient flexibility in responding to local day-to-day operational changes.

The risks associated with database access via a VPN include the reliance on both the third party provider and having a central computer system.

The plan was to use spare capacity on the Wide Area Network of the national rail company. The rail company would need to give assurances regarding:

(i)   the future capacity on the WAN

(ii)   the reliability of the system

(iii)   the security of storing and transferring what could be sensitive information

(iv)   provision for contingencies in the event of the failure of the system eg, establishing adequate back-up facilities, because system failure could effectively disrupt the whole of the country's criminal justice system.

With the VPN, the plan would be to hold all local information centrally with remote access being available from all courts even though it is unlikely that this information would be needed by the central administration on such a frequent basis. Local courts would be reliant on the central computer for all the information they require, placing a heavy workload on it. The increased workload could contribute to a higher risk of systems failure.

The risk of a systems failure is another of the problems when an organisation relies on a central computer system. In the event of a failure local courts would be unable to operate effectively unless backup facilities could be guaranteed.

ANSWERS TO PILOT PAPER

PILOT PAPER ANSWERS

Answer 48 (Answer 1 of Pilot Paper)

(a)

Porter's five forces technique can determine the intensity of competition and profitability of a company and be used at Q.NET to choose the strategic options to give them a competitive advantage. The five forces are as follows:

♦ **Competitive rivalry** - competitors are organisations making similar products or offering similar services and selling them in the same market. Q.NET's competitors are all booksellers. To achieve an advantage over their competitors, Q.NET needs some way of reducing costs, providing a better service, improving their marketing or achieving product differentiation.

Cost leadership can be exploited by information technology (IT) eg, supporting just-in-time systems. Q.NET could also change the basis of competition by setting up new communications networks and forming alliances with complementary organisations for the purpose of information sharing.

Customer service can be improved if additional investment in the IT infrastructure, and closer links with book suppliers, bring about more efficient operations in ordering, stock control and dispatch. The end result could be a reduction in the time between a customer placing an order and the delivery of that order. However, book suppliers also require some additional benefit for linking to a re-seller in some way. Decreasing the time taken to pay suppliers may be an appropriate means of gaining this incentive. Q.NET can also offer a better service by improving differentiation. Additional information is available on all books from Q.NET's database but further investment is required in the IT infrastructure to provide this information for customers.

Q.NET could improve marketing by storing book, customer and transaction data in a database and building a customer profile to use for competitive purposes. Tailored information could be presented to a customer on accessing Q.NET's website, encouraging the development of a long-term relationship and also differentiating Q.NET from traditional booksellers.

♦ **Threat of new entrants** - as new book re-sellers become established in the market, they could attract customers away from Q.NET. Given the high capital costs experienced by Q.NET, this situation does not appear to be very likely although changes in technology or a fall in price of existing technology may reduce the entry barrier and allow this to happen. The establishment of a strong brand and reputation, combined with competitive pricing policies will form the most effective long-term barrier for Q.NET.

The establishment of a close relationship with suppliers, using mutually beneficial systems such as EDI links would limit the possibility of new entrants coming into the market because, to compete effectively, any new entrant would need similar EDI links to offer a timely service. Providing a quicker service would also challenge existing bookshops by making shopping for books on the Internet more convenient.

♦ **Threats from substitutes** - substitutes are alternative services/products that serve the same purpose. Alternatives to buying books over the Internet include purchasing from a bookshop or book club, borrowing books from libraries, buying magazines, hiring videos or buying the material on CD-ROM, to be viewed on screen with a hard copy printed off if required. Books and other paper-based products are under threat from the new digital communication forms. It is possible to access and read printed material on a website, or download it from a website to read on a hand-held computer. A hybrid product, combining a book, a CD or DVD and on-line links is likely to become the norm in some areas of publishing.

Q.NET can use its IT systems to make its Internet service more attractive to customers by reducing delivery times, providing more customer specific information and passing on cost savings achieved as a result of using IT eg, lower staff, storage and office costs.

♦ **Threats from the power of buyers** - buyers can make an industry more competitive by forcing prices down, bargaining for higher quality or improved services and/or playing competitors off against each other.

For Q.NET, as books are a relatively low value, non-essential product, collective action by buyers is unlikely; the deciding factor for the customer will be a combination of price and service. The main power of buyers in this market is the ease by which they can change supplier. Buyers can switch to other websites within seconds to compare book prices and delivery times so, as well as price and service, further incentives such as 'book miles' or 'loyalty discounts' for repeat purchasers may be justified.

Interactive information systems add value by providing an extra service to an existing product eg, personalised suggestions can be offered by matching with previous purchasing history, current requests and similar purchasing habits of other customers.

♦ **Threats from the power of suppliers** - publishers of books are often in a monopoly position with regard to the supply of an individual book and Q.NET cannot therefore threaten to switch suppliers to obtain a better price. In this type of situation suppliers can squeeze profitability out of an industry by raising prices or reducing the quality of their goods and services. However, if Q.NET can buy similar books from more than one supplier, it will limit the extent of monopoly profits that can be obtained.

Using computerised JIT stock systems can forge strong links with suppliers. This partnership approach should benefit the competitive position of both Q.NET and the supplier. Offering a standard commission based on book sales may be another viable alternative.

(b) **High sales and support staff turnover**

There are several reasons why sales and support staff turnover could be high.

Alienation - perhaps there is no sense of belonging, with employees perceiving Q.NET simply as an organisation that sends them work and pays them at the end of the month. There is little employee consultation regarding the direction of the company or information on the organisation's current goals and achievements. Actual commitment to the organisation could be extremely low, simply because each employee cannot see (and therefore be part of) the aims of Q.NET. A lack of commitment to the company may result in dissatisfaction and work not being carried out efficiently or effectively.

Another problem arising from working at home is the lack of social interaction between colleagues and not being involved in the everyday events of the company. If employees are isolated ie, no Intranet connections or meetings, this lack of contact could mean that they are unable to share problems and concerns and to find out if other sales and support personnel are facing similar problems. Where employees feel there is a lack of peer group support and they miss it, they might be inclined to look for the type of employment where this support is available.

Many employees find home working quite difficult in terms of dividing their time effectively between office and home and because of the distractions from family, friends and general neighbourhood noise. There is always ample opportunity to browse the Internet to alleviate boredom and look for alternative employment.

Lack of job variety - using a computer for most of the day to either answer e-mails or make changes to the Web site database is likely to be quite monotonous, because there is insufficient job variety. Maintaining concentration levels and motivation for any significant amount of time will be difficult. Employees are, therefore, likely to become bored easily and may seek other jobs that seem more interesting. A related issue are the problems associated with the continued use of technology, which can lead to repetitive strain injury (RSI) and vision defects. Because employees will be using the technology all day, they may well end up suffering from these conditions and be encouraged to leave the company.

No personal customer contact - all communication is via e-mail and is consequently very impersonal with little opportunity for employees to build up a service relationship with a customer. Although there are ways of personalising e-mail, employees will be receiving messages concerning problems encountered by ordering from Q.NET. Because the mail is likely to be negative in content, employees will be subject to the stress that complaints bring but will not experience the praise from satisfied customers. Responding to problems and queries all day through an impersonal system can be de-motivating and lead to employees wanting to leave of their own accord or to leave because their performance is not considered acceptable.

Improving staff retention

Q.NET can encourage interaction with other employees as a partial solution to the problem by providing e-mail and telephone connections so that they can share problems and simply talk socially. If the problem is one of lack of commitment to the organisation, the answer could be to hold meetings and/or social occasions so that the employees can get together, share problems and experiences and hopefully see that Q.NET is taking more of an interest in their welfare. However, this may not be feasible where employees are geographically dispersed because frequent meetings are likely to be impossible in terms of time, distance and cost.

Periodically changing the tasks given to staff (work rotation) may also help to alleviate some of the boredom. For example, employees could answer e-mails and provide input to the Web pages on alternate days.

Because home working is becoming more expensive, due to the hardware movement and recruitment costs, the Board at Q.NET may wish to restructure the sales and support team and consider whether home working is actually an acceptable solution. It may be more appropriate, and even cheaper, to expand the office space and actually locate staff in one building.

(c)   Purpose of an information strategy

The main purpose of an information strategy (IS) in a commercial organisation will be to ensure information is best used to facilitate customer services and to support business operations and the overall business strategy.

Customer services - the IS may be used to provide information to decision-makers outside the organisation eg, customers use information to make a purchase decision from the organisation. The amount of information required will vary depending on the nature of the product or service. For Q.NET, customers may only want to check the availability of a book or they may need to know the range of publications offered on a specific topic. Part of the organisation's information system will therefore be externally focused to ensure that appropriate information is given to customers.

Business operations - another purpose of an information strategy is to provide relevant information to individual user departments. Having set an overall business strategy and provided strategic level information, more specific operational level information will be required by managers of individual user departments to ensure that the business strategy can be met.

The IS of the organisation will ensure that operational managers receive the information that they require. For example, if the business strategy is to provide good customer service, then the IS will need to ensure that operational information about stock and lead times are available on-line.

Supporting the business strategy - the corporate strategy will identify what that organisation wants to do and how it will be achieved. The IS will support it by providing appropriate information on customers, products, and production etc, to the decision-makers in the business. It should be geared towards the specific goals and strategies outlined by the organisation.

(d)   The effectiveness of the IT system

The effectiveness of the IT system at Q.NET can be measured in terms of how well it provides the information to meet the objectives of the IS.

Customer services - Q.NET seems less than effective in its provision of information for customers because the IT system does not always provide them with the information on each title that is available. More information on each individual book is available on Q.NET's database, although the IT system will not allow this information to be accessed. This is a weakness because people are more likely to buy a product if they have sufficient information to reassure them. The lack of information will soon become an issue if Q.NET loses competitive advantage to competitors who are providing this information.

Supporting business operations - the information system could also be failing suppliers because customer purchase information cannot be analysed for their benefit. If customer demand patterns are given to suppliers, then those suppliers can calculate the ongoing demand for books more accurately. Seasonal demand will be apparent allowing the correct decisions to be made. Book production and delivery can be modified to meet specific sales requirements, supporting the core function of getting books to customers as quickly as possible.

Supporting the business strategy - the IS cannot provide detailed customer history information after more than six weeks. This could be harming management's ability to make marketing and purchasing decisions. Removing this information from the hard disk to save space may be a valid reason but it does mean that detailed customer histories for book purchases, and cumulative information of book purchases by type of customer, cannot be built up. Q.NET is handing a competitive advantage to booksellers able to target customers appropriately and build up a detailed purchase history.

The lack of information will become an issue when competitive advantage is lost, especially if Q.NET fails to provide special offers to customers based on their previous purchasing history, or management make incorrect purchasing decisions because demand for a particular book is estimated incorrectly.

Answer 49 (Answer 2 of Pilot Paper)

REPORT

To	Board of HB Ltd
From	Management accountant
Subject	Investment in IT system
Date	12 June 20X0

This report will explain some of the benefits of implementing a new computer-based production monitoring system. It will firstly show how the movements in contribution and fixed costs, highlighted in the main graph provided by the consultant, can be achieved, and then will go on to discuss other ways in which the system will help the organisation gain a competitive advantage. The two main areas of improvement were shown to be an increase in contribution from each unit of cement sold and a decrease in the fixed costs of the company.

Increase in contribution per unit

Increased contribution can be achieved by either lowering the variable costs of production or by increasing the selling price per unit. In the production process of cement, HB Ltd's variable costs comprise raw materials used, machine time and usage and labour cost. The labour cost could be a fixed or stepped cost, because the number of production workers is only likely to change with significant changes in the level of production. The variable element of labour is due to overtime levels of existing staff.

There are several ways of using IT to produce a shift in the contribution line shown in the graph.

Reduce waste - Computer aided measurement of raw materials will reduce the raw materials used in the production process. The present system of weighing inputs manually results in errors being made, especially where products can only be weighed to the nearest 100 kg because of a lack of accurate weighing equipment. If precise measurement reduces raw material usage, it will reduce the costs per unit and increase the contribution per unit of cement.

Reduce the cost of the labour content of production - the increased automation of the weighing and monitoring process, previously undertaken by manual labour along with the accuracy of the production process should reduce the number of hours that production workers need to produce the same volume of cement. This means that the actual labour cost per unit produced should fall.

Reduce repair and machine down time costs - machines will be monitored automatically and the computer system will examine the production process and build up a profile of the accuracy of each cement-mixing machine. Where individual machines start to show a history of producing poorer products or breakdowns, preventative maintenance can be undertaken to minimise time lost, either through adjusting or servicing broken machines. Minimising machine downtime will help to decrease the machine cost per unit and so increase contribution made.

Improved product - The company could use IT to monitor the input mix and production process to increase the quality of the cement being produced. Rather than relying on the skill and judgement of the production staff, precise quantities of raw materials can be input to each process with the mix itself being monitored and sampled as the cement is produced. Producing higher quality cement will enable HB Ltd to charge a premium price for the product, which will in turn increase contribution per unit.

Focus on more profitable lines - another way of increasing the contribution per unit could be via the product mix. The system will provide more accurate costing information making it possible to monitor the contribution obtained from each type of cement with a greater degree of accuracy. Subject to demand considerations, production can be focused on higher contribution-making types of cement. Alternatively, prices may be amended to increase the contribution of lower margin cements if the competitive position allows. If this is not sustainable, HB Ltd may consider stopping production of those cement types.

Decrease in the fixed costs of the company

Fixed costs are those that remain constant at any production level. HB Ltd's fixed costs include staff in all departments, rent, rates, factory overheads and marketing activities.

Staff - investing in IT will increase the number of staff required to run the computer system. However, the increases could be more than offset by savings in employment costs in the production process.

Production overheads - it is possible that in the longer run production of cement may require fewer machines, especially if production time falls as a result of a decrease in machine downtime, and machines are used more efficiently as a result of computer planning of machine usage. This could lead to fewer machines, and possibly a smaller amount of factory space, being required. Fixed costs may fall if factory rent and rates fall because less factory space is required. However, this will only happen if the excess factory space can be sold or let.

Distribution costs - an investment in IT could be used to schedule deliveries and optimise the distribution of the product because the inclusion of customer and distribution details in the system will allow for better co-ordination of deliveries. Distribution costs may fall if deliveries to customers in a similar geographical area can be scheduled for the same day. More precise computer monitoring of orders and production may allow this efficiency in the delivery system to be utilised. The overall number of delivery vehicles and drivers could be reduced, with the result that fixed costs also fall.

(b) Other ways of obtaining competitive advantage in sales and marketing activities

The investment in IT systems will allow HB Ltd to increase sales when compared to competitors and to obtain competitive advantage in the following ways:

♦ *Providing more information to managers* - to help them make decisions and adopt strategies to capture a share of the specialist cement market. The technology will outline the feasibility of either switching production to cover the full range of cement products or of specialising in one type of cement eg, coloured cement for bicycle-only lanes on roads. If information can be provided to demonstrate that their products can match the needs of customers requiring high quality control and guaranteed delivery times, they can sell to these customers with confidence.

♦ *Providing better information to customers* - investment in IT will mean that customers can be kept better informed concerning the progress and the expected delivery time of each order. This could mean winning new customers and retaining existing ones. The manual system is not able to provide this information because of uncertainties in the production process. However, with computer scheduling and monitoring of production, a more definite delivery date can be given. Customers are likely to favour HB Ltd over other producers because they can plan work around definite delivery dates.

♦ *Building up customer profiles* - the computerised system will facilitate the production and maintenance of a database containing the history of orders from each customer. This database can be searched for order trends such as repeat orders or specific types of cement being ordered in the same month each year. Targeting customers and offering discounts or other favourable terms on particular types of cement will help to generate customer loyalty and repeat orders. Where competitors are still using manual systems, they may find it difficult or uneconomic to maintain this information and HB Ltd will gain a significant competitive advantage.

Answer 50 (Answer 3 of Pilot Paper)

(a)   **Refining or amending the information system**

There are several actions that could be taken to limit the information being received

Divert all incoming telephone calls via a secretary - Interruptions by telephone calls and personal visits on a regular basis do not allow the accountant time to concentrate on the main job role. A secretary or administrator should be allocated to take telephone messages and meet personal visitors, only putting through calls of significance and admitting visitors that require immediate attention. This filtering technique will be effective so long as the accountant provides instructions concerning the messages that must be relayed, and trusts the secretary to carry out those instructions.

Filter e-mail - programs within the e-mail system have the ability to review and re-direct messages based on the message content, priority, sender and/or intended recipients. The accountant may decide only to review messages that are sent as urgent or which contain specific text, such as a client name. The non-selected messages could be copied to a selected person, or just redirected to a non-urgent inbox for review later.

Use software intelligent agents - the accountant normally spends a lot of time reviewing specific websites for amendments to information. This entails finding the correct pages and trying to identify what changes, if any, have been made since the page was last checked. Once the criteria is set down as to what should be retrieved, the use of agents would reduce the amount of time the accountant would need to spend reviewing websites. Intelligent agent applications can organise, filter, and structure the information, leaving the accountant just reviewing specific sites rather than a long list. It will also store both the old and new pages in memory and compare them to find the precise nature of any change.

Delegate contact with specific clients - some decisions taken by the accountant may not require the consideration of such a senior person. Ongoing routine contact with clients ie, the tactical and operational decision making, can be delegated to one of the more junior managers, who will only need to refer to the accountant in situations where strategic decisions affecting the service to that client need to be taken. As long as the accountant trusts the judgement of the manager, this will be an extremely effective method of both limiting the information received by the accountant, and providing a better service to the client via a dedicated manager.

Subscribe to a press cutting service - the reviewing of journals for relevant information is time-consuming. A press cutting service will limit the information to specific topics by reviewing relevant journals and newspapers and forwarding via e-mail copies of those articles that meet specific criteria, such as the names of specific clients or topics eg, IT systems development.

(b)   **Information characteristics**

The accountant has a strategic decision-making role within the organisation, which involves planning the organisation's overall objectives and strategy and measuring whether they are being achieved. The type of information will include the profitability of the main business segment, investment appraisal studies and the availability and prospects for raising long-term funds.

At this planning level, information is unpredictable and relates to wide organisational aspects. It should be summarised and not contain a high level of detail. The accountant will require an overview of any situation, rather than the detail; however, the detail may be available in the form of appendices should this be required.

Information given to the accountant should have most of the following characteristics:

Complete - so that all the information that can affect a decision is received and reviewed.

Timely - information can only be of use if it is received in time to influence the decision-making process. In many situations, circumstances may change quickly, with the result that information goes out of date rapidly. It may therefore be appropriate to present information in an electronic document, which can be amended quickly, rather than in a paper-based report.

Relevant - keeping information simple and understandable means highlighting the significant factors and screening out any facts that are not important enough to affect the decision-making process. The concept of relevance is closely linked to those of understanding and significance. Information that is easy to understand is more likely to produce action.

Communicated via an appropriate channel - information should be provided using the relevant media. For example, the use of graphs and diagrams in particular will ensure that the accountant can assimilate numeric information easily.

Well presented - the method of presentation should help understanding. If information is presented in the form of a lengthy report, a table of contents and summary of the report's findings should be provided at the beginning. The report should also have appropriate paragraphs and headings and use clear language. This will help the accountant to understand the purpose of the report and see the points that the author wants to make before the whole report is read. The information may also be posted on the company's Intranet, assuming that the contents are not confidential and the Intranet is used efficiently by those who need to view the information.

Answer 51 (Answer 4 of Pilot Paper)

REPORT

To	Board of SN plc
From	Management accountant
Subject	Maintaining information systems
Date	12 June 20X0

As requested by the board, the systems for providing information to the company's professional sales staff are evaluated in this report. Specific weaknesses are identified and recommendations made to show how these weaknesses can be alleviated.

Non aligned corporate and IT strategies

The IS/IT strategies should be developed so that they support the overall objectives of the business. However, at SN plc there seems to be no alignment of IT strategy to the overall business strategy. The head of IT communicates to the board but there are no channels of communication open to other functional departments or to the other decision-makers in the organisation.

To address this weakness, management must define a framework for IT in terms of overall direction, allocation of resources, rate of implementation and level of financial investment.

Lack of strategy review

The head of IT produces the overall IT strategy for SN plc, but there are no checks to ensure that any new information system projects are in alignment with this strategy. While this may not be an issue in some situations, there is a danger that a new system may be implemented which cannot be supported by the company's IT strategy. IT is an expensive investment that requires co-ordination and management to ensure the best value is obtained.

To avoid this problem, a process should be introduced whereby the head of IT must review all proposed projects to ensure they are consistent with and complementary to the IT strategy.

Where conflicts are found, then appropriate changes must be made to the project at the design stage so that the delivered systems are in line with the company's overall IT strategy.

No steering committee

There appears to be no overall control of the design and maintenance of the information systems. The functions of specifying the information systems, overall authorisation of each system, writing each system and final implementation are all carried out by different departments with little or no ongoing contact or feedback controls. The lack of control may mean that projects become late, are cancelled or lack the necessary prioritisation, to the overall detriment of the organisation.

Implementing a steering or design committee with representatives from all interest groups within the organisation would help to maintain an appropriate project schedule and achieve overall control of the information systems.

Insufficient direct user input

User input is essential for most projects to ensure that any revised or new system does what users need it to do. Unfortunately, the main users of the information systems at SN plc are not involved in the development process; user input is not obtained until a new system is ready for implementation. This is far too late - the system should be built to meet user requirements, not built and then presented to them.

This approach makes it very difficult for the users to take ownership of the information systems or the data held on them. Because they will feel that the systems are imposed on them, there will be little or no incentive to use those systems or ensure that the data on them are actually up-to-date. At SN plc there is a very good chance the new system will be rejected by users because it does not fully meet their requirements. Even if a reasonable system is offered, the chance of user-acceptance is small, as users generally do not enjoy having systems imposed on them without having been involved in their development.

The main method of ensuring that user requirements are met is to involve them in the design of the system - from initial specification through to implementation, provide more detailed training and explain the benefits of the new systems in more detail. Setting up the steering committee would help to achieve this objective.

User training problems

The provision of a comprehensive user manual does not constitute user training because it is unlikely that staff will have the time, motivation or necessary information to work through it. This means that they will probably not understand what any new system can do, nor be able to resolve queries when using it. There is also the danger that the system will not be used correctly, resulting in incorrect or inaccurate data being held and decisions being taken that may result in financial loss to the company if the wrong advice is given.

Defining a framework for IT will ensure that the resources are available to achieve the objectives of the organisation. The financial investment to ensure the smooth implementation of these critical systems should include the training process. A training plan must be drawn up and implemented as a matter of urgency.

IT department isolated from users

There are some advantages in having the IT department in a separate location - programmers spend their time programming rather than answering users' minor queries. However, there are significant disadvantages to this arrangement, for example:

♦ the IT department is seen to be complacent and a 'them and us' mentality seems to have developed;

♦ being isolated from users means they have limited contact with users and trainers;

♦ it is difficult to monitor and test completed modules with user input; and

♦ the IT department has a reputation within the company of not meeting user requirements in a timely manner.

Moving the IT department to one of the company's main buildings would make user-programmer liaison easier, and provide physical evidence that this is a joint effort requiring input and co-operation from all concerned. Directing ongoing queries from users regarding software to a specific Help Desk will also help staff in the IT department to focus on the task of writing new programs rather than answering minor queries from users.

Answer 52 (Answer 5 of Pilot Paper)

(a)   Adopting e-commerce as part of the business strategy

When deciding whether to adopt e-commerce as part of their business strategy, the two types of organisation can be compared using six different perspectives:

♦   Overall business strategy
♦   Objectives of the organisations
♦   Customers
♦   Competition
♦   Expertise available
♦   Legal issues

Overall business strategy - when undertaking any activity an organisation should first ensure that it is consistent with the overall business strategy. By contrasting and comparing the product/service range, market segment, competitor and customer characteristics of the two organisations, we can consider whether e-commerce would support the strategy of the organisation.

Product/service range - from financial advice being provided to a range of garden products being supplied, the ranges of both organisations are likely to be both diverse and wide - many types of financial advice and many types of garden products. A website would therefore be a useful tool in the dissemination of product information. For the international consultancy supplying financial advice, it would help them to avoid sending out printed financial information that would quickly become out-of-date. For the supplier of garden plants and accessories, the web site would allow them to show the types and prices of goods and the geographical area they supply.

Market segment - both organisations appear to have a clearly defined market segment. They know what goods they want to sell and where they will be sold. The profit margins associated with each organisation are very different. Selling products or services with higher margins eg, financial advice, may be more attractive to e-commerce because more profit is made per sale than for garden products. This means that fewer Internet transactions would be required to recover the outlay of establishing and maintaining the website. Because of the lower margins on its products, the garden centre will have to sell many garden accessories to make the same profit, compared to the multinational organisation selling a single pension scheme. The market segment of the international organisation may, therefore, be more suited to e-commerce.

Competitor and customer characteristics - the competitors of the international organisation will also be large organisations whereas the garden centre's competitors are likely to be other local outlets. It is much more difficult for an international consultancy to reach their potential customers than it is for the local customers to visit the different garden centres easily and compare prices and product quality using traditional means.

Customers looking for financial advice would require full and detailed information and expect a multinational financial organisation to provide an informative website. This assumption would be based on the size and reputation of the organisation, and the fact that similar organisations would invariably have such a site. The selling of financial products online may also be expected. There is no physical product, so the transaction could be completed electronically (although a signature on documentation will probably be required to finalise the transaction).

Establishing an Internet site with e-commerce may not be beneficial to the garden centre because there is no real value over competitors. As customers may not expect to use the Internet for their gardening requirements, it appears that e-commerce is more likely to support the strategy of the financial advice organisation than the garden centre.

Objectives of the organisation - these will be more specific and define the short and long-term goals/objectives of the organisation. Typical objectives will include profit maximisation and growth. Other objectives may be employee satisfaction or environmental impact.

Profit maximisation and growth - for the international organisation, achieving profit maximisation and growth will mean utilising sales opportunities where the net revenue from those sales is positive (over a given number of years). If organisations providing financial advice use 'increase in profit' and 'absolute growth' as performance indicators, and if e-commerce is shown to increase sales and profit, then this selling medium will be adopted. The garden centre will also require sufficient profit to justify the capital tied up in the business. Growth may be less important, depending on the long-term strategic aims. As long as an adequate return on capital is achieved, other objectives, such as customer and employee satisfaction, may be more important. So, unless e-commerce can be used to provide an adequate profit, or increase customer satisfaction, it is unlikely to be part of the overall strategy of the garden centre.

Employee satisfaction or environmental impact - employee satisfaction may be of greater concern to a garden centre than with the multi-national organisation, as closer relationships often develop in small locally focused retail outlets. Environmental impact should not be too much of an issue with garden centres as they have a relatively green and friendly image that should be fostered. These objectives may have less effect on determining whether the international organisation uses e-commerce. If e-commerce is chosen the organisation will be required to ensure proper employee welfare under the Health and Safety at Work Act. There may be a slightly positive environmental impact if sending documents electronically decreases the amount of paper used in the organisation.

The large multi-national financial organisation would be able to utilise e-commerce to achieve greater profitability and growth but e-commerce would most likely not contribute enough to the local garden centre's goals to justify the expenditure required.

Customers - the buying habits of customers will probably have an effect on whether e-commerce becomes part of the business strategy of an organisation. Situations where customers normally use the Internet, or expect information on a particular product or service to be available, will prompt an organisation to decide to make e-commerce available. Large multinational organisations will definitely expect to find out information on suppliers from the Internet.

Individuals who want to purchase financial services are likely to be in higher income brackets and therefore are more likely to have Internet access at home or work. They will also expect a well-known, well-established and trustworthy provider of financial advice to have a web site providing detailed information on the organisation and products. Use of e-commerce therefore would complement the service provided by a provider of financial advice, and should become part of the business strategy.

Although purchasers of garden products will be representative of most social groups, there might perhaps be a slight bias towards middle-aged to older people - a group that is not yet strongly represented among current Internet users. Garden products are tangible products and most people will want to see what is being purchased and choose from a selection. Providing an Internet site for this type of customer will be less important, although a web site may be useful if it provides an overview of product availability and illustrations that may entice customers to visit the garden centre. However, the e-commerce aspects of the site will be restricted where customers want to see what is being purchased or where they live more than 20Km away from the garden centre.

Competition - The garden products' supplier is selling a generic type of product where specialist selling skills and customer contact are not likely to be important to the customer. There are likely to be many competitors in the surrounding area. Large, bulky and low value products tend to have a limited geographical market. Additional sales potential is limited due to the small area they can sell into. E-commerce may have very little effect on any garden centre. There is no need to establish a site simply to remain competitive and given the cost of setting up a website (consultant's time, ISP hosting fees etc) and the limited benefits it appears unlikely that a garden centre would find e-commerce profitable.

Multinational, international and domestic competitors in the financial advice market, on the other hand, will almost certainly have a website and use e-commerce. Establishing a website is necessary to match the service offered by competitors, and reinforce the organisation's standing. As already noted, the selling of financial advice may be appropriate via e-commerce because the product is not tangible. However, the importance of the product to the customer may mean that a high proportion of them want some direct contact with a representative before making a purchase. The customer's hand-written signature will also be required on various documents, requiring either some face-to-face contact or the posting of documents for signature.

Expertise available - one of the main supports of the strategy for any organisation is having access to the required expertise ie, appropriate staff to implement and maintain that strategy.

A large organisation is more likely to be able to afford to set-up a website and to start using e- commerce. The cost of setting up and maintaining the site can be offset against a larger sales value and administrative staff costs become a smaller proportion of total costs. If the expertise is not available internally, the fee charged by an external organisation could be met and justified, even if revenue does not immediately cover costs.

A smaller organisation will find the expense of setting up and maintaining a Web site a bigger drain on its resources, due to smaller sales volume and the difficulty of attracting expert staff to a small organisation with potentially lower salaries and fewer staff benefits. Internal staff are unlikely to possess the necessary expertise and an agency may not produce exactly what the client requires. The costs of an external consultancy would probably not be justified in light of the limited benefits the site would bring.

Legal issues - if e-commerce is adopted as part of the strategy of an organisation, then various legal issues must be considered. At the very least, the organisation will need to ensure that no national laws are broken and that the products or services they are selling are not banned from being sold. The supplier of financial advice will be selling products and services in a diverse market and, where the different personal requirements and different laws and regulations of each market must be met, it may mean some product customisation is required. The adaptation of the website to prevent the sale of certain products to people that are not eligible may also be required.

Because the supplier of garden products will probably only be selling to customers in a small geographical area, if e-commerce is adopted by this organisation, then there will only be the requirement to meet the law of the country it is operating in. Sales to other countries can be banned, although it is unlikely that people in other countries would purchase bulky goods of low value anyway, due to high transportation costs.

(b) Organisations that benefit from e-commerce

The supplier of financial services, which is a large international organisation, is likely to see the Internet as being part of their overall strategy and e-commerce as a means of achieving faster growth and profit. It is more likely to benefit from e-commerce because:

♦ it has a wider potential market and an intangible product that can be explained efficiently on a website;

♦ the market is not hampered by the need to deliver large and bulky items;

♦ the targeted higher income groups and companies are more likely to have Internet access;

♦ the IT strategy, aligned with its overall business strategy, is directed to finding new sources of sales;

♦ sales could fall if e-commerce is not made available because customers can access competitors' Internet sites easily.

The garden centre has some persuasive reasons for not making a significant investment in e-commerce at this stage, such as:

♦ insufficient financial resources;

♦ size - each one is too small to warrant setting up and maintaining a costly web site;

♦ lack of resources in terms of skilled staff;

♦ lack of appropriate business objectives (profit or growth) to require e-commerce to be part of the business strategy;

♦ customers may not require it.

May 2001 Exam Answers

Answer 53 (Answer 1 of Exam Paper)

<table>
<tr><td rowspan="4">Tutorial note:
Required</td><td>(a)</td><td>A report to the Board of Directors of MB Ltd critically evaluating the proposed new system described in the scenario, with a recommendation.</td></tr>
<tr><td>(b)</td><td>Discuss the relationship between investigating MB's parts ordering system and its IT strategy.</td></tr>
<tr><td>(c)</td><td>Identify and discuss the information needs of MB's car managers and relate this to the Directors' information needs.</td></tr>
<tr><td></td><td></td></tr>
<tr><td rowspan="3">Not Required</td><td>(a)</td><td>A general discussion about implementing a new system.</td></tr>
<tr><td>(b)</td><td>An explanation of how you would investigate MB's stock ordering system.</td></tr>
<tr><td>(c)</td><td>A general discussion about information required by managers.</td></tr>
</table>

(a)

To: Board of Directors MB Ltd   9 February 20XX

Report: The Proposed Implementation of a New Component Ordering System

---

I have investigated the proposed implementation of a new component ordering system for MB Ltd and have identified the following potential benefits and problems it may create.

Potential Benefit

Back Up

The new system will be developed jointly with three much larger car manufacturers who will all have the same purchasing system. If MB suffers a systems failure it might be possible to use one of the other manufacturers systems. This will avoid the need to arrange alternative expensive back up facilities or the negative impact on production of a systems failure.

Reduced Costs

MB LTD and the three other manufacturers will share the system's development design and operational costs. The new system should also reduce the purchasing lead-time and improve production efficiency. This will also result in reduced operational costs for the company.

Supplier Support

Using the same purchasing system as other manufacturers will standardise MB's purchasing procedures. Suppliers who might otherwise not want to trade with other small manufacturers operating a non-standard system in the future will prefer this.

Potential Problems

If the implementation of the proposed system goes ahead, the following problems might occur:

♦ Dispute with other manufacturers

The costs of the proposed system will be shared by MB Ltd and the other larger manufacturers involved. In the future these other manufacturers might use their stronger bargaining power to impose a larger share of costs onto MB Ltd and obtain priority over the company in dealings with suppliers. This will create a conflict between the company and other manufacturers.

♦ Inaccessibility of information

The new system will store data in a dedicated database that will not allow access by car managers directly. The car managers are important systems users who will not be able to obtain information from the system.

♦ Duplication of data and input

The proposed system will be kept in a separate database from the rest of MB's data; this will result in the duplication of data stored and input. If MB developed its own purchasing system it could be integrated with the rest of its data.

♦ No consultation with car managers and other users

The new system has been developed without consulting the car managers and other users. It is unlikely it will satisfy their information needs and there is a high risk they will resist its introduction.

♦ Dependence on the large manufacturers

The new system will make MB Ltd more dependent on the large manufacturers and their suppliers. This could compromise the company's independence in the future.

Conclusion

The proposed new system has a number of serious potential problems as well as many benefits. The implementation of the system should only go ahead if some of these problems can be eliminated. The car managers and other users should be consulted before a decision is made.

Signed   A N Other
Management Accountant
MB Ltd

(b) An undertaking such as MB Ltd will have a corporate strategy that covers all activities. This will be formalised in a mission and statement of objectives. An IT strategy is a functional strategy that should relate the information technology function to the corporate strategy. The corporate strategy is set first then the IT strategy is developed so that it fits the corporate strategy.

An important feature of all organisational strategies is that they are compatible ie there is no conflict between them. The development of MB's component ordering system has been carried out independently and is not related to the rest of the undertaking. This has resulted in a number of weaknesses that can be attributed to its failure to fit the company's corporate strategy. These are:

♦ A structural weakness will occur as there is no facility provided to link the system with users outside the purchasing and accounts departments. This will result in communication barriers and cause a communication failure. This will weaken MB's value chain.

♦ Sub-optimisation will occur.

The interests of the purchasing department, which is a support activity, will be put before the interest of the line functions of the company. This might result in stock outs of components occurring causing a delay to production.

♦ The IT strategy is supplier driven.

The current strategy is customer driven, as the focus is high quality, high priced custom-built cars. The new system will compromise the quality of service currently provided and is likely to result in being perceived by customers as a reduction in service quality.

The IT strategy should be consistent with MB's corporate strategy and should contribute to achieving the company's corporate objectives. Where a conflict occurs one of the strategies will have to be revised. The investigation of the purchasing system should be conducted with the objective of providing the best system that serves the needs of all the users within the company, suppliers and customers at the same time. It is likely that the current system needs some updating and improvement.

(c)   The car manager's main information requirement will be operational. This will focus on:

♦ A short-term time horizon of one or two months.

♦ Detail relating to resources available and specific customer orders.

♦ Control information such as progress reports on each customer order.

The emphasis will be on gaining access to the system instantly and obtaining up to date information of a specific and predictable nature eg the estimated completion date of a specific customer order.

MB Ltd's Board of Directors' information requirements will be completely different from that of the car managers.

The directors will require information:

-     that relates to the long-term time horizon of up to five years. This will mean that much of the information will be in the form of forecasts.

-     that is about the whole of MB Ltd. The directors will require information about all of MB's functions, including finance, production and marketing. This means that their information requirement is much broader.

-     that provides feedback. A lot of information used by the directors will be in the form of performance reports such as budget variance reports indicating where targets have not been hit.

-     that is summarised and does not contain detail.

It can be seen from this that the information requirements of MB Ltd's Board of Directors is very different from that of the car managers.

Answer 54 (Answer 2 of Exam Paper)

Tutorial note:		
Required	(a)	A straightforward discussion about the benefits and disadvantages that might result from applying cost benefit analysis to assessing the value of information.
	(b)	Identify and justify types of information that will be required to evaluate the new system described in the scenario.
Not required	(a)	A description of how a cost benefit analysis assignment is conducted.
	(b)	A description of the information that will be stored on the company's website.

(a)   Cost benefit analysis focuses on financial costs and benefits.

Benefits

An organisation using cost benefit analysis to evaluate its information system could obtain the following benefits:

♦   Most organisations have economic objectives based upon profit or cost reduction. Cost benefit analysis will calculate the net financial benefit of information to the organisation. This will enable the contribution of information to achieving the organisation's financial objectives to be assessed.

♦   Monetary value is a measured yardstick against which actual performance of an information system can be measured. Cost benefit analysis is a useful tool for evaluating the operating performance of an information system and to determine whether it is worth producing information.

♦   Users easily understand financial costs and benefits. Cost benefit analysis can be used to explain and justify the production of information eg a particular report cannot be justified as the costs of producing exceed its value.

♦   Expenditure on systems that produce information will include the need to make substantial capital investment. Cost benefit analysis will evaluate financial risks and separate costs between capital and operational elements. This will enable an organisation to arrange for the finance of capital expenditure in advance.

♦   Cost benefit analysis can be used as an input into producing budgets for information systems.

The use of cost benefit analysis for evaluating information has many limitations including:

♦   Cost benefit analysis requires financial forecasts to be produced and is subject to forecasting error. Users of the analysis may place too much reliance on what it shows, assuming it to be accurate.

♦   Some costs will be indirect and difficult to relate to the production of information. An example of these is the time-based costs relating to an information system such as hardware maintenance costs. It will be impossible to make a precise charge of indirect costs to the production of specific information reports.

♦   Most benefits from producing information will be non-financial and will not be included in a cost benefit analysis exercise. The benefits of producing good quality information and information required by people that it was previously not possible to produce give many valuable benefits that cannot be quantified.

Examples of these are:

-   More effective planning and decision-making.

-   Increased employee morale because employees have instant access to accurate and up to date information.

♦   Some benefits might not be separately identifiable as the benefits of improvements to an information system. An example of this is when an organisation has invested in improving its customer accounting system and undertaken an advertising campaign at the same time.

♦   Hidden costs will not be identified. These are costs that cannot be financially valued and include eg resistance to changes to an information system by employees and increased security risks.

(b)

> **Tutorial note:**
>
> You should produce a well-structured answer covering five key issues.

The information required to evaluate the success of Eagle Inc's new web-based ordering system includes the following:

♦ Website upgrade

Eagle Inc currently has its own website so the provision of website facilities for customised ordering will require the existing site to be upgraded. The costs incurred in upgrading the website will have to be calculated. It will be useful to produce a budget estimating the hardware, software and other costs. These can then be compared with the benefits and actual costs. Other performance indicators such as user satisfaction and access times can also be used.

♦ Production Facilities

The proposed system will have an impact on Eagle Inc's production processes. The question states that these can be easily adapted to produce shoes for each customer's specific needs so there should be few practical problems. The cost of making any changes to the production system should be assessed together with efficiency levels before and after the changes. Internet ordering may improve production efficiency by using up any existing idle time or it might result in increased costs by lost production economies of scale, as Internet order units will be much smaller. Production costs might also increase if existing production technology has to be upgraded eg a CAD/CAM system has to be introduced.

♦ Marketing

The proposed system of website ordering will have marketing implications that must be evaluated. Potential customers must be informed of the service. Eagle Inc will need to undertake a marketing campaign including advertising to create customer awareness of the new system. Additional marketing costs should be monitored and feedback obtained on sales made via the website. Customer satisfaction of the new service should also be evaluated. This can be done by placing a customer questionnaire on Eagle's website and asking customers to make comments on the service received.

♦ Customer Account Profitability

The new system is a form of job costing. A method of measuring customer account profitability should be established to report on the profit or loss on each customer account and each customer order. This will provide an accurate measure of increased contribution earned by the new system.

♦ Systems Reliability

The reliability of the new system in terms of failure to deliver service should be considered after it is operational. An acceptable failure rate should be determined.

Answer 55 (Answer 3 of Exam Paper)

Tutorial note:			
Required	(a)	An explanation of Porter's Generic Strategies.	
	(b)	Describe how a holiday provider can add value to its business using the Internet.	
Not required	(a)	An explanation of Porter's five competitive forces model used to assess a business's competitive position.	
	(b)	A description of the value chain.	

(a)   Porter identified three strategies that he claimed could be used by organisations to gain competitive advantage.

 ♦   Cost leadership
 ♦   Differentiation
 ♦   Focus

Cost Leadership

This strategy requires an organisation to continuously strive to reduce its costs without compromising quality. The objective of cost leadership is for an organisation to have a lower cost structure than its competitors thereby gaining advantage. An organisation with the lowest cost structure has a number of advantages over its competitors.

 ♦   It will earn higher profits making it easier and cheaper to raise capital and borrow.
 ♦   A company's shareholder value will rise.
 ♦   It has the scope to reduce its selling prices offering customers more value for money.

Costs can be reduced many ways eg by improving efficiency, outsourcing, locating operations where costs are low and obtaining greater economies of scale.

Some organisations might find that using Internet can reduce its costs. The Internet can be used as a cheap means of communicating information to stakeholders and as a method of direct selling avoiding the need to invest in decentralised premises. Sales and distribution can be centralised keeping costs low. Cutting out retailers and wholesalers can also shorten the distribution chain.

This can also be extended to the value chain by using the Internet to provide an automated link to suppliers. An example of a cost saving this will achieve is reduced stockholding costs. The book trade is an example of a business sector that has achieved cost leadership using the Internet.

Differentiation

This involves giving an organisation or its products a uniqueness that will enable consumers to:

 ♦   Distinguish the business and its products from its competitors

 ♦   Have a preference for one product or the products of one organisation to those of competitors.

A differentiation strategy can be created by building a strong brand name or corporate identity or by providing a range of products and services that are better than those provided by competitors.

Providing facilities on Internet can contribute towards a differentiation strategy by:

♦ Promoting a brand name. Consumers may obtain information and make comments at a specific organisation's website eg Tesco's.

♦ Busy consumers using state of the art technology to obtain information and make purchases, eg a specific airline, can save time. Some consumers expect an Internet facility.

♦ Additional services can be provided that competitors do not provide eg personalised Internet shopping and fast delivery.

Focus

This strategy involves an organisation concentrating its resources on a niche market so that it doesn't spread its resources too thinly and can maximise the benefit it obtains from economies of scale. This allows the organisation to focus on a core activity or market so it can build a critical mass in which it has core competences. A focus strategy enables an organisation to provide an excellent service in a specialised market gaining an advantage over its competitors.

It is difficult to see how the Internet will contribute to a focus strategy.

(b) The following information could add value to a holiday company by using an Internet site.

♦ Additional information about each resort can be provided eg video images.

♦ Details about each holiday site can be described with graphical images eg entertainment, views, sports facilities and staff.

♦ Information can be kept up to date.

♦ Consumers can ask questions that can be replied to using Email. Experts can be used to reply to these questions.

♦ Information can be provided about special offers and other promotions together with holiday availability.

Other features that can be provided by a holiday provider's Internet site should include the following:

♦ Bookings can be accepted direct from customers. This will cut out travel agents and save the commission that would be paid to them.

♦ Bookings can be made for optional extras such as sightseeing tours, car hire and airport transfers.

♦ A customised holiday service could be provided matching facilities to the individual needs of a customer eg holidays coinciding with sporting events.

♦ Comparisons can be made with similar holidays provided by competitors. These can cover price and other inclusive facilities and 'value for money' comparisons.

Answer 56 (Answer 4 of Exam Paper)

Tutorial note:			
Required	(a)		An examination of the social and technological barriers to the planned introduction of SH Co's new system.
	(b)		Discuss the key contractual issues relating to the network supplied by ADO.
Not required	(a)		A general discussion about social and technological issues.
	(b)		A general discussion about entering into business contracts.

(a)   The following issues could prevent SH Co reaching its mobile telephone customer target of 500,000 by June 2002.

Social Issues

♦   Customer Acceptance

SH Co has forecast that 500,000 customers will want to use mobile phone services by June 2002. The actual number wanting the service may be less than this. This will result in an adverse volume variance.

♦   Security

The new telephone banking system must guarantee to be 100% secure to protect customer's assets and the privacy of information about them. A failure in the system's security could result in SH Co receiving bad publicity, which would destroy the credibility of the system.

♦   Lack of Physical Evidence of Transactions.

Transactions carried out using the mobile phone system will not have any documentary evidence. No proof of a transaction will exist so disputes between a customer and the bank will be difficult to resolve. This problem could deter customers from using the system.

♦   SH Co plans to close one half of its branches as a result of introducing its mobile phone banking service. 1.6 million customers are not expected to use the service; these customers will oppose the closure of the branches and see the move as a reduction in the personal service offered by SH Co. The mobile phone service will not provide customers that use it with a complete range of banking services, eg cash withdrawals and deposits. The branch closure programme is likely to adversely affect the bank and this has not been considered in the forecast, eg loss of customers.

Technological Issues

♦   Cost

The new system will be expensive to install and operate. Currently the mobile phones to be used are expensive so initial costs will be high. Unit costs may later fall due to greater economies of scale if a lot of customers use the system. Benefits must be quantified and be offset against the costs. A detailed cost/benefit analysis should be undertaken by SH Co.

♦   Insufficient Supply of Hardware Units

Current production levels of mobile phone units are only 15,000 a month. If this cannot be increased only 180,000 units will be available by June 2002 giving an expected shortfall of 320,000 units. To meet the target for new customers, production output will have to be substantially increased.

♦ Systems Reliability

New technological systems often suffer from unreliability when first introduced. The new system's credibility will be destroyed if reliability problems occur. This will stop many would be customers using the system.

♦ Network Coverage

The preferred system provided by ADO only covers 85% of the country. This is not sufficient for SH Co to provide a good service to its customers. A telephone banking service should cover 100% of the country's landmass.

♦ Telephone Standards

The country SH Co currently operates in has a national Country Specific Security Standard and Wireless application Protocol. A global standard application has not yet been developed so this will restrict the service to SH Co's country of residency.

A risk in the future is that when a global standard is introduced it might not be compatible with the country's current standard.

(b)   The following issues should be considered by SH Co when negotiating a contract with ADO:

♦ Cost

The contract price should be discussed during negotiations. The contract's duration will be three years so the cost over this period must be considered. The negotiations should consider exactly what is to be provided at what cost and cover terms for payment and penalties for poor quality service.

♦ Network Coverage

ADO's current coverage of the country is 85%. The precise areas of coverage will need to be discussed together with ADO's plans to increase coverage to match its competitor's service. The standard of service provision should also be considered.

♦ Quality Control

Measures to be taken to maintain quality control of the service should be considered together with responsibility for maintaining quality control. Access to ADO's system by SH Co's internal auditors will be a very important issue as will be the provision of a back up service should ADO's system fail or be destroyed. These issues must be discussed with ADO.

♦ The credibility of ADO as a supplier

The contract will be for three years duration. Research should be carried out to obtain information that can be discussed with ADO during negotiating a contract. Financial information must be obtained eg copies of past accounts and ADO's trade reputation should be established. Details of the users of ADO's mobile phone systems should be obtained so that they can be contacted.

♦ Benchmark for service provision

SH Co should consider other suppliers systems and find out what they can offer and at what price. The systems and terms being offered by ADO can then be compared with other suppliers systems.

Answer 57 (Answer 5 of Exam Paper)

Tutorial note:			
Required	(a)		Explain the steps involved in information processing and discuss the benefits of using human beings to process information over the use of computers.
	(b)		Compare the problems of finance directors and junior management accountants relating to the processing of information.
Not required	(a)		A description of manually operated information systems.
	(b)		A discussion about the disadvantages of using people to process information.

(a)   Information processing has four basic stages:

- ♦   Input
- ♦   Process
- ♦   Output
- ♦   Action

In relation to human beings this process can briefly be described a follows:

- ♦   Input

Data is collected by human beings in various formats eg visual and audible or input into a person's mind.

- ♦   Process

The data is then processed mentally by a person and stored in his or her memory. Data entered can be manipulated using other data that has already been memorised.

- ♦   Output

Information is then produced and given meaning. Output can be represented many ways eg in a written report, using symbols or oral communication.

- ♦   Action

Information is then acted upon.

Using human beings to process information has many advantages, including the following:

- ♦   Spontaneity

Human beings do not have to be programmed in advance to do something. Computers can only process information that they have been programmed for. The need for information using computers has to be determined in advance. Human beings can think and act spontaneously and deal with ad hoc situations.

- ♦   Mobility

Human beings have the natural ability to go anywhere, thinking and taking action wherever they are. A computer does not have such a facility. Humans are mobile information processors.

- ♦   Independent of a power supply

Human beings are not dependent upon a power supply to do work.

♦   Ability to conceptualise

Human beings are able to apply concepts when processing information. They can see a much broader picture of events than a computer can establish and think of new ideas. An example of this is in design work.

Human designs can be original and unique. Computer designs are standardised and functional.

♦   Ability to rationalise

Human beings can apply rational judgement to input and information. They can work out solutions when data is missing and can identify errors because information 'doesn't look right' or 'this can't be right'. Computers do not have the ability to do this.

(b)   The finance director and a junior management accountant work at different levels in the organisation. The finance director is a member of a company's top management team working at a strategic level; a junior management accountant is an operational manager.

A finance director will be using information produced from a multitude of sources both internal and external. He or she will rely a lot of other people to do the routine processing. Information used by the FD will be both quantitative and qualitative. A junior management accountant will be using information from a few sources and the work will be of a routine nature. This person's work will be less interesting so errors might be made through boredom or through familiarity with a routine. The financial director is more likely to be vigilant in detecting errors.

The financial director is more likely to make errors of omission, as it will be difficult to know if information is complete as the information produced is of a more subjective nature. The junior management accounts work is of a more precise nature and information omitted will be quickly identified.

The financial director is more likely to suffer from overwork and stress at certain times. This is because the nature of his or her duties will result in them dealing with many different reports at the same time. He or she is more likely to confuse information at times resulting in errors. The junior management accountant has a much narrower range of duties and is likely to be only working on one or two reports at a time so is less likely to make this type of error.

November 2001 Exam Answers

Answer 58 (Answer 1 of Exam Paper)

> **Tutorial note:**
>
> | Required | (a) | (i) | Recommend and justify the use of performance indicators relating to the Critical Success Factors of CLB. |
> |---|---|---|---|
> | | | (ii) | Explain the information system required to provide feedback on the achievement of the PIs described in your answer to a(i). |
> | | (b) | | Recommend and justify a structured decision making procedure to update CLB's information system in order to solve the problem of falling brand awareness of its products. |
> | | (c) | | Describe and evaluate an appropriate information system for communicating information between CLB's factories and its centralised warehouse. |
> | **Not required** | (a) | (i) | A description of Critical Success Factors. |
> | | | (ii) | A general description of an Information System |
> | | (b) | | A general description of the decision making process. |
> | | (c) | | A discussion of various methods of communication used in organisations. |
>
> You must focus your answer on the three Critical Success Factors given in the scenario. At least two PIs per CSF need to be described.

(a)   (i)   **CSF – Maintaining a Gross Profit margin at 40% of sales**

Performance Indicators

Total Gross Profit to Total Sales Ratio

This should be calculated periodically based upon data from CLB's financial statements.

Comparisons can be made with:

- the target at 40%

- previous periods gross profit, this will allow the trend in gross profit margins within the company to be analysed.

- the gross profit margins of competitors to act as a benchmark.

Gross Profit to Sales ratio per product line

The gross profit margin for each of CLB's product lines should be measured. This will enable the performance of each product line to be independently analysed; poor performing and high performing product lines can be identified so that decisions can be made relating to investing resources.

CSF – Improving Customer Satisfaction

Performance Indicators

Number of Returns Per Number of Goods Sold

Customers return goods to CLB for a reason. Measuring the number of goods returned and relating it to the number of goods sold during a period eg each month will show trends. For example, if this ratio is increasing, customer dissatisfaction might also be increasing. The reasons for returning goods should be recorded and analysed.

Customer Survey – Percentage of Satisfied Customers

Customers can be asked how satisfied they are with CLB's products and service by completing a questionnaire or by telephone. The results of this survey can be analysed and monitored over a period of time. The results will indicate whether customer satisfaction is increasing or decreasing.

Tutorial note:

Many other PIs could be given to answer this question, eg number of customer complaints.

Performance Indicators

Number of day's production in raw material stock

This is a commonly used performance indicator for evaluating stock used for analysing CLB's working capital cycle. The most benefit can be obtained by calculating this for each of CLB's product lines. The results can be compared with a target, trends analysed and weaknesses identified ie products with a high number of days stock of raw material.

Raw material stock as a percentage of cost of sales

This performance indicator can be calculated monthly to show trends. An increase will draw CLBs management's attention so that the cause can be investigated. To achieve this CSF these PIs will need to be closely monitored. Each survey could contact all of CLB's customers or just a sample depending upon the situation. Customer satisfaction can then be measured and compared with a standard.

Tutorial note:

The best way to answer this part of the question is to follow the pattern established in part (i).

(ii)   **CSF – Maintaining a gross profit margin of 40% of sales**

Performance Indicator

Total Gross Profit to Total Sales Ratio

The information required to calculate this PI will be provided by CLB's financial accounting system. A cut-off point to each period must be specified eg the end of each calendar month. The company's cost of sales, sales and gross profit must be accurately recorded. The actual gross profit margin should be compared with the 40% target.

Gross profit to sales ratio per product line

The basic requirement to provide information to calculate this PI is to establish each product line as a profit centre. The sales price for each product must be recorded together with the production cost. This should be based upon actual cost. The gross profit margin can then be calculated for each product and compared with a standard margin; variances will then be calculated and reported.

CSF – Improving customer satisfaction

Performance Indicators

Number of returns per number of goods sold

The information system to report on this PI will require each sales return to be recorded with reasons why. CLB's sales department should already record sales orders. This ratio can then be calculated on a periodic basis eg monthly. A report should be produced analysing returns by reason so that those attributable to customer complaints can be identified.

Customer Survey – Percentage of Satisfied Customers

To establish this PI some customer research will need to be undertaken. CLB's information system should record details of each customer eg name, address and telephone number.

Customers will then need to be contacted using questionnaires or by telephone and asked to comment on the degree of satisfaction with CLB's products and service. This should be done annually so that changes can be monitored. Each survey could contact all of CLB's customers or just a sample depending upon the situation. A measure of customer satisfaction can then be measured and compared with a standard.

CSF – Minimising raw material inventory cost

Performance Indicators

The information required to calculate this PI will be obtained from CLB's raw material stock control system and its production records. The company's stock and production records must be accurate and up to date. The cost of raw materials consumed by production during each period will be calculated and compared with the value of closing raw material stock at each period and expressed in days. This PI should be calculated for each stock item.

Raw material stock as a percentage of cost of sales

The information to calculate this ratio will be obtained from CLB's management accounting system. The cost of producing each product line should be recorded and broken down into direct material cost, direct labour cost and production overhead. The recording of this information accurately is very important.

Tutorial note:

The examiner gives the starting point for this answer in the scenario – a decision trigger.

The directors of CLB could use the following structured decision making procedure to solve the problem of falling brand awareness.

(1)   Decision Trigger

The first stage of the process is to identify the need to make a decision. The fall in brand awareness has triggered the decision making process as it has been identified as a problem. CLB's breakeven point is $600 million p.a. current turnover is $650 million p.a. This gives a low margin of safety of $50 million. The company also has adverse budgeted sales variances and is losing ground against its competitors. Urgent remedial action is needed.

(2)   Collect Information

The next stage in the decision making process is to collect relevant, accurate and up to date information. The directors are concerned about the problem but the information they have is limited, it is based upon historic financial accounts and a trade journal. The company needs to conduct market research to establish brand awareness amongst customers and people in the market who are not customers (these may be potential customers).

The market research survey needs to ask a series of questions relating to income, spending and brand awareness now and in the future. Questionnaires, telephone interviews and other interview methods should be used to collect information.

(3)   Analysis of Information

The information collected during the previous stage will now be processed and classified using various techniques. Much of the work done at this stage can be done by a computerised system. CLB's existing information system will have to be updated or the work could be outsourced to an organisation which already has the software needed. Decision Support Software should be used to identify and use additional information such as the impact of findings on other parts of CLB's business eg employee morale. Future trends can be forecast.

(4)   Evaluation of Results

During this stage the various courses of action that can be taken will be identified and each one evaluated. Decision making criteria for evaluating each of the options needs to be established such as cost/benefit analysis and risk evaluation. The information system used to do this must have the information and software capability. The directors must consider the use of a centralised system of stock control as an option despite the objections from the HR and IT directors. The directors at this stage should keep an open mind.

(5)   Decide on the optimal course of action.

The directors of CLB then decide upon the best course of action. It is important that the directors agree on the action to be taken and take into account all of the relevant information including financial and non-financial. The action decided upon will result in changes to the company's existing system.

(6)   Implementation

The action decided upon must now be implemented. It is important that this is carefully planned and will involve:

♦   Consulting with and keeping informed employees affected by the changes.

♦   Ensuring all staff involved are properly trained.

♦   Ensuring that any new components are tested to ensure reliability.

♦   Date transferred to the new system is accurate.

♦   Some form of backup is available during the changeover period eg the new system is run in parallel with the existing system.

(7)   Review

After implementation the new system should be monitored closely to ensure that no unforeseen problems arise and that it is achieving expected levels of performance.

(c)   Recommended Information System

A central database should be installed at CLB's central warehouse. This should initially process information relating to raw materials, stock, production and finished goods for the ten factories and the central warehouse. Data communication links will have to be established between each of CLB's factories and the central warehouse. It is likely that existing telephone lines can be utilised for this.

Data can be entered interactively at each factory and the central warehouse providing a real time information system.

This system can be developed at a later stage to provide links between the factories.

Benefits

The benefit of a centralised database system to CLB and its managers and employees will be:

♦ Up to date information on the stock of raw materials, production and finished goods will be available to staff when required. This will improve decision-making and result in better stock control.

♦ A view of the whole of CLB's business position will be available, as this system will integrate the activities. This will result in more effective planning.

♦ Improved stock control can result in lower stock levels being held with lower stock holding costs and less materials wastage through less risk of obsolete raw material stock.

♦ Sales staff will have more accurate and up to date information to give customers. Customer satisfaction should improve and sales increase.

♦ Reduced lead-time for customers waiting for finished goods.

♦ Less time will be spent by staff trying to obtain reports they want. Various analytical reports will be available on demand based on individual manager's needs. Greater user satisfaction should result.

Disadvantages

The main disadvantages of the recommended system are:

♦ Local production managers will see the centralised system as a transfer of some of their power so some resistance is likely.

♦ The system is opposed by CLB's HR and IT Directors who may do as much as they can to ensure it is not successful

♦ There is a risk of the centralised system suffering the effects of a disaster eg a fire at CLB's central warehouse. An expensive backup provision will be required to avoid CLB losing its information systems facility.

♦ A communication link between one of CLB's factories and the central warehouse might fail cutting off that factory from the centralised system, denying it access.

Answer 59 (Answer 2 of Exam Paper)

Tutorial note:		
Required	(a)	Identify and explain the weaknesses in the information system of MSV as described in the scenario.
	(b)	Identify and justify the reasons why introducing a new information system in MSV will be difficult.
Not required	(a)	Identifying any strengths in MSV's information system.
	(b)	A general discussion about introducing or implementing a new system and its problems.
The best way to structure your answer is to classify the weaknesses into two groups – external and internal.		

(a)

External Information

MSV Company's current information system provides very little information to its Board of Directors about the external environment. The main external deficiencies are:

♦ No information is provided about the company's competitors. No information is available relating to who they are, what their strengths and weaknesses are and the threat they pose. This means that MSV's Board of Directors must make decisions without knowledge of competitors eg what their reaction will be. MSV will not know what its competitive position is.

♦ Information required for benchmarking is not available. This will make setting performance targets difficult and limit the value of performance evaluation as an input to the decision making process of MSV.

♦ No long-term information is available so no long-term forecasts are produced. The only external forecast is for the next five years sales.

This will reduce the reliability of decisions made by the Board of Directors.

♦ No information is available about changes occurring to global climates and weather patterns. These are changing, which affects the growth rate of trees. This will make using past information on tree growth rates obsolete.

♦ No information is available about substitutes for timber. Technology changes will result in new and possible cheaper substitutes becoming available in the future. This will reduce the reliability of information used for decision-making eg sales forecasts.

♦ No scientific information is available. Trees are affected by disease, so any new scientific developments relating to trees might have an impact on MSV. The Board of Directors will need information on such developments to assess scientific developments when making decisions.

Internal Information

The following internal deficiencies occur in MSV's current information system.

♦ Inaccuracies caused by the destruction of records 45 years ago.

After the fire that occurred forty-five years ago MSV's data was lost and was not recovered. This resulted in errors and omissions occurring which have been carried down the years and still exist in the current system. Decisions relating to trees that are more than forty-five years old will not be reliable.

♦ No attempt has been made by MSV to introduce an integrated system. Each of the forecasting offices keeps its own set of records. This will result in duplication of work and make it difficult to obtain co-ordinated reports. This will waste a lot of MSV's directors' time.

(b)

Before a new information system is introduced by MSV Company, the following difficulties will have to be overcome:

♦ MSV is an old business and has a mature information system. It will probably have a traditional culture the existing information system has developed on a piecemeal basis over the years. This means that there will be a high risk of resistance to introducing a new information system by MSV Company's managers and employees. This resistance will have to be eliminated beforehand.

♦ Lack of External Information

MSV has very little information about its external environment. This information will need to be collected and entered into a new system to provide maximum benefits. This will take time and require a lot of resources.

♦ No Information Strategy

The current system's inaccuracies caused by the fire forty-five years should be put right before a new system is introduced otherwise the new system will have errors at take on and will still provide inaccurate information.

♦ Rapidly changing environment

MSV's external environment is changing rapidly. This will make predicting future needs difficult.

♦ Many of the benefits of the new system will be qualitative and will be difficult to quantify in financial values eg improved management decision-making.

Answer 60 (Answer 3 of Exam Paper)

Tutorial note:		
Required	(a)	A critical evaluation of Intelligent Agents relating to data mining.
	(b)	A discussion about the government of Xanadu benefits and limitations of collecting data using roadside scanners to obtain data on vehicle movements.
Not required	(a)	A detailed description of Intelligent Agents and data mining.
	(b)	A discussion about using roadside scanners to collect road tolls.

(a) An Intelligent Agent is a computer program that will search for, locate and analyse specific data stored in a database. When the task specified is complete or additional information is required the program reports back to the use.

Data mining is the analysis of data within a database to identify relationships and patterns amongst the data.

Within the context of data mining the use of Intelligent Agents has the following benefits:

Speed

IA's can review vast quantities of data very quickly. This saves user time and ensures results can be produced while the data is still current.

Automatic Operation

IA programs once set up need very little operator intervention unless additional information is required. This allows operators and users to get on with other work; no operator is needed to link the program to data mining.

Review of Additional Data

Continuous operation of IA's is possible so that additional data can be reviewed as it is entered. New relationships between data will be immediately identified.

Identification of New Trends and Relationships

An IA might identify a trend or relationship between events that was previously unknown.

Limitations relating to the use of Intelligent Agents

♦ High Cost

The development and installation costs of the system will be high the benefits will be relatively greater for larger organisations with large amounts of data in their databases.

♦   Unreliability of Data

An IA will only be as good as the data it reviews. Inaccuracies in data stored will result in inaccurate reports.

♦   Over Reliance on Results

Reports will be based upon the data stored and instructions given. Users will rely on relationships identified and reports provided and will be unlikely to look at the data themselves. Some relationships will be missed by the IA and will never be identified because users rely solely on the IA to find them.

♦   The IA will relate some data because two trends have the same cause, but the events they relate to are unrelated.

(b)   The strategic benefits to the government of Xanadu obtained from collecting data about vehicle movements includes:

♦   Changes to traffic patterns can be monitored and related to causes, eg the impact of the climate on need usage can be assessed.

This will require the data recorded to be related to other data.

♦   Long-term trends in usage can be identified and extrapolated. This can be used for planning future road networks for the country.

♦   The motor vehicles of people driving to attend meetings and concerts will be recorded; this might make controlling major events easier.

♦   Crime Detection

Information about vehicle movements can be given to Xanadu's police force. This will make police work in the detection of crime easier. The movement of vehicles will be recorded so that when a crime is reported the police can see what vehicles were in the vicinity at the time and trace their owners

Collecting information on vehicle movements will also have a number of limitations including:

♦   Using the data to collect tolls for road usage will result in many vehicle drivers using alternative routes to avoid paying tolls.

♦   The drivers of vehicles will not be recorded so disputes will arise with legal implications for the government eg a vehicle owner who was not in the car might dispute any liability.

♦   The system will not directly provide information on the cause of changes to traffic patterns eg sudden increases in traffic levels.

♦   Trends can suddenly change in the future. The system will not predict future changes to traffic pattern trends.

♦   The system will not record the number of people in each vehicle so actual attendances at meetings will not be recorded. The system also excludes people travelling around the country using other methods of transport.

♦   The system will not be 100% accurate so disputes may arise over errors, again this will cause legal problems. Eg if a wrong vehicle is recorded and the owner can prove that the vehicle was elsewhere at the time.

Tutorial note:

Part (b) is a very subjective question.

Points given in your answer must be justified.

Answer 61 (Answer 4 of Exam Paper)

Tutorial note:			
Required	(a)		Comment on the strengths and weaknesses of ZX's current system explaining where using an Intranet will eliminate any problems.
	(b)		Identify and explain any reservations you would have about using an Extranet to share information between pharmaceutical companies.
Not required	(a)		An explanation of how an Intranet works.
	(b)		A general discussion about the use of Extranets.

(a)   An Intranet will allow each department and group of employees within ZX to establish its own database and make each of these and any other files accessible to all staff using the intranet.

An evaluation of ZX's current system identifies the following strengths and weaknesses.

Strengths

The current system has been designed to ensure data is accurate and complete so users can rely upon it.

Weaknesses

◆   The current system uses hard copy as the main method of producing reports, which are then transmitted from one location to another. This results in delays and documents becoming lost and mislaid. The use of an Intranet will allow reports and other information to be transmitted electronically. This will save time and if a report is lost a copy can immediately be retrieved by the user.

◆   The current system does not run tasks in parallel even though a facility exists. An Intranet will allow groups of employees to carry out work simultaneously to other groups, each group being able to obtain information from others this will reduce the time it takes to complete new research projects.

◆   There are currently no integration facilities so that without asking for and receiving printed reports one group is not able to obtain information from others. As work is carried out in four different locations logistic problems occur. The use of an Intranet will overcome these logistic problems.

◆   In ZX's current system there doesn't appear to be a facility for the central manager to interrogate local information systems. He or she must wait for reports to be received from employee groups. An Intranet will allow the central manager to obtain reports when required.

Overall the use of an Intranet could reduce the time taken to complete R & D projects will benefit both the company and its customers.

(b)   Using an Extranet to share information between different pharmaceutical companies has the following limitations:

◆   Confidentiality

The competitive edge of pharmaceutical companies is dependant on constantly developing new products, which result form substantial investment in research and development. Sharing information via an Extranet may enable competitors to obtain confidential information, such as new product development.

♦ Security

Linking a company's system to an Extranet creates security risks from imparting errors and viruses from other systems. Measures will have to be taken to protect a system against such risks but none of these will be completely secure.

♦ Incompatibility

It is unlikely that all systems linked to the Extranet will be compatible. This will make exchanging information difficult. Any information that is exchanged will be unreliable

♦ Lack of Trust

For the exchange of information to benefit participating organisations, trust between them must exist. It is unlikely that companies competing on the same market will trust each other. This will create a communications barrier between the companies.

Answer 62 (Answer 5 of Exam Paper)

Tutorial note:		
Required	(a)	Explain the stages involved in developing and implementing an Intranet banking system.
	(b)	Discuss the benefits and potential problems that might result from SPV outsourcing he writing and maintenance of its Intranet banking web site.
Not required	(a)	An explanation of the stages of a system's analysis and design project.
	(b)	A textbook learnt list of the advantages and disadvantages that result from outsourcing.
A good answer should follow a structured format.		

(a)   SPV should adopt a structured approach to develop and implement an upgraded Internet banking system. This should be as follows:

♦ Define SPV's corporate strategy.

A new Internet banking system will require the allocation of substantial resources and its success or failure will affect the whole business. It is important that the Internet banking system fits in with the overall corporate objectives of SPV.

♦ Set clear objectives for the Internet banking system. In order for the project to be successful it will need to be controlled during its development and implementation and when it is operational.

The development project should also be carefully planned using various techniques such as PERT Critical Path Analysis and cost scheduling.

♦ The external environment of SPV relating to Internet banking will need to be analysed. Research will need to be undertaken to establish particularly the likelihood of customer acceptance, technological developments and competitor's systems. This will reduce the risk of the new system becoming obsolete or not being accepted by customers.

♦ Internal Analysis of SP's current system. To introduce a new or upgraded system the existing system and resources available need to be carefully analysed to identify current strengths and weaknesses. An upgrade should be based on exploiting current strength and eliminating current weaknesses. People involved in SPV's current system especially its users need to be consulted during and before this stage.

♦ The options available to SPV should be identified and evaluated using various criteria such as cost benefit analysis and risk analysis. The solutions offered by various suppliers should be compared and assessed. The system that best achieves the objectives of SPV is then selected. The banking services to be provided by Internet should be determined at this stage.

♦ System's Specification

A formal system's specification should be produced; this should specify the exact requirements of SPV for its Internet banking.

♦ Implementation

The new system should now be introduced. This stage will be complex as Internet banking is a new service to be provided by SPV. The service will have to be marketed so customers are aware of it. Information will have to be provided on how to use it. Great care must be taken to avoid any problems. It might be appropriate to introduce the new system on a pilot basis in one part of the country to test its reliability.

♦ Review

After its introduction the Internet banking system should be monitored closely to ensure it is reliable, secure and kept up to date.

(b)   SPV could obtain the following benefits form outsourcing the writing and maintaining of its Internet banking web site.

♦ Reduced Costs

It is likely that a considerable cost saving will be achieved, as SPV will not have to recruit and train its own employees. This will avoid learning curve costs.

♦ Expediency

The outsource supplier should already have employees with considerable expertise in setting up web sites and maintaining them. SPV will not have to invest resources in trying to find and recruit experts.

♦ Increased Efficiency

SPV will not have to worry about finding employees other work to do when writing the new system is finished. The outsourcer will only be paid for work done.

There are a number of problems or disadvantages that could arise if these tasks are outsourced by SPV including:

♦ SPV will have no direct quality control over work done by the supplier. Measures must be taken to set and maintain standards of accuracy and reliability.

♦ Inflexibility

The outsource agreement will only cover work specified by contract, normally for a fixed period. It could be difficult for SPV to later change any terms of the contract, as there will be legal implications.

♦ Once the web site is set up and operational SPV will be more dependent on the outsource supplier, this will increase the suppliers bargaining power over the bank.

♦ There is a risk that the supplier may go bankrupt. This will leave SPV with no one to maintain its web site and little knowledge of it. The business will have to take on the responsibility for the site itself.

♦ A very serious concern is the security of the SPV's web site. SPV is a bank and the web site will be used for Internet banking the site must be guaranteed to be one hundred per cent secure from fraud and information must be held with absolute confidentiality. Using an external supplier could increase the risk to SPV's security unless exceptional measures can be taken and guaranteed by a supplier. Security measures must also be operated and checked by SPV and its auditors.

May 2002 Exam Answers

Answer 63 (Answer 1 of Exam Paper)

Tutorial note:

In part (a) there are three options to discuss but all of them require an understanding of the advantages and disadvantages of outsourcing.

Part (b) - the Examiner has been very explicit in the requirements - even outlining the framework to use. You should have been prepared for a question on the grid - it tends to come up quite regularly.

There are two parts to (c); the first is a question on communication channels - a different slant to this popular subject. The second part is a tricky question where you are asked to look at the problems with the proposed Internet site. It is very tempting to give an opinion based on the current scenario and not take into account how quickly the movement towards Internet use in the UK has escalated over the past five years.

(a)   There are three alternative development methods currently under consideration for updating the database and implementing the on-line system. These include:

   1   **Extending the existing outsourcing arrangement**

         The main reason for continuing to use an outsourcing arrangement is that LC does not seem to have the staff, management time or expertise to organise their substantial data processing requirements. The service provided by DD so far has helped LC to avoid the shortage of IT staff and keep up with technological changes.

         The main difficulty with outsourcing from LC's point of view is the lack of control over the system, which will be exacerbated if the contract is extended.

         The scenario does not give any information about whether DD has the necessary resources and expertise to carry out the new work. They might find the transfer too complicated or difficult to actually perform in the time allowed (only 24 weeks), especially considering the untrained users who will be accessing the database.

   2   **Establishing a new IT department in LC**

         There are two options here. The first is that LC can keep the current arrangement with DD for maintenance and service and set up a new department in LC to transfer the database and write the software. This would cause problems because it would mean that effective interfaces between the two systems would also be required. The alternative is to alter the entire IT provision within LC and provide access and maintenance in-house.

         There would be problems with the in-house solution. Once a company has handed over its computing to an outsourcing firm, it is locked into the contract and the decision might be very difficult to reverse. Taking back control will involve a long and complicated changeover process. The effort and expense that LC would have to incur to rebuild its own computing function and expertise would be enormous and may be a barrier to implementation of the new system.

   3   **Employing PP (another government agency, where a similar system is already in place) to establish the database, which DD would maintain in-house.**

         This solution would make sense if DD and LC were unable to establish the database; especially as PP have experience of a similar system. However, it would mean another contract having to be drawn up and managed, with additional reliance on outsourcing companies.

Conclusion

Examination tip: You must justify your choice of strategy. However, this does not mean that there is a correct strategy. The Examiner will be looking at the arguments for and against the alternatives.

The new system will mean a shift in the core activity of LC to one of providing and maintaining the database and the choice made will effectively lock it into outsourcing or in-house provision for many years. The best option would be in-house provision. However, without experienced staff **and** the time constraint of 24 weeks, outsourcing the development with a company that has experienced staff already available to work on the new system seems the least-risk option. The choice between PP and DD would depend on DD's ability to cope with the development work within the time scale. Management at LC have found that DD tends to make changes according to its own timetables rather than meeting specific requests.

(b)   We can use McFarlan's Application Portfolio Theory to evaluate the situation at LC.

Examination tip: There is no need to draw the grid but it can often help to remind you of the strategic impact associated with each segment.

Strategic impact of

	Low	future systems	High

Low **Strategic impact of current systems** **High**	<u>Support</u> Applications which improve management and performance but are not critical to the business	<u>Turnaround (high potential)</u> Applications which may be of future strategic importance
	<u>Factory</u> Applications which are critical to sustaining existing business	<u>Strategic</u> Applications which are critical for future success

Examination tip: You need to illustrate your arguments with examples from the scenario

Support - IT has a support role for a business where information systems have little relevance to a firm's existing or future success and require below average investment and little management attention. This is obviously not the case at LC - the current systems are critical to the business.

Factory - this role means that existing IT applications are important but future IT developments are not anticipated to be relevant. At LC, the existing systems are important, especially to a large proportion of their callers who have no access to the Internet, are not computer-literate - and perhaps have no intention of being - and who may not understand English. However, management have decided that Internet access is the way forward and that information will have a high impact on future systems.

Turnaround - this role exists where current IT is not important, but future developments are likely to have a significant impact. In this case, IT is becoming more important. Its role and profile in the organisation is being enhanced and the organisation is preparing itself for change. Here again, this does not totally fit the situation at LC. At present, staff must access the database system to provide the relevant information to the callers. This makes the strategic impact of their current system very important. However, recent developments in communications technology have made it possible for information held on the LC database to be made available over the Internet. 45% of callers to LC already have access to the Internet, and it is generally increasing over time. The current system will be developed to give LC an Internet site so that citizens of Xanadu can access the database. There will be a shift in LC's core activity to one of providing and maintaining the database.

Strategic - this role exists where current and future developments are at the heart of the company's future success. This describes the situation at LC - the current strategic impact of IT is high - systems are used to store, collate and provide information for the call centre employees. LC plans to develop a significantly enhanced system that allows access to the whole LC database via the Internet. This means IT has a very important future role.

(c) (i) To be considered an appropriate communication channel, the database and Internet site must equal or improve on the current method of providing the information and should encourage the dissemination of information.

As with any new technology, there will be some people in Xanadu that take to the new system very well, while others will feel disappointment to have lost the call centre with helpful staff to give them the information they want. Only 45% of current callers have access to the Internet, and the majority of the citizens are not computer literate and would find using any database very difficult - this leaves them without the means to access the information easily. The citizens must be aware of the change and informed about the Web site. An advertising campaign plus reminders and re-direction from the current call centre staff should guide the users to the site.

Once at the site, the format must be user-friendly with translation from one language or terminology to another as part of the design of the site because only 90% of the callers have a basic qualification in English and Web browsers cater mainly for English-speaking people. Depending on the type of link to the Internet that people have, the speed of access and download time might be much slower than the telephone call.

We are not told about the cost of the Internet in Xanadu and how it compares with the telephone, but 60% of the current callers are manual workers and if they find the cost higher using the Internet, it may be a barrier to accessing the information.

At the present time, the Internet may not be the best method of communication, because of the access and computer literacy problems. However, situations change and LC must provide for the users of the future.

(c) (ii) Design and implementation issues include the following:

- How open is the system? - A combination of the numbers of current users having access to the Internet, the lack of user education and experience in computing, English and using a database via the Internet, with some resistance to change means that the usefulness of the website is limited and fewer people may be accessing the Internet. The reason for implementing the website will have to be explained clearly, so that users can learn to accept it.

- Communication between the system and its users - this includes the design of the input, dialogue and output. Serious thought must be given to the input of the data onto the database - the volume, range and seasonality, as well as its accuracy, security and completeness. Hackers could change this data eg, changing competitors' details unfavourably, which could reflect very badly on LC. Also, the threat posed by a viral attack is considerable, given the mobility between computerised systems and the sharing of resources and data. The dialogue and output design needs to take into account the age distribution of users - older users may be able to verbally communicate their information requirements but may not have the necessary computer skills to search a database, whereas young users may not know what information they require, but will quite happily search using the computer to initiate a search. It may be that none of the age ranges will be ideally suited to this form of communication. Graphics to dispel technofear must be kept fairly simple because the time taken to download will cause concern over the cost for some users and cause impatience and frustration in others.

- To what extent does the methodology facilitate participation? - It may be difficult to find a representative sample of users to test the site on and the lack of input may mean that the site is not designed with the majority of users in mind. The users' information requirements and potential requirements should determine the type of data collected and the way it is presented.

207

♦ Does it generate alternative solutions? - The website must be easy to use, with on-line help to navigate through the pages to find the information required. The alternative is to provide additional telephone support.

Answer 64 (Answer 2 of Exam Paper)

Tutorial note:

The Internet is a popular topic in both the academic and the business worlds. You can identify with the senior partners in this scenario and feel their frustration at the lack of standard software and systems in the different locations and the communication difficulties identified while working from more than one office.

Part (b) is a little vague in its requirements because, apart from them finding difficulties with the different computer systems, we are not given much information about the likely reactions of the staff towards a new system being implemented. The Examiner will expect a variety of answers to this part of the question.

(a) The deficiencies of the XYZ system, highlighted by knowledge of the Internet, include the following:

♦ E-mail - the Internet has become the most important e-mail system in the world because it connects so many people worldwide. It is a very fast method of communication with messages being sent and received within seconds, although they can be stored and opened to suit the recipient. Attachments such as documents, photos, and plans can also be sent with the message. The cost of e-mail and other Internet connections tend to be lower than the equivalent voice, postal or overnight delivery.

The communication channels available at XYZ are disappointing in comparison. Messages and documents cannot be transferred between offices very easily and the staff probably rely on the telephone and post. The deficiencies associated with these methods are the relative slowness of the post and the uncertainty of leaving a message on the telephone if the call cannot be taken.

♦ Information retrieval - users are able to search many thousands of databases and gather information on almost any topic. The Internet can also be used to access a remote computer and retrieve files from it using File Transfer Protocol. Some companies transmit corporate data using a Virtual Private Network (VPN), which is a low-cost alternative to a private WAN. Sharing information so easily would be a bonus for the staff at XYZ. The individual offices are not networked so accessing shared documents presents quite a few difficulties.

♦ Universal standards - the Web is a system with universally accepted standards for storing, retrieving, formatting and displaying information using client/server architecture. It combines text, hypermedia, graphics and sound, using graphical user interfaces for easy viewing. At XYZ, no standards are specified. A variety of software has been purchased by the offices individually. Moving from one location to another means learning new systems, commands and screen layouts.

(b) *Examination tip: Think how you would feel if you were in a similar situation. The software applications available for accountants are very varied (as they are for surveyors) and if you were used to working with a particular system and had to change to a completely different one, imagine how it would affect you.*

The problems involved in implementing a suitable information sharing system in XYZ include the following:

♦ Partnership objectives - it seems there has not been a lot of discussion on the needs of the business. Although the partnership has gained some significant contracts recently, which have sparked the dissatisfaction with the current system, we are not told whether they are long-term contracts or whether the partnership will revert back to its previous ways of working soon and have no need for a new system. The partners need to draw up a business case for the change. Could they actually justify the cost of a new system for the sake of a few shared files and inconvenient communication channels?

- Choosing the system - there are two main options available to the partnership - a WAN or the cheaper option of a VPN. All the staff who were previously involved in making decisions on the software purchases must be consulted so that the new system will be suitable for all the users' needs

- Information sharing - decisions will need to be taken on the information that is going to be shared. Will the information be kept and updated in a central location? Who will be responsible for the backup of the files? Will sensitive or personal data be transferred? Suitable security controls, including encryption, will have to be implemented.

- Storage and retrieval - because the current system at XYZ does not normally allow for information sharing, the different offices will have their own methods of storing and retrieving data. The new system will mean transferring data from various formats into the new one, which might cause difficulties at the changeover.

- Integration - the software and databases will need to be standardised. Some software will have to be dumped and this will cause problems, and hurt feelings, for employees who have to learn new applications because their chosen software is not suitable for the new network. Imposing a common database of information may cause resentment unless training is provided to help staff accept the new system.

- Cost - the new system is likely to be very expensive and time consuming to implement. The ongoing cost of operating and maintaining the system must also be taken into account. The partners do not seem to have any experience in this field, so an analyst may have to be involved in the planning, design and implementation stage. Estimates should be obtained from several sources and agreed at senior level before committing the partnership to this change.

- Resentment - a shared system will mean that individual offices will no longer have their own autonomy. People get used to working in a certain way and change is very rarely welcomed. Learning how to use different applications and dealing with different types of communication, as well as coping with an increased workload, may result in poor customer service, a lowering of standards of work and inefficiencies. Poor morale could lead to resignations and problems with recruitment.

Answer 65 (Answer 3 of Exam Paper)

Tutorial note:

The first part of this question would probably deter a lot of students from answering it. As there are ten marks available, knowing three or four characteristics would earn you a pass mark.

Part (b) is the type of question on intelligent agents that you might have prepared for. Keep your answer moving. Try and discuss a range of points, rather than focussing on one or two specific ones.

(a) Intelligent agents are software programs that carry out specific, repetitive, and predictable tasks for an individual user or business process. The agent uses a built-in or learned knowledge base to accomplish tasks or make decisions on behalf of the user.

Autonomy implies that agents should be able to act without the direct intervention of humans or other agents - the program works with some degree of independence and takes decisions. Autonomy here does not mean that the agent must be fully independent but that the agent can automatically ask for the assistance and service of other agents or human beings whenever necessary.

Additionally, intelligent agents should have the following features:

Examination tip: If needs be, make up your own list using properties derived from human examples eg, intelligence, knowledge, rationality, mobility, learning, communication and action.

Flexibility - an intelligent agent should be able to learn, to reason, to adapt to the environment and to solve problems.

Pro-activeness - the program takes initiative with goal directed behaviour. Agents have objectives to achieve and are driven towards them. However, they should not simply act in response to their environment, but should also expose possible solutions, and by way of their own initiative choose the optimal one.

Reactivity - the agent is able to perceive its environment and respond in a timely fashion to changes that occur in it.

Continuous - agents are continuous because they continue to run regardless of the presence of a user or a network connection.

Social Ability - the program interacts with other programs using some agent communication language and solves problems collectively. They may communicate with the user, system resources and other agents as required in order to perform their task. More advanced agents may co-operate with other agents to carry out tasks beyond the capability of a single agent. Finally, as mobile or even active objects, they may move from one system to another to access remote resources or even meet other agents and co-operate with them.

(b)   The e-mail support system at R&G has just been upgraded with intelligent agent software to assist the work of the support staff. The benefits include the following:

  ◆   The agent can review the content of e-mails by matching key words - because it has access to the technical support database, and potentially many other sources and agents, it is able to organise, filter, and structure this information so that it can answer queries posed in the e-mails. Finding a solution to a query might involve the agent accessing alternative information sources over a network or over the Internet This will help support staff by decreasing manual search time and by providing quicker customer service.

  ◆   The agent can navigate through external and internal networks, remembering short cuts and book marking interesting sites. It can highlight appropriate additions to the databases, which can be verified by support staff before setting up the necessary links.

  ◆   Using keywords the agent can allocate specific types of fault or queries to specialist staff members to answer. This will help prioritise faults, build up a knowledge base and ensure good customer service.

  ◆   It can monitor the number and type of e-mails and telephone calls answered by each member of the support staff. This will help assess the productivity of individual support staff.

  ◆   The agent can manage the storage, deletion and backup of information and perform virus detection. Queries on new faults, with no existing links, can be identified and referred to the appropriate staff member prior to being added to the database.

  ◆   Some agents can recommend a course of action without the intervention of staff. They are collaborative and need many profiles to be able to make an accurate recommendation but certain questions eg, FAQ's can be treated in this way.

As well as benefits there will also be a few problems associated with the agent's use.

  ◆   Unless staff are reassured regularly, they may be concerned that their work is being de-skilled by the agent finding the required database pages.

  ◆   Although one of the benefits of the agent is its ability to filter the information and reduce overload by removing unwanted data, unless the key words that the agent picks up match those in the database, there will inevitably be retrieval problems.

◆ Another of the benefits is the matching of key words and finding the information from the database. But, if the agent misunderstands the query and obtains the wrong information or allocates the query to the wrong staff member, it may turn out to be a disadvantage and waste staff time where incorrect help pages are displayed.

◆ When recommendations are made by the agent that turn out to be wrong, staff may lose confidence in the software and concentrate on finding the information themselves - not considering the agent.

◆ If and when the employees find out that their work is being monitored, they will be angry and resentful that they were not consulted. They would probably argue that, even with a grading system to determine how long an individual query should take to answer, the software could not accurately identify reasons for some queries taking longer to respond to and it would therefore provide inappropriate assessments of productivity.

Answer 66 (Answer 4 of Exam Paper)

Tutorial note:

Knowledge management is highly topical and a prime candidate for exam questions. A detailed understanding of the technology is not required for this question but you do need to be able to explain that, like any other valuable resource, information and knowledge must be managed effectively.

For part (b) of the question you should be able to identify the types of system used for knowledge sharing.

(a)   The barriers to sharing knowledge in the AHM Company can be divided into three areas.

Organisational

These barriers exist because there are no policies or strategies on information or communication and the structures to aid knowledge transfer are not in place. The speed of information transfer is also hampered by the infrequency of planned meetings.

To remove the barriers, the company needs to move away from its bureaucratic structure with its hierarchies, defined roles within 'functions' and lack of formal and informal systems for transferring information. Decentralised structures allow decisions to be taken where critical knowledge is located and reduce duplication of IS and research projects, resulting in fewer instances of inefficiency within the organisation. Flexibility allows information sharing and movement of personnel to respond to opportunities (or problems). Useful ideas generated either on the shop floor or in the boardroom could be brought to the attention of R&D staff and used to improve the overall quality of the finished product.

Examination tip: *Remember to comment on the impact of the barriers on the efficiency of information transfer.*

Social

These barriers exist because there is very little communication between the three factories and between departments. None of the groups are aware of the information available from others and no group seems willing to share its knowledge. This has come about because of the lack of contact with other staff - people are less likely to share information with their colleagues if they cannot identify with them on a personal level.

In addition to the changes in organisation structure, management should create environments and activities to discover and release tacit knowledge and devise systems that stress the importance of shared ownership, shared culture, vision and values and rewards for knowledge sharing.

Technological

The main technological barrier to sharing knowledge is the lack of any groupware system. The telephone and mail systems are not ideal for sharing ideas and plans. Maintaining three separate R&D departments, combined with the lack of suitable information transfer links between the locations, prevents information sharing and results in duplication and inefficiencies.

Better access to operational knowledge distributed widely throughout the organisation can speed processes, reduce duplication and reveal new competitive opportunities. Staff must be integrated and taught to co-operate and communicate so that useful ideas and potential improvements to models can be identified in future.

Introducing groupware to support shared activities is one of the ways to remove the technological barriers. The software provides functions for collaborative work groups, allowing information to be sent electronically, and providing a user-friendly form of communication.

(b)   The systems that can be used to facilitate the sharing of knowledge between the three groups of research staff include the following:

Examination tip: There are different systems that you could have mentioned. The most important one is groupware because the features cover most of the systems anyway.

- ♦   Groupware
- ♦   An intranet
- ♦   Knowledge work systems

To implement these types of system, the company would need to invest in the appropriate hardware and software to provide the network support system.

Groupware is a term used to describe software that provides functions for the use of collaborative work groups. Some of the features of groupware are:

- ♦   Messaging - allowing users to send and receive e-mails from different locations. Messages can be sent to one person, sent sequentially to a number of people, who may add to it or comment on it before passing it on, or sent to everyone on a distribution list at once. Messages can include attachments, which may be documents, photos or technical drawings. Hyperlinks can be added to guide the recipient directly to a Web page or file server. The software tracks any changes made within documents and co-ordinates responses.

- ♦   Assigning tasks - the groupware keeps the status of the task up-to-date on a task list.

- ♦   Access to shared databases with views of the information held on them that can be used to standardise the way information is viewed in a workgroup.

- ♦   Group scheduling - to keep track of members of the team.

- ♦   Video conferencing - participation in on-line discussions with others and removing constraints such as travelling time and costs.

- ♦   Workflow management - moving and tracking documents created by groups.

An Intranet - is an internal network used to share information. Intranets use Internet technology and protocols. The firewall surrounding the intranet fends off unauthorised access.

Intranets and other network technologies provide a set of tools for creating collaborative environments in which members of an organisation can exchange ideas, share information and work together on common projects and assignments regardless of their physical location.

These tools include e-mail, fax, voice mail, teleconferencing, videoconferencing, data conferencing, chat systems and news groups.

Knowledge work systems - provide knowledge workers, such as the research staff, with tools such as:

♦   Analytical tools
♦   Powerful graphics facilities
♦   Communication tools
♦   Access to internal and external databases
♦   A user-friendly interface

Answer 67 (Answer 5 of Exam Paper)

Tutorial note:

In part (a) any framework can be used to identify the types of IT system and how they would be prioritised.

Part (b) The first part is a straightforward comparison of two types of process and the second part gives you an opportunity to explain why it would be important to WOWR. Structure your answer around situations that bring about radical changes in an organisation.

(a)   WOWR will identify many different types of application that they need. However, it is not always feasible to develop all the applications at the same time and therefore it will be necessary to prioritise the applications. One way of doing this is by building an application portfolio - a development of the McFarlan Strategic Grid or Peppard's can be used to look at the portfolio of systems.

Strategic importance in the
competitive environment

	Low	High
High Strategic importance in the predicted competitive environment	High potential	Strategic
Low	Support	Key operational

Examination tip: Other frameworks can be used as a basis for this answer. Wiseman developed a strategic options generator. Another was put forward by Davenport. Earl identified a few different types of framework that could have been explained to answer this question.

Like McFarlan, Peppard suggests four classifications. WOWR would use the grid to target those applications within its portfolio that have the greatest strategic potential. The four categories are as follows:

Support - applications that improve management effectiveness but are not critical to the business eg, accounting systems, payroll systems, spreadsheets and legally required systems. WOWR have already implemented these systems but development of existing applications may be required because investment has been limited in recent years. This may include developments in MIS.

Key operational - applications that are critical to sustain the existing business. They generally support core organisational activities eg, inventory control, production control and order management.

Strategic - applications that are critical to future business. The Board at WOWR needs to identify the mission and CSF's to support the strategies. For example, a new system could make more effective use of the historical sales data by linking past sales trends with demographic information to try and forecast sales for new publications. Other areas might include Internet systems eg, web design techniques, expert systems, or multimedia.

High potential - applications that are innovative, and might be of future strategic potential Areas for innovation may include direct links from customers to the sales systems to plan their purchases better. A sales database may be established using data mining techniques or intelligent agents to identify trends in that data to assist in forecasting future sales.

(b)   (i)   **Business Process Reengineering** (BPR) is the fundamental rethinking and radical redesign of business processes to achieve dramatic improvements in critical, contemporary measures of performance, such as cost, quality, service, and speed. What constitutes this dramatic change is the overhaul of organisational structures, management systems, employee responsibilities and performance measurements, incentive systems, skills development, and the use of information technology. BPR can potentially impact every aspect of how WOWR conducts business.

BPR is often undertaken in response to dramatic changes in the external environment eg, a paradigm shift, that apply considerable pressure on the ability of the organisation to fulfil its mission, improve its competitive positioning, or to even survive as an entity. BPR actions are radical and transforming and virtually all functions within the organisation are affected.

Process Innovation is the envisioning of new work strategies, the actual process design activity, and the implementation of change in its entire complex technological, human, and organisation dimensions. Process innovation is more drastic than BPR and has a greater chance of adding value to an organisation, because it supports the creation of new processes. It is likely to be a much more radical approach and may involve cultural changes.

(b)   (ii)   There are usually three types of situations where a company would undertake process innovation and BPR and these are when the company is:

- ♦ **In trouble and has no choice** - where costs are higher than the competition or customer service is poor and custom is being lost, these organisations are re-engineering to survive and need to take drastic actions to achieve rapid results in a very short time-scale. Cost savings may arise from the provision of better information or the automation of administrative functions. Although WOWR are not in trouble, they could make cost savings by linking IT systems in the supply chain. The sales database could be improved to give more reliable information on forecast sales volumes, so that more effective decisions can be made on production schedules.

- ♦ **In a turnaround or threatened position** - these organisations have the foresight to see trouble coming and are able to take action in advance to avoid adversity. Trends could indicate changes in customer requirements and perceptions of quality. New competitors maybe entering the market or changes to the regulatory or economic environment may be looming. Technological change can prompt process innovation, especially where competitors start using new technology eg, if WOWR are not using the Internet for ordering or selling goods and their competitors are, then they may lose sales. BPR can also make radical changes to work practices and produce productivity gains. Staff savings and a reduced and more adaptive workforce could provide WOWR with the ability to respond more effectively to the requirements of the customer.

- ♦ **In peak condition** - even these organisations undertake re-engineering because it gives an appropriate focus to the business and encourages a long-term strategic view of operational processes. They view re-engineering as an opportunity to gain competitive advantage by improving their lead over competitors and making it even more difficult for new entrants or existing competitors to take control of the market. By focusing on entire processes BPR can streamline activities throughout the organisation. WOWR could completely change the on-line ordering service before its competitors, giving the organisation some competitive advantage, and forcing competitors to do the same.

November 2002 Exam Answers

Answer 68 (Answer 1 of Exam Paper)

XL

Tutorial note:

All four parts of this question are based on the scenario.

Part (a) - short questions appear to be deceptively easy on first read, and then more difficult when you try and think of sufficient content for 12 marks. For this part of the question, try and think of some of the qualities of good information in a plan, referring back to the scenario so that you can do the comparison, before writing out the answer. This will help you to ensure that a sufficient number of points are included in the answer.

In part (b) you need to know the different sources of information that are required to make strategic decisions and to highlight the lack of internal and external information within the existing information systems.

Part (c) is tricky - you need to put yourself in the position of receiving too much information and think what you would do to reduce it to a manageable level. There are several methods of summarising and filtering information prior to use by the recipient.

For part (d) you need to stress that any model will have some limitations, mainly relating to uncertainty regarding the future. However, you must explain those uncertainties in the context of strategic planning at the Board level of XL.

(a)   An information system can improve the efficiency of management by providing timely, accurate, well-presented, relevant information tailored for the user. The type of information presented will vary according to the management level receiving it. For example, the petrol station manager will require detailed information while the Board will need information in summary format.

Good information possesses certain qualities - these will be interpreted differently for the petrol station manager and the members of the Board

Examination tip: *You can remember these qualities by means of the mnemonic ACCURATE.*

- ◆ Accurate - information must be reliable enough to facilitate meaningful decisions. The degree of accuracy required will vary e.g., the Board only requires a summary of the profit, probably to the nearest hundred or thousand pounds, whereas the manager requires a high degree of precision in balancing the sales account.

- ◆ Complete - information should not be more complete than is required. For example, if a company is looking for a new supplier of one of its raw materials, it would be impossible for them to contact all possible UK suppliers; instead a representative sample would be chosen.

- ◆ Cost effective - the overriding consideration is that the cost of obtaining information should not exceed its value to the user. All of the managers seem to have quite a basic cost effective transaction-processing system to provide the necessary information. The cost compared to the benefit derived from the EIS that supplies strategic information to the Board is more difficult to calculate.

- ◆ Understandable - information that is easy to understand is more likely to produce reasoned decision-making and action. The manager needs information to identify problems in allocating staff or to remind him/her to order stocks whereas the Board need exception reporting on whether certain budgets are being met.

♦ Relevant - information should be screened to remove any factors which are irrelevant to making decisions. The manager will need to know the prices of the flowers but this information is irrelevant to strategic decision making

♦ Adaptable - as the organisation evolves, management's needs for information are constantly changing. The petrol station manager needs information about the type of customer buying goods so that he/she can alter the mix of goods sold to meet the customers' requirements. The board members will need information on road building policy to decide on future requirements.

♦ Timely - information can only be of use if it is received in time to affect the decision-making process. The manager makes decisions on a daily basis and needs specific information for operational control. The Board will probably only need to analyse the information monthly

♦ Easy to use - information should be clearly presented and sent using the right medium and communication channel.

(b)   ***Examination tip:*** *Try to think about a SWOT analysis to give you some ideas on the extra environmental information required.*

To make more informed decisions regarding the siting of new petrol stations, the Directors need to update and amend the EIS to provide additional information. The new software uses statistics to forecast the future profitability of the organisation but does not take into account important environmental information or enable the Directors to monitor results from individual petrol stations to ensure they are fulfilling their objectives. Updating the EIS to provide a GUI and immediate access to the TPS, as well as access to more environmental information would help them in their decision-making. The extra environmental information should cover:

♦ Customers - the demand for petrol is linked to car ownership and information on this is available from Government publications and car manufacturers. If a significant number of people switch to public transport then the industry will be faced with fewer customers and spare capacity. Market research could establish public opinion on the continued use of motors, which will help indicate future demand for fuel.

♦ Competitors - the shift in emphasis away from road building means rivalry amongst competitors will become stronger. Plans to expand will need more than the limited information previously required. The Directors need to know where competitors are building or withdrawing from the market to identify suitable sites for future development. Links with the AA and RAC, planning departments of local authorities, as well as publications regarding businesses for sale, will help them keep abreast of developments in the market.

♦ Suppliers - with the current uncertainty in world production of oil, information on supplies would help with capacity planning for existing and new petrol stations and also with the forecast income and expenditure of the FB division, based on the estimated price of petrol.

♦ Technology - as pollution and congestion become more of an issue, innovations in powering vehicles will be important. The directors must have access to information on alternative fuels to include in their planning discussions.

♦ Government action - on emissions, road charging, road building, landfill, recycling and road and fuel tax will affect the future demand for petrol. Access to information on these areas is critical for forecasting three years into the future.

♦ Monitoring activities - information from the TPS, along with the published financial accounts of competitors will help identify which petrol stations are under performing, which areas have the most potential for future growth and whether the new petrol stations are meeting the objectives regarding the increase in market share. Information on the cost of building a new petrol station and the returns in revenue from it can show the overall break-even position.

(c)   Some systems struggle at times to deliver the right information to the right people on time and in the correct analysed format. Information overload generally means that individuals are in receipt of so much information from a variety of sources (such as e-mail, telephone calls, verbal reports from staff, clients and the company's databases) that they are unable to assess what is and what is not important.

The Directors of XL are concerned about the reduction in focus on key operational areas as a consequence of information overload. An information system can be designed to prevent information overload occurring for the Board of XL using tools to summarise and provide exception reports in EIS, as well as filtering and intelligent agents.

The Board are currently receiving a lot of information from their three divisions and the EIS can automatically summarise data and highlight important trends and ratios. Information can be grouped by critical success factors to maintain focus on the main activities and help the members of the Board track the company's results quickly and easily. The system can be designed in such a way that although much detailed information can be built into it, users can have the ability to enter it at a higher, summarised level but 'drill down' for additional information should they require it. Good screen design using graphs, charts and hyperlinks will help in this process.

The problem of information overload can also be overcome by exception reporting. Filters can be used to show either the totals from combining some of the variables and/or exceptional items depending on some specific criteria.

Examination tip: *Try not to get too carried away with intelligent agents because they* might not be the most suitable way of resolving the information overload problem at XL.

A Web browser is a cumbersome method of scanning the external environment and becomes more unwieldy as the quantity of information grows. Having to search through database after database to make sure that you do not miss the information you need, gets to be tedious and time consuming. The promise of an intelligent application that operates in lieu of user intervention on the Web is finally becoming a reality. Described as 'intelligent agents', these applications organise, filter, and structure this information on the user's behalf, even though the user is not assigning the tasks proactively. These tasks range from mundane information filtering, through active negotiation to actually reacting to new information.

(d)   The limitations of this model lie in the lack of environmental information used. The software 'attempts' to analyse the divisions without information on competitor activity, innovations, government actions or specific rates of inflation for the petrol-chemical industry - all of which will have an impact on the future of XL. As with all planning systems, the model will become less accurate the further into the future that the system forecasts for. But this highlights the dilemma for XL because the economic viability for drilling and extracting will be calculated over the life of an oilfield, which might be more than ten years.

For the drilling and extraction division, producing a forecast for three years may be insufficient, because of the extended timescales and uncertainty involved. New oilfields or problems in the Middle East may affect the price of oil, rendering the forecast less reliable. Assessing the viability of a new deposit using discounted cash flow techniques and general interest rates will not give the Directors a fair approximation of the return from investments.

The refining division operates worldwide. There could be a choice of locations for the refining and a choice in the mix of products. Without market information, what factors are used to make that choice? There may be improved techniques of refining or alternative sources of fuel - building further inaccuracies into the model the longer the period into the future of the forecast.

The retail division is undergoing the most change, but the model is not able to predict the actions of competitors or the affect of changes to their supplies, which would undoubtedly affect demand forecasts for new petrol stations.

Unfortunately, the model would not provide accurate results even if more environmental information were used because the complexities of the industry make forecasting changes difficult.

Answer 69 (Answer 2 of Exam Paper)

Expert Systems

> *Tutorial note:*
>
> Part (a) is reasonably straightforward and hopefully your knowledge of Expert Systems will extend to their use in helping to manage strategic information.
>
> There are two parts to (b) - you need to distinguish between the social and employment effects of both expert systems that are involved.

(a)   An expert system is a computerised package designed to allow non-expert users to make expert decisions. This is based on the concept that an expert's knowledge can be captured and held in computer storage, usually based on a set of rules. Others can then use this knowledge e.g. to diagnose a situation where there is a considerable degree of uncertainty. Expert systems can be used at a variety of different levels. At the simplest level they can give factual answers to technical questions. At a more complex level they can suggest how a decision should be made, recommending a course of action. They are similar to DSS but where the DSS functions by modelling how a manager believes a problem should be solved, expert systems offer new 'intelligence' to that manager, and should also be able to explain the line of reasoning they have pursued.

In the management of strategic information, the ES can deal with highly structured problems in a specific knowledge domain. It may be used for technical advice and to assist with recurring decisions such as checking on legislation, assessing taxation implications and selecting equipment. In this respect, if the knowledge base is extensive and kept up to date, an ES may well perform better than the human experts.

Unfortunately, an ES will not be appropriate in the management of strategic information. Most of the decisions taken at strategic level are risky because the strategic decision-makers generally make one-off decisions e.g., whether to invest in an ES, and the knowledge base is incomplete. Information on the external environment is often the most uncertain and disorganised and generally takes a long time to collect and analyse. The environmental issues affecting strategic decisions are quite complex and cover a variety of influences including social, technological, ecological, political and economic, which are not well formulated.

(b)   The SZ hospital has introduced two new expert systems. System A reviews the performance of doctors and system B is a diagnostic ES. The social and employment effects of System A include:

♦   resistance - people fear change and motivation will be affected if the ES are unpopular.

♦   job security and status - some staff will lose their jobs; others will use the ES and become more productive.

♦   skill levels - tasks that are highly structured and rule based, such as monitoring the performance of doctors, are the most susceptible to de-skilling. The expert system is used to make decisions rather than the administrator.

♦   task variety - ES can either increase or decrease task variety. If the system automates boring tasks that used to account for a large part of the day, then staff will now be able to spend more time on other tasks. If however, the ES eliminates many tasks thus focusing attention on just a few tasks then the impact of the ES will generally be negative.

♦   operational efficiency - identifying decreases in efficiency raises awareness and reduces errors. Monitoring the trends is also likely to be faster than using reviews performed by staff.

♦   disruption of social system - the ES might disrupt the established team spirit in the office. Individuals who are used to working with each other might be separated into different groups. Doctors acting competitively to improve recorded performance might try and see more patients than their colleagues and not pay enough attention to diagnosing their illnesses.

- stress - lack of consultation with staff regarding actual implementation has led to doctors and their professional union rejecting the system because it causes them stress. Staff may be afraid that the system will reduce them to being operators - losing the ability to introduce the 'human touch'. The ES can reveal weaknesses in the previous system, putting people under pressure by the revelation of deficiencies.

Examination tip: *Although the examiner does not expect you to distinguish between the two ES, you might find it easier to do it this way as you re-read through the scenario.*

The social and employment effects of System B include:

- resentment - staff may feel that the death of the patient could have been prevented. It gives them another reason to dislike the ES.

- skill levels - staff autonomy is reduced as the ES makes the decisions. Junior doctor's jobs may be less attractive and the hospital may have difficulty recruiting.

- uncertainty and fear - staff may be uncertain about the value of the system. Not knowing where the liability lies when there is a fault in an ES that is relied on for decision-making could cause much anxiety. It could be the programmer, the expert or the user of the ES.

- redundancy - the proposed decrease in the number of junior doctors has only been postponed while the software supplier carries out a more detailed investigation.

Answer 70 (Answer 3 of Exam Paper)

RR University

> *Tutorial note:*
>
> Requirement *(a)* is in two parts. For the 7 marks allocated to part (i) you need to evaluate the use of data at the University. This means looking at the positive and negative aspects of it - even though it is difficult to find the good points.
>
> Part (ii) focuses on the necessity to ensure that revisions to an IS link to the CSFs of that system.
>
> *Part (b)* is quite difficult because we tend to only think of the advantages of data. However, recognising its disadvantages helps to ensure that only appropriate systems are specified.

(a)   (i)   Although individual systems succeed in meeting the specific information needs of each department, they are incompatible with each other. This means that there is duplication of data and it cannot be shared or transferred between departments or the central University database - updating general data into the central database will be more difficult as more than one copy of each field is likely to exist and data may not be equally up-to-date on all information systems There are other problems that stem from the data duplication. Maintaining duplicate systems is expensive; it is an inefficient use of resources and involves more inputting of data, more computers and software and it needs more storage space.

The way that the systems are organised means that data integrity is lost - all users cannot access the same data and inconsistencies between data might exist. Also the data is not program independent - a wide range of software is used. This reduces the flexibility of processing.

(ii)   **Revising the current IS**

The Board of Management could use Critical Success Factors in revising the current information system in the following way:

- There must be a clear and shared understanding of what the CSFs of the University are and a recognition throughout the organisation of the need to integrate with the overall business objectives. The new system must be designed with these CSFs in mind. Each department must know how they can contribute to satisfying these objectives.

♦ Although the existing systems currently meet the requirements of the different department heads, they should be checked to ensure that no changes are necessary before the individual CSFs are decided.

♦ Once the CSFs have been established, the developments that provide the maximum support to these factors can be identified. A comparison between the current systems and the desired one will determine the IS gap. Revisions to existing IS, or completely new systems can then be specified to meet the information gap.

♦ The CSFs should have known and reliable performance measures. They will be used to monitor the actual success of each factor and make it easy to identify the information required.

(b) Data warehousing involves setting up a central corporate database in which all or most of the organisation's data will be held. The University data warehouse would store data from current and previous years extracted from its 35 operational databases, as well as information from various external sources such as other Universities and private training companies. It would be a central source of data that was screened, edited, standardised and integrated so it could be accessed and used to support business analysis, market research and decision making.

Examination tip: Most of the information you require to answer this question is in the scenario.

The main disadvantage of data warehousing in this scenario is that the operational data resides in many different types of systems and the process of collecting the data into the warehouse needs to be customised and automated so that it can then be made available to all authorised users via their workstation. This would cause the following problems:

♦ The University does not currently have an integrated system and to access the proposed warehouse new hardware and software would have to be installed. This would be very costly.

♦ As data is stored in different formats in the various departments, much of it will need altering to be able to store it in a common format within the warehouse. All data must be consistent in format and codes and the data input routine should eliminate any inconsistencies. Because of the different requirements for data access and report generation, this may involve writing in many report formats.

♦ The case would have to be made for having so much extra data available and users would need training to be able to access it and avoid information overload.

Although the data warehouse system will provide the University with historic data, there will be an understandable reluctance to destroy any of the data contained in the systems that, although may not be used on a daily basis, provides them with a record of their experiences and growth. The Board members need to ensure that the warehouse software can cope with the volumes and expand to meet the future requirements. They must also ensure that backup systems are installed.

Answer 71 (Answer 4 of Exam Paper)

IT strategy

Tutorial note:

This question focuses on the service sector

In part (a) you will need to know the reasons for having an IT strategy in an organisation and be able to explain that IT may take on more of a support role.

Part (b) is one of those questions where, if you know the subject, you could write more than is necessary to gain the full marks. Hopefully, you will recognise the model and be able to visualise the matrix to help with the discussion.

(a)   IT can be described as 'the use of computers, microelectronics and telecommunications to help us produce, store, and send information in the form of pictures, words or numbers, more reliably, quickly and economically. For any type of organisation the IT strategy will identify the key areas that can benefit from an investment in IT. It will further outline the type of investment that the organisation will make, and how the strategically important units will effectively use the technology.

Examination tip: You do not have to choose a firm of accountants but, as it is a profession that you are familiar with, it gives you a better chance of answering the question fully.

For a large international firm of accountants, the IT strategy is needed for the following reasons:

◆   To align the IT resources with corporate objectives - it is normal within an organisation for the IT strategy to support the overall business strategy. This could be to improve electronic commerce with their partners and to achieve electronic connectivity with their clients. Appropriate hardware and software systems will have to be implemented to provide senior partners with access to information concerning their partnership and to provide remote access to centralised databases for accountants working at clients' premises.

◆   As a strategic weapon - it is unlikely that an organisation will gain a competitive advantage from the incorporation of IT per se, but rather will gain an advantage from what IT enables it to do or offer. Computers with modems enable people to work from home, or communicate from client's premises - reducing the cost of travel and office space. An extranet could allow clients to access the firm's technical databases for information on legislation or taxation.

◆   For the allocation of resources - how much would the system cost in terms of: software; hardware; management commitment and time; education and training; conversion; documentation; operational manning; and maintenance? Portable PCs and communication equipment can be very expensive and mistakes or omissions can be extremely costly, the IT strategy helps to plan and control the expenditure. Where IT is used in a collaborative venture, it can change the basis of competition by setting up new communication networks and forming alliances with complementary organisations, such as investment bankers, to share information. E-mail or workgroup software will be required to provide this communication system.

◆   Developing standards - the IT strategy will enforce standards for current systems and also ensure that future changes are compatible with the existing IT infrastructure. Most organisations rely on IT and, where there is constant and sometimes rapid change, having an IT strategy helps to ensure that all the relevant aspects work together. IT will provide common work platforms for exchanging documents and writing standard reports.

◆   Developing the 'knowledge base' by training - part of the IT strategy will look at the implications for the existing workforce. It will identify the requisite skills and identify training needs. This helps ensure that there are no major disruptions in introducing the new system.

(b)   *Examination tip:* It isn't necessary to draw the matrix - except that it might help to jog your memory.

Porter and Millar's information intensity matrix provides a basis to identify the potential of information systems to provide a competitive advantage for the organisation. The axes of the matrix show the following:

		Information content	
	Low	of the product	High
High **Information intensity** **of the value chain**	Oil refining Legal services **Information is important**		Newspapers Banking Education **Information is crucial**
Low	Cement Bricks **Other factors are** **dominant**		Fashion **No evidence**

On the *x*-axis - the extent to which information is a component part of the product or service offered. This is very low in a product such as cement, but very high in newspapers or financial services. When the information in the value chain is high, it implies that sophisticated information systems are required to manage the linkages optimally.

On the *y*-axis - the number of information exchanges that must take place in order for a transaction to take place. This is low in fashion but high in oil refining or airlines.

By positioning an organisation in a given segment, advice can be 'read off' as to where information systems are going to be critical to business activities. This model can be used to provide measures of the business importance of IS but it can also refine the crude view into a more detailed picture of where and how it holds that business importance.

Of course, when Porter and Millar described this model they were not able to consider the effect of the Internet. The technological environment has been transformed since 1985. Many of the companies that would have been placed in the lower sections of the intensity grid might now be using EDI, intranets and e-commerce.

However, most service industries - including accounting firms would still be rated high on each axis. They provide a service in which information is a crucial component because it provides information enabling the client to make informed choices. As far as the value chain is concerned, how the firm provides the service is intimately connected with the information it actually gives. It cannot offer information if this is not entered to the system and processed in some way for it to be of use. This means the information content of the value chain is also high.

Answer 72 (Answer 5 of Exam Paper)

VNS

Tutorial note:

In part (a) you need to identify the positive and negative aspects of using an Extranet. Most of the information is useful in the scenario to guide you towards the answer the Examiner wants.

Part (b) needs you to think of other information sharing systems and suggest alternative systems that could be used in this situation.

(a)   An Extranet is an Intranet that is accessible to authorised outsiders. It can be used by the VNS charity to inform and exchange information with hospital staff, members of the public and the suppliers of information. It should improve customer service and make significant cost savings and, assuming it provides a good service, it may also increase the income generated from donations.

Examination tip: *Evaluate means looking at both the negative and positive aspects.*

The main advantages are that it can provide:

♦ Various levels of accessibility - only those outsiders with a valid username and password can access an extranet, with access rights enabling control over what people can view.

♦ Secure e-mail - enabling the charity to share news of common interest exclusively with hospital staff and privileged users.

♦ Web access - this can provide information about the charity and the benefits to society to encourage browsers to make donations or share information on certain diseases. It can also provide hyperlinks to the information database for authorised users and information on registration for those who are not.

♦ Access to information at all times - people can have queries resolved on a timelier basis using the Extranet. The Extranet also allows better use of the knowledge held by facilitating access to it. Users' forums could be established to share information and give answers to frequently asked questions.

♦ Cost savings - we can assume that supplying statistical information to the hospitals is produced on paper, requires frequent updates and generally incurs volume-related, high printing costs. Transferring these communications to an Extranet could result in better service and substantial cost savings.

♦ Collaboration with other organisations on joint development efforts - research staff in hospitals can be involved in updating the databases.

Introducing the system will give staff time to devote to charity activities, because there will be fewer people telephoning the charity.

The main disadvantages associated with this technology for VNS are the time required for staff to re-input the information and vet applications to use the Extranet and the costs of purchasing additional hardware and employing more staff to maintain its reliability.

Other shortcomings include:

♦ Confidentiality and security - it may not be appropriate to place some information on the Extranet. The information must not relate to individuals or breach any confidentiality. Firewalls and other security arrangements must be installed to protect sensitive information and prevent hacking/unauthorised access to the Extranet.

♦ Arrangements for people needing advice or without Internet access - There may be a requirement to explain or clarify the information provided on the Extranet and provision should also be made for clients without the technology; both groups should still be able to obtain the information they require directly from the charity. Live interaction can be essential for clients who have a strong preference for human contact.

♦ Staff motivation - there are currently problems with staff retaining information deliberately, which may not be resolved by introducing the Extranet. People react to changes differently and it may take time to persuade staff of the system's benefits.

(b)   ***Examination tip:*** *There are two parts to this question - identify and evaluate - make sure you do not miss out on easy marks by forgetting to evaluate one of the alternative systems.*

Other information sharing systems include:

♦   **A website** can be set up by VNS on one of its own computers, which could be permanently on-line. The provision of information on the Internet means that the client can retrieve it quickly and relatively cheaply provided they have access to a computer and telephone connection. It can be more dynamic than a paper-based catalogue, using text, pictures, graphs, and moving images as well as sound to illustrate the various recommendations.

Having a website means that staff would not have to vet Extranet users but they would still receive telephone calls, so it is unlikely to reduce the workload of the staff. Keeping the site up-to-date can also be a chore unless it is properly documented and supported by appropriate resources and an out-of-date website can give the wrong impression of the charity.

♦   **E-mail** removes the need for writing letters or using the telephone - queries can be answered when convenient for staff. Messages can be delivered immediately with proof of delivery, a feature that usually requires a premium payment using traditional posting methods. Distance and weight are not a consideration, unlike conventional surface mail. Thus, the charity can distribute the latest statistics and recommendations to individuals or identified user groups instantaneously without laborious reproduction and expensive postage costs.

However, e-mail may not be sufficient as a communications route, especially if it involves a delay before replies or acknowledgements are forthcoming, which may result in adverse publicity for the charity.

♦   **CD-ROM** - is used by some manufacturers to keep their customers up-to-date with the product database. It can be viewed on screen with a hard copy printed off if required. Using this option the staff would send the information to the clients at their location, removing the need to contact the charity in any way.

The problems with this type of communication are the time taken to produce and distribute the disks, diverting resources away from the charity's key activities. Mistakes or losses in the post could lead to clients having out-of-date information creating limited or misleading use.

Exam Kit Review Form

CIMA PAPER 14 KIT – MANAGEMENT ACCOUNTING – INFORMATION STRATEGY

We hope that you have found this Kit stimulating and useful and that you now feel confident and well-prepared for your examinations.

We would be grateful if you could take a few moments to complete the questionnaire below, so we can assess how well our material meets your needs. There's a prize for four lucky students who fill in one of these forms from across the Syllabus range and are lucky enough to be selected!

	Excellent	*Adequate*	*Poor*
Depth and breadth of technical coverage			
Appropriateness of coverage to examination			
Presentation			
Level of accuracy			

Did you spot any errors or ambiguities? Please let us have the details below.

Page	Error

Thank you for your feedback.

Please return this form to:

The Financial Training Company Limited
Unit 22J
Wincombe Business Park
Shaftesbury
Dorset SP7 9QJ

Student's name: ....

Address: ....

....

....